KIDS ♥ LOVE Virginia

Your Family Travel Guide to Exploring Kid-Friendly Virginia 600 Fun Stops & Unique Spots

Michele Darrall Zavatsky

Dedicated to the Families of Virginia

© Copyright 2023, Kids Love Publications

For the latest major updates corresponding to the pages in this book visit our website:

www.KidsLoveTravel.com

All rights reserved. No part of this book may be reproduced or transmitted in any form or by any means, electronic or mechanical, including photocopying, recording or by any information storage and retrieval system without the written permission from the authors, except for the inclusion of brief quotations in a review.

Although the authors have exhaustively researched all sources to ensure accuracy and completeness of the information contained in this book, we assume no responsibility for errors, inaccuracies, omissions or any other inconsistency herein. Any slights against any entries or organizations are unintentional.

REMEMBER: Museum exhibits change frequently. Check the site's website before you visit to note any changes. Also, HOURS and ADMISSIONS are subject to change at the owner's discretion. If you are tight on time or money, check the attraction's website or call before you visit.

INTERNET PRECAUTION: All websites mentioned in KIDS LOVE VIRGINIA have been checked for appropriate content. However, occassionally sites get hacked, usually off season. Report this to your server and let us know so we can find a safer website to point folks to.

Kids Love Virginia ~ Kids Love Publications, LLC

TABLE OF CONTENTS

General Information..Preface
(Here's where you'll find "How to Use This Book", Maps, Tour Ideas, etc.)

Chapter 1 – NORTH EAST AREA **(NE)**..1

Chapter 2 – WASHINGTON, DC AREA **(NE-DC)**................................41

Chapter 3 – NORTH WEST AREA **(NW)**...63

Chapter 4 – SOUTH CENTRAL AREA **(SC)**......................................101

Chapter 5 – SOUTH EAST AREA **(SE)**..131

Chapter 6 – SOUTH WEST AREA **(SW)**..203

Activity Index.. 217
(Amusements, Animals & Farms, Museums, Outdoors, State History, Tours, etc.)

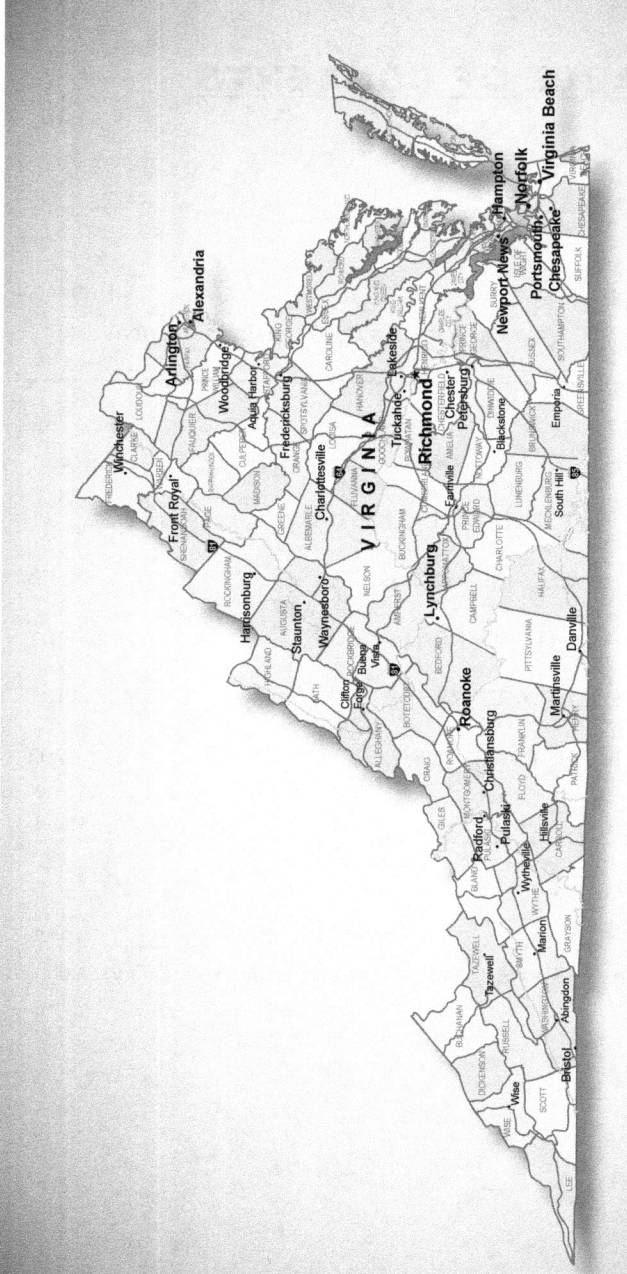

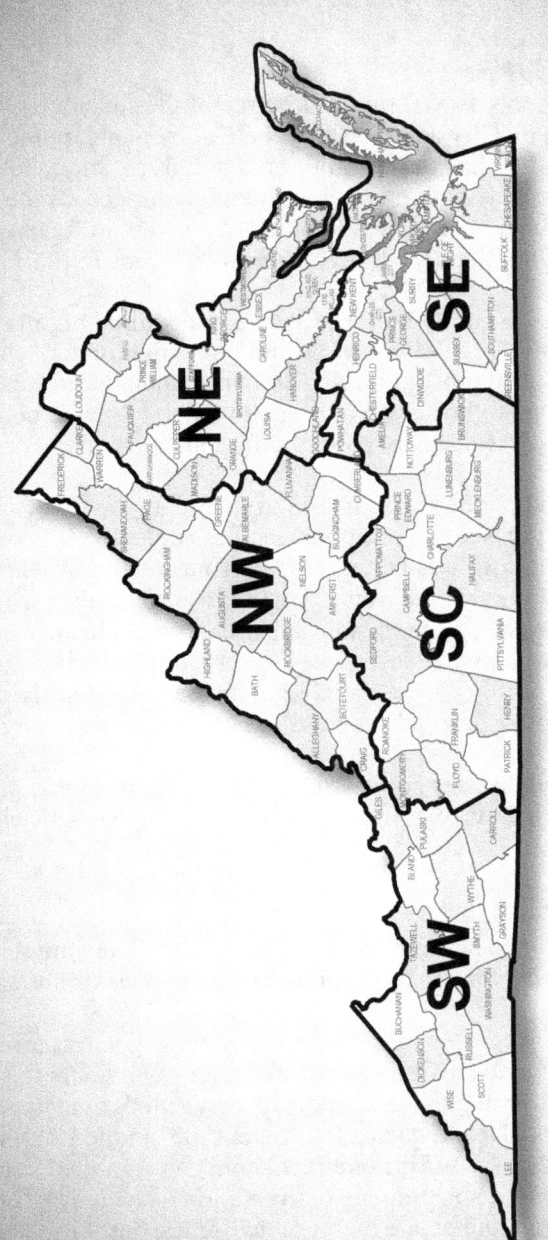

Chapter Area Map

(Chapters arranged alphabetically by chapter name)

HOW TO USE THIS BOOK
(a few hints to make your adventures run smoothly:)

BEFORE YOU LEAVE:
* Each chapter represents a two hour radius area of the state or a Day Trip. The listings are by City and then alphabetical by name, numeric by zip code. Each listing has tons of important details (pricing, hours, website, etc.) and a review noting the most engaging aspects of the place. Our popular Activity Index in back is helpful if you want to focus on a particular type of attraction (i.e. History, Tours, Outdoor Exploring, Animals & Farms, etc.).
Begin by assigning each family member a different colored highlighter. At your leisure, begin to read each review and put a highlighter "check" mark next to the sites that most interest each family member or highlight the features you most want to see. Now, when you go to plan a quick trip - or a long car ride - you can easily choose different stops in one day to please everyone.
* Know directions and parking. Use a GPS system that you trust.
* Most attractions are closed major holidays unless noted.
* When children are in tow, it is better to make your lodging reservations ahead of time. Every time we've tried to "wing it", we've always ended up at a place that was overpriced, in a unsafe area, or not clean. We've never been satisfied when we didn't make a reservation ahead of time.
* If you have a large family, or are traveling with extended family or friends, most places offer group discounts. Check out the company's website for details.
* For the latest critical updates corresponding to the pages in this book, visit our website: www.kidslovetravel.com. Click on Updates listed by state.

ON THE ROAD:
* Consider the child's age before you stop at an exit. Some attractions and restaurants, even hotels, are too formal for young ones or not enough adventure for teens.
* Estimate the duration of the trip and how many stops you can afford to make. * From our experience, it is best to stop every two hours to stretch your legs or eat/snack or maybe visit an inexpensive attraction.
* Bring along travel books and games for "quiet time" in the van. (see tested travel products on www.kidslovetravel.com) As an added bonus, these "enriching" games also stimulate conversation - you may get to know your family better and create memorable life lessons.

ON THE ROAD: (cont.)
* In between meals, we offer the family snacks like: pretzels, whole grain chips, nuts, water bottles, bite-size (dark) chocolates, grapes and apples. None of these are messy and all are healthy.
* Plan picnics along the way. Many Historical sites and State Parks are scattered along the highway. Allow time for a rest stop or a scenic byway to take advantage of these free picnic facilities.

WHEN YOU GET HOME:
Make a family "treasure chest". Decorate a big box or use an old popcorn tin. Store memorabilia from a fun outing, journals, pictures, brochures and souvenirs. Once a year, look through the "treasure chest" and reminisce.

WAYS TO SAVE MONEY:
* Memberships - many children's museums, science centers, zoos and aquariums are members of associations that provide FREE or Discounted reciprocity to other such museums across the country. AAA Auto Club cards offer discounts to many of the activities and hotels in this book. If grandparents are along for the ride, they can use their AARP card and get discounts. Be sure to carry your member cards with you as proof to receive the discounts.
* Supermarket Customer Cards - national and local supermarkets often offer good discounted tickets to major attractions in the area.
* Internet Hotel Reservations - if you're traveling with kids, don't take the risk of being spontaneous with lodging. Make reservations ahead of time. We don't use non-refundable, deep discount hotel "scouting" websites unless we're traveling on business - just adults. You can't cancel your reservation, or change them, and you can't be guaranteed the type of room you want (ex. non-smoking, two beds). Instead, stick with a national hotel chain you trust and join their rewards program (ex. Choice Privileges) to accumulate points towards FREE night stays.
* State Travel Centers - as you enter a new state, their welcome centers offer many current promotions.
* Hotel Lobbies - often have a display of discount coupons to area shops and restaurants. When you check in, ask the clerk for discount pizza coupons they may have at the front desk.
* Attraction Online Coupons - check the websites listed with each review for possible printable coupons or discounted online tickets good towards the attraction.

> Check out these businesses / services in your area for tour ideas:

AIRPORTS - All children love to visit the airport! Why not take a tour and understand all the jobs it takes to run an airport? Tour the terminal, baggage claim, gates and security / currency exchange. Maybe you'll even get to board a plane.

ANIMAL SHELTERS - Great for the would-be pet owner. Not only will you see many cats and dogs available for adoption, but a guide will show you the clinic and explain the needs of a pet. Be prepared to have the children "fall in love" with one of the animals while they are there!

BANKS - Take a "behind the scenes" look at automated teller machines, bank vaults and drive-thru window chutes. You may want to take this tour and then open a savings account for your child.

CITY HALLS - Halls of Fame, City Council Chambers & Meeting Room, Mayor's Office and famous statues.

ELECTRIC COMPANY / POWER PLANTS - Modern science has created many ways to generate electricity today, but what really goes on with the "flip of a switch". Because coal can be dirty, wear old, comfortable clothes. Coal furnaces heat water, which produces steam, that propels turbines, that drives generators, that make electricity.

FIRE STATIONS - Many Open Houses in October, Fire Prevention Month. Take a look into the life of the firefighters servicing your area and try on their gear. See where they hang out, sleep and eat. Hop aboard a real-life fire engine truck and learn fire safety too.

HOSPITALS - Some Children's Hospitals offer pre-surgery and general tours.

NEWSPAPERS - You'll be amazed at all the new technology. See monster printers and robotics. See samples in the layout department and maybe try to put together your own page. After seeing a newspaper made, most companies give you a free copy (dated that day) as your souvenir. National Newspaper Week is in October.

PETCO - Various stores. Contact each store manager to see if they participate. The Fur, Feathers & Fins™ program allows children to learn about the characteristics and habitats of fish, reptiles, birds, and small animals. At your local Petco, lessons in science, math and geography come to life through this hands-on field trip. As students develop a respect for animals, they will also develop a greater sense of responsibility.

PIZZA HUT & PAPA JOHN'S - Participating locations. Telephone the store manager. Best days are Monday, Tuesday and Wednesday mid-afternoon. Minimum of 10 people. Small charge per person. All children love pizza – especially when they can create their own! As the children tour the kitchen, they learn how to make a pizza, bake it, and then eat it. The admission charge generally includes lots of creatively made pizzas, beverage and coloring book.

KRISPY KREME DONUTS - Participating locations. Get an "inside look" and learn the techniques that make these donuts some of our favorites! Watch the dough being made in "giant" mixers, being formed into donuts and taking a "trip" through the fryer. Seeing them being iced and topped with colorful sprinkles is always a favorite with the kids. Contact your local store manager. They prefer Monday or Tuesday. Free.

SUPERMARKETS - Kids are fascinated to go behind the scenes of the same store where Mom and Dad shop. Usually you will see them grind meat, walk into large freezer rooms, watch cakes and bread bake and receive free samples along the way. Maybe you'll even get to pet a live lobster!

TV / RADIO STATIONS - Studios, newsrooms, Fox kids clubs. Why do weathermen never wear blue/green clothes on TV? What makes a "DJ's" voice sound so deep and smooth?

WATER TREATMENT PLANTS - A giant science experiment! You can watch seven stages of water treatment. The favorite is usually the wall of bright buttons flashing as workers monitor the different processes.

U.S. MAIN POST OFFICES - Did you know Ben Franklin was the first Postmaster General (over 200 years ago)? Most interesting is the high-speed automated mail processing equipment. Learn how to address envelopes so they will be sent quicker (there are secrets). To make your tour more interesting, have your children write a letter to themselves and address it with colorful markers. Mail it earlier that day and they will stay interested trying to locate their letter in all the high-speed machinery.

General State Agency & Recreational Information

Call *(or visit websites)* for the services of interest. Request to be added to their mailing lists.

- ☐ Virginia Tourism Corporation. (804) VISIT-VA or www.virginia.org
- ☐ Virginia Historical Society. www.virginiahistory.org
- ☐ Virginia Time Travelers. A program which encourages students to visit historic sites in Virginia. www.timetravelers.org
- ☐ Virginia Civil War Trails. (888) CIVIL WAR or www.virginia.org/listing/virginia-civil-war-trails/19049/
- ☐ Virginia State Parks – Richmond. (800) 933-PARK or www.dcr.virginia.gov
- ☐ Virginia Campground Directory. https://arvc.org
- ☐ Virginia Game and Inland Fisheries. (804) 367-1000 or www.dgif.virginia.gov
- ☐ Virginia Marine Resources Commission. (757) 247-2200 or www.mrc.state.va.us
- ☐ Virginia Trails Association. www.dcr.virginia.gov/recreational-planning/virginia-trails

---

- ☐ **NE** – Alexandria CVB. (800) 388-9119 or www.visitalexandriava.com
- ☐ **NE** – Arlington CVB. www.stayarlington.com
- ☐ **NE** – Fredericksburg Tourism. www.visitfred.com
- ☐ **NE** – Prince William County / Manassas CVB. (800) 432-1792 or www.visitpwc.com
- ☐ **DC** – Washington, DC CVB. https://washington.org/
- ☐ **DC** – Fairfax County CVC. www.fxva.com
- ☐ **NW** – Charlottesville / Albemarle County CVB (877) 386-1103 or www.visitcharlottesville.org
- ☐ **NW** – Lexington CVB. (877) 4LEXVA2 or www.lexingtonvirginia.com
- ☐ **NW** – Staunton CVB. (540) 332-3865 or www.staunton.va.us
- ☐ **NW** – Winchester/Frederick County CVB. (877) 871-1326 or www.winchesterva.com
- ☐ **SC** – Lynchburg Regional CVB. (800) 732-5821 or www.DiscoverLynchburg.org
- ☐ **SC** – Roanoke Valley CVB. (800) 635-5535 or www.visitroanokeva.com
- ☐ **SE** – Hampton Conventions & Tourism. (800) 487-8778 or https://visithampton.com/
- ☐ **SE** – Jamestown-Yorktown Foundation. www.historyisfun.org
- ☐ **SE** – Newport News Tourism. (888) 493-7386 or www.newport-news.org
- ☐ **SE** – Norfolk CVB. (800) 368-3097 or www.visitnorfolk.com
- ☐ **SE** – Portsmouth CVB. (800) PORTS-VA or https://portsvacation.com/
- ☐ **SE** – Richmond CVB. (800) 370-9004 or www.visitrichmondva.com
- ☐ **SE** – Virginia Beach Tourism. (800) VA-BEACH or www.visitvirginiabeach.com
- **SE** – Williamsburg Area CVB
- ☐ (800) 368-6511 or www.visitwilliamsburg.com
- ☐ **SW** – Heart of Appalachia. (888) 798-2386 or www.heartofappalachia.com

Chapter 1
North East

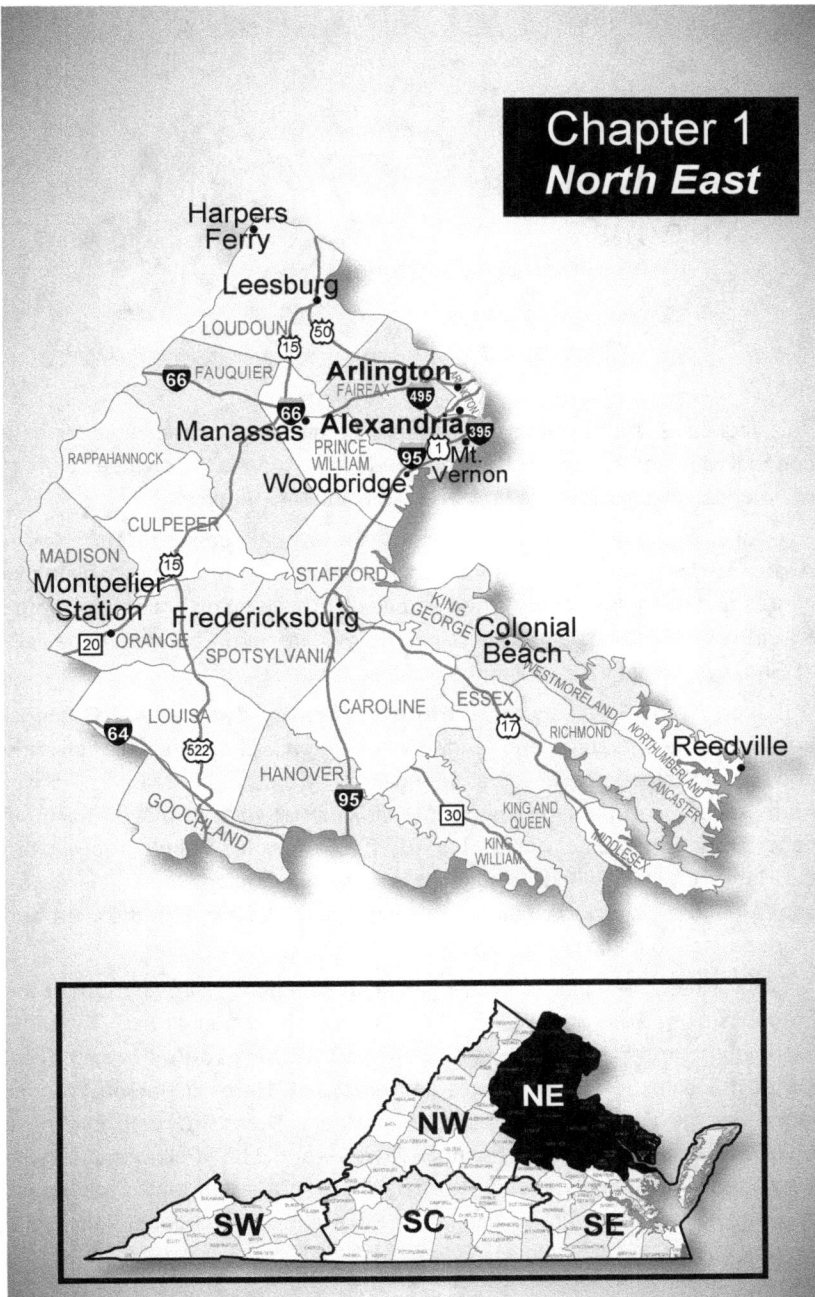

A Quick Tour of our Hand-Picked Favorites Around...

North East Virginia

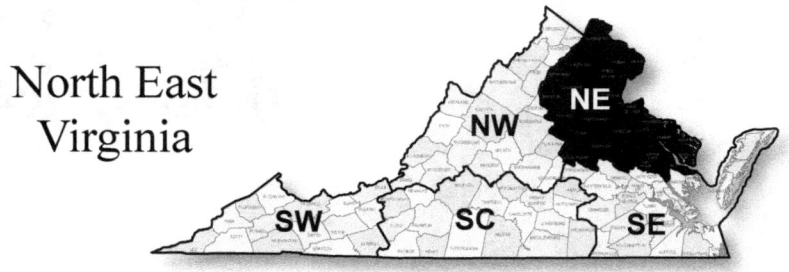

Virginia is synonymous with American history. For those seeking to connect with their history and heritage and to experience the diverse richness of American culture, there is no place like Northeast Virginia.

Take a moment to journey back to an 18th-century **Old Town Alexandria** tavern, hotel, apothecary or church where famous historical figures and everyday people dined and slept. "Touch points" of many George & Martha Washington haunts are found everywhere here – but most especially at Gadsbys, Christ Church and the Apothecary.

Just south of Alexandria is **Mount Vernon Estate** and Gardens, beloved home of George and Martha Washington. Although smaller children don't usually stand still for tours, they can enjoy the nature trail and Pioneer Farmer site full of heritage animals. Most kids will want to move at a good pace through the actual house, but, for sure, every kid will want to explore the Hands-on History Tent (seasonal) and the Orientation Center. Here, you can "Measure Up" to Washington or learn about Washington, the man and grandpa, not so much the president.

Encounter the richness of the American experience at every turn in the Fredericksburg Area and walk in the footsteps of Presidents and Generals. Start your tour of Fredericksburg at **George Washington's Ferry Farm**, the boyhood home of the nation's first president. Here, in Parson Weems' fable, George Washington cut down his father's cherry tree and threw the silver dollar across the Rappahannock River — or did he? Follow that up with a wonderful **Fredericksburg Trolley Tour** of the old town. You'll pass many sites you may want to visit later. Several historic national battlefields are just outside of Old Town.

For updates visit: www.KidsLoveTravel.com

Take Rte. 1 south paralleling the Potomac River until it meets the Chesapeake Bay. Many historic homes dot your trip and some are available to tour. Our favorite way to enjoy this area is by cruise across the **Chesapeake Bay** from historic Reedville at the tip of Virginia's Northern Neck to quaint **Smith Island**, only 13 miles away, yet a world apart. You'll see the crabbers and the fascinating soft shell crab "farms" as you come into Smith Island.

Head west of the Capital area to study the Civil War at places where it began. At the **Manassas National Battlefield**, what started as a picnic turned serious quickly. Of particular interest are the cute lights on the lighted battlefield model (easy for kids to understand and follow) and the fact that General Jackson got his Stonewall name here. Even further west, John Brown believed he could free the slaves, and he selected **Harpers Ferry** as his starting point. Some say this is really where the Civil War truly began. The site interpreters do an excellent job of absorbing you into history and teaching you little known facts of the mid-to-late 1800s - all at one site. Be careful though, not to bombard the kids with too much history. Take a break and grab a smoothie or a cone at one of the snack shops in the old town. Or, plan a hike or boat trip to the river nearby.

Sites and attractions are listed in order by City, Zip Code, and Name. Symbols indicated represent: 🍽 Restaurants   🛏 Lodging

Alexandria

FORT WARD MUSEUM & HISTORIC SITE

Alexandria - 4301 West Braddock Road (I-395, Seminary Road exit) 22304. Phone: (703) 838-4848 or (703) 838-4831(park). www.fortward.org. Hours: Museum: Thursday-Saturday 11:00am-4:00pm, Sunday 1:00-5:00pm. Park: Daily, 9:00am-Sunset. Admission: FREE. Online gift shop coupon. Note: Occasional informal encampments are held on the grounds.

The museum, patterned after a Union headquarters building, houses a Civil War collection and exhibits. When in the Museum, be sure to stop at the three-dimensional model of Fort Ward to see a small scale version of how the site looked during the Civil War. Also see the large map which outlines the extensive ring of forts comprising the Defenses of Washington, called "Mr. Lincoln's Forts." An orientation video provides an excellent overview of the history of Fort Ward, the best preserved of all the Civil War forts around Washington, and the wartime defense of the Union capital.

The Fort's Northwest Bastion has been completely restored and the grounds also feature a reconstructed ceremonial gate (decorated with cannonballs) and Officer's Hut. Climb the stockade into the fort and check out the cannon as you pretend to live the everyday life of Civil War soldiers and civilians. After duty in the Defenses of Washington, many were sent to serve in southern campaigns where the conditions of army life were considerably harsher than in the forts and camps around Washington.

CHRISTMAS IN CAMP OPEN HOUSE

Alexandria. Fort Ward Museum. (703) 838-4848. Learn how the holiday was observed during the Civil War with living history interpreters, period music, a Civil War period Thomas Nast Santa Claus, and light refreshments. Admission. (December, second Saturday)

GREAT WAVES AT CAMERON RUN REGIONAL PARK

Alexandria - 4001 Eisenhower Avenue (I-95/495 exit 3A) 22304. Phone: (703) 960-0767. www.novaparks.com/parks/cameron-run-regional-park Hours: Pool: (Memorial Day weekend - Labor Day). Batting cage and Mini golf: (mid-March - October). Hours vary. Peak season hours generally between 11:00am-7:00pm. Admission: Pool is $11.00-$15.00. Batting and Mini Golf are $1.00 or more added to pool price. Note: Concessions and picnic areas.

This park offers something for everyone - waterslides, wave pool, lap pool, Play Pool (climb on snakes or alligators in shallow waters), Tad Pool, batting cages and miniature golf.

ALEXANDRIA SEAPORT FOUNDATION

Alexandria - 1000 South Lee Street, Jones Point Park (waterfront, south of Founders Park) 22313. Phone: (703) 549-7078. www.alexandriaseaport.org. Hours: Weekdays 9:00am-4:00pm Admission: Observation FREE. Special programs or events - call for details.

Doing Big Things with Small Boats! Through the building and use of wooden boats, the Alexandria Seaport Foundation helps young people turn their lives around and provides families, community groups, and schools with meaningful educational, social, and recreational experiences. This floating museum includes a boat building shop, a marine science lab and traditional boats on the water. Volunteers build boats, teach boat building to youths, restore old boats, skipper and crew the 42' dory boat and the 15' Federalist, teach rowing and sailing, conduct marine science courses and offer boat rentals and boat-building classes on weekends.

For updates visit: www.KidsLoveTravel.com

ALEXANDRIA ARCHAEOLOGY MUSEUM

Alexandria - 105 North Union Street, #327 (on Potomac River @ the corner of King & Union Streets. - Torpedo Factory Art Center, 3rd Floor) 22314. Phone: (703) 838-4399. www.AlexandriaArchaeology.org. Hours: Wednesday-Friday 11:00am-4:00pm, Saturday 11:00am-5:00pm, Sunday 1:00-5:00pm. Closed most holidays. Admission: FREE.

Want to go on an archaeology dig? Learn from the experts at an authentic site! Interact with the City archaeologists and volunteers working in the public laboratory (and occasional public dig days). This small space will surprise you. You might first notice a small dinosaur skeleton - but is it really a dino? - not! Hone your archeology skills doing the Plate Puzzle: try to put the broken plate back together similar to what one might find on a dig.

The Alexandria Archaeology Museum offers Family Dig Days, where everyone can participate and learn secrets from the experts. Experience Alexandria using maps, oral history, heritage through exhibits, self-guided tours, and hands-on discovery kits. View the latest finds from current excavations where archaeologists reconstruct history.

ALEXANDRIA SYMPHONY ORCHESTRA

Alexandria - 1900 North Beauregard Street (Schlesinger Center & Various locations (indoors and out) around town 22314. www.alexsym.org. Phone: (703) 845-8005.

Charismatic virtuosity has guided the ASO through critically-acclaimed performances full of passion, power and emotion. They have an annual Children's Holiday Concert and Children's Art Festival each year. Students are inspired to create beautiful artwork while listening to the music.

ALEXANDRIA COLONIAL TOURS

Alexandria - 221 King Street (Ramsay House Visitors Center) 22314. Phone: (703) 838-4200. https://www.alexcolonialtours.com/historytours   Admission: $15.00 adult, $10.00 child. Parking: Obtain a FREE pass at the Visitor's Center. Tours: Daily tour departs Friday-Sunday at 2:00pm from the garden. (March-November) weather permitting.

KING STREET TROLLEY: Runs 11:00am-11pm daily, this FREE trolley runs between N Union Street and the King Street Metro station, making stops for hopping on and off along Old Town's streets.

A 60-minute tour walking by many of Old Town's significant landmarks, as well as little known sites. Learn history beginning from the French / Indian War even through current events. Questions will be answered about: Why are there "snowbirds" on roofs? Why are some of the drainpipes marked, Alexandria, DC instead of Virginia? During the Civil War, how was Alexandria used by Union troops? Why is Christ Church considered, "in the woods" even though it is located right in town? Where did the first Union soldier die in the Civil War? Where did Washington stay when he was in town? Where did he hold birthday parties? Be sure to look for a "busybody" and the sign of the "pineapple story". It is presented in a fun way to hold your attention by some very enthusiastic and energetic tour guides! Note: The 1½ tour is delightful for about 4th graders and up (who have studied American History). Younger children (particularly without strollers) will tire quickly.

CHRIST CHURCH

Alexandria - 118 North Washington Street (Olde Town) 22314. Phone: (703) 549-1450. www.historicchristchurch.org. Hours: Wednesday 1-4:00pm, Thursday/Friday 9:00am-4:00pm, Saturday Noon-4:00pm, Sunday, 2:00-4:30pm plus visitors are welcome to attend services at 8:00am, 9:00am, 11:15am, and 5:00pm. (Visitors can actually sit in the Washington family pew - first come, first served). Admission: FREE, donations accepted.

Men and women from the parish serve as docents and welcome visitors to Christ Church throughout the year. The docents point out the church's most interesting architectural features and history. Built in 1773, George Washington attended church here (pew #60) and Robert E. Lee was also confirmed here. In the early days, rent was charged for a family pew in lieu of tithes (and if you didn't show up for church...everyone knew!). Notice the wine goblet shaped pulpit with a sounding board overhead. No microphone was used - then or today. The Union army took over this church during the Civil War. Although the structure suffered no serious damage, the grave markers were removed and stacked to make room for the camps. No records exist of where the markers were...so it's anybody's guess if the graves are now correctly marked. Find the grave that shows a woman living to be 156 years old...really?

For updates visit: www.KidsLoveTravel.com

FREEDOM HOUSE MUSEUM

Alexandria (Mason Neck) - 1315 Duke Street (old town, near outskirts, King Street Metro is 3 blocks away) 22314. Phone: (703) 836-2858. https://nvulypn.wildapricot.org/Visit-the-Museum   Hours: Thursday- Friday 11:00am-4:00pm, Saturday 11:00am-5:00pm, Sunday & Monday 1-5:00pm. Self-guided tours. Guided tours by appt. Admission: FREE.

Once headquarters for the slave-trade operations in this area, the historic building now houses this museum. Franklin, Armfield & Co. were the largest domestic slave trading company in the country. Thousands of men, women, and children passed through these doors on the horrific journey to lives of bondage and hard labor in the deep south. Black wire mannequins stage the sad state slaves were reduced to. Learn why they needed so many slaves.

FRIENDSHIP FIREHOUSE MUSEUM

Alexandria - 107 South Alfred Street, Old Town 22314. Phone: (703) 838-3891. http://oha.alexandriava.gov/friendship/.   Hours: Open one Saturday per month 11:00am-5:00pm. Closed New Years and Christmas. Admission: $2.00.

The Friendship Fire Company was established in 1774, and was the first volunteer fire company in Alexandria. The current firehouse was built in 1855, remodeled in 1871 and renovated in 1992. The Engine Room on the first floor houses hand-drawn fire engines, leather water buckets, axes, sections of early rubber hose and other historic fire-fighting equipment. Fun to look at for a quick trip inside, out of the hot sun.

FRIENDSHIP FIREHOUSE FESTIVAL

Alexandria. Friendship Firehouse grounds. The popular family event features antique fire apparatus, craft booths, displays by Alexandria merchants, and live music. In addition to the day's outdoor events, festival participants enjoy visiting the Friendship Firehouse Museum, originally built as a firehouse in 1855. Look for the hand-drawn fire engines, leather water buckets, old axes and antique fire truck. Food and beverages are available. Children receive free fire helmets, meet a real Dalmatian, and are treated to a supervised visit inside the City's fire trucks. FREE. (first Saturday in August)

GADSBY'S TAVERN & MUSEUM

Alexandria - 134 North Royal Street (Olde Town) 22314. Phone: (703) 838-4242, Restaurant: (703) 548-1288. www.gadsbystavern.org. Hours: Museum: Thursday - Friday 11:00am-4:00pm, Saturday 11:00am-5:00pm, Sunday 1:00-5:00pm. Restaurant: 7 days for lunch/dinner. Colonial entertainment in the evenings. Admission: Museum: $5.00 adult, $3.00 child (5-12). Restaurant prices: Lunch $15.00. Child's menu $10.00 all day. Dinner prices: Average $25.00.

Guided Tours: offered most days right before/after lunch through afternoon. Tours start at a quarter after hour and a quarter before the hour, lasting approx 30 minutes. $8.00 per person. On summer Friday nights they offer tours by lantern for the family. Note: Stairs on tour.

Take a moment to journey back to the 18th-century tavern and hotel where famous historical figures and everyday people dined and slept. "General Washington's steward had recommended me an inn kept by Mr. Gadsby..." This is the place if you're in the mood for authentic colonial dining (fresh fish, crabcakes, Virginia ham and pyes - potpie puff pastry) that is served by a costumed wait staff who speak old English. The museum is in the 1770 City Tavern and City Hotel where many political and social events occurred (even Washington's birthday parties). Notice the ice well where they kept ice all year long and could serve cold beverages in the heat of summer (something very few establishments could do). Notable guests and stories of visits included on tour are Washington, Jefferson, Robert E. Lee, and their wives.

HISTORIC CANDLELIGHT TOURS

Alexandria. Gadsby's Tavern. Take a break from the pace of the season & experience the charm and history of Old Town with this holiday celebration. Tour Carlyle House, Gadsby's Tavern Museum, Lee-Fendall House and a special guest site by candlelight and enjoy decorations, entertainment and refreshments. Reservations are recommended. Admission. (second Saturday in December)

OLD TOWN SCAVENGER HUNT

Alexandria - (pick up hunt page 105 N. Union Street) 22314. Retail store: (703) 548-2829.   https://www.scavengerhunt.com/locations/Old_Town_Alexandria_Scavenger_Hunt.html. Tours: You can purchase your Scavenger Hunt online or at the store. (near the Ramsay House Visitor Center). Open daily. Cost $12.99 per player (5 & older). Educators: The hunt is geared towards ages 8-11 who are studying early American history.

Young Adventurers, you will hunt through the brick-lined streets of historic Old Town Alexandria. Discover clues and facts about George Washington and his seaport hometown. The Hunt is a self-guided walk. On the Hunt you will search for historic places and literally walk in our first President's footsteps. Each hunt takes about 45 minutes. The Hunt is fun for families to take together - split into teams and see who wins!

POTOMAC RIVERBOAT COMPANY

Alexandria - Union & Cameron Streets (City Marina) 22314. Phone: (703) 548-9000 or (877) 502-2628. www.potomacriverboatco.com. Admission depends on tour chosen. Tours: 5 times daily (each way) - Tuesday-Sunday, 11:30am-9:00pm (May-September). Plus Monday Holidays and Weekends (April & October).

Some of the tours offered include:

- **SEAPORT** - 50 minute, narrated sightseeing cruise of Alexandria's historic waterfront. Water taxi from $17.00.
- **MOUNT VERNON** - cruise from "old town" to the Mount Vernon Estate. 50 minutes each way. (Mt. Vernon admission included in ticket price) from $55.00.
- **MONUMENTS** - round trip, 60 minute cruise (each way) past Washington's majestic landmarks. Can get off in Georgetown and catch a later boat. From $15
- **PIRATES ON THE POTOMAC CRUISE** - During this 40-minute cruise, children of all ages will be entertained with music and tales of piracy on the Potomac River. This cruise features Alexandria's historic seaport and its landmarks. May through September, Friday, Saturday, and Sunday.

All tours are narrated with fun facts, history and legends. Sailing schedule is subject to weather and river conditions. Contact by website, brochure or telephone is suggested to obtain current sailing schedule. Some younger children may prefer this method of touring.

STABLER-LEADBEATER APOTHECARY MUSEUM

Alexandria - 105-107 South Fairfax Street, Old Town 22314. Phone: (703) 838-3852. http://oha.alexandriava.gov/apothecary/ap-mission.html. Hours: Wednesday - Friday 11:00am-4:00pm, Saturday 11:00am-5:00pm, Sunday 1:00-5:00pm. Closed: New Year's Day, Thanksgiving, Christmas. Admission: $5.00 adult, $3.00 youth (11-17). Children under 11: FREE.

When the Apothecary closed during the Depression, in 1933, the doors were simply locked, preserving the contents for history. The building re-opened as a museum in 1939. Over 8,000 objects, including pill rollers, mortars and pestles, drug mills, and hand-blown medicine bottles with gold-leaf labels, were left in place. Medicinal herbs and paper labels remain in their wooden drawers. Large show-globes from the mid-19th century remain in the windows. Original apothecaries created their medicine onsite using herbs and other ingredients. The names of famous customers appear in several original documents, including Martha Washington, James Monroe, and Robert E. Lee. According to an 1802 letter from Mount Vernon, "Mrs. Washington desires Mr. Stabler to send by the bearer a quart bottle of his best Castor Oil and the bill for it." Tours of the museum show how the apothecaries plied their trade and give a glimpse into the "drug stores" of early America. Funny how remedies of the past are now creeping back into modern herbal remedies…

TORPEDO FACTORY ART CENTER

Alexandria - 105 North Union Street 22314. www.torpedofactory.org. Phone: (703) 838-4565.   Hours: Daily 10:00am-5:00pm. Closed on Easter, July 4th, Thanksgiving, Christmas, and New Year's Day. Admission: FREE.

Constructed in 1918 for the manufacturing of torpedoes, the factory now serves as working studios for over 82 professional artists. Visitors can purchase wares onsite or simply watch the creative process in action. Gaze at the dozens of studios and ask a question of the artist working on something unusual. Watch anything from sculpture, to painting, jewelry, stained glass, weaving, printmaking, ceramics, to photography being created.

UNITED STATES PATENT & TRADEMARK OFFICE/NAT'L INVENTORS HALL OF FAME

Alexandria - 600 Dulany Street (in the atrium of the Madison Building, take King Street and Eisenhower Metro stop) 22314. https://www.invent.org/museum/plan-your-visit Phone: (571) 272-0095. Hours: Monday-Friday 10:00am-5:00pm, first Saturday of the month 11:00am-3:00pm. Admission: FREE. Parking: Find convenient parking in the East Garage at 551 John Carlyle St. for max $10 fee.

For updates visit: www.KidsLoveTravel.com

Looking at the exhibits, you will realize how you take advantage of inventions and rely on trademarks every day of your life. Intellectual property is found in the routines you follow at the beginning of the day, in methods you use for travel, in medical innovations you rely upon for good health, and in the different ways you relax and play. Look over videos, interactives, artifacts and touch-screem technology featuring patents, trademarks, inventors and inventions. Every season, they change displays of famous patents-like Michael Jackson's anti-gravity boots or Edison's first record. The Talking Gallery of famous inventors is interesting and whimsical but kids really get inspired by the 7-minute movie shown about modern inventors of extreme sports equipment! Buy a cute invention in the gift shop as a souvenir.

JUNETEENTH COMMEMORATION

Alexandria - Black History Museum. www.alexblackhistory.org. On June 19, 1865, slaves in Texas first learned of their emancipation more than two years after Lincoln's Emancipation Proclamation. Juneteenth commemorates a joyous day in African-American history. This family-oriented celebration includes music, a reading of the Emancipation Proclamation, entertainment and food. Admission. (June 19th)

USA & ALEXANDRIA BIRTHDAY CELEBRATION

Alexandria - Oronoco Bay Park, Pendleton & Union streets. Celebrate with a concert by the Alexandria Symphony Orchestra, food, including birthday cake, and fireworks. Festivities start at 4:00pm with entertainment beginning at 6:00pm and the grand finale fireworks at 9:30pm. www.alexandriava.gov/recreation. (second Saturday in July)

CAMPAGNA CENTER'S SCOTTISH CHRISTMAS PARADE WALK

Alexandria - The Campagna Center. www.scottishchristmaswalk.com. This parade honors the city's Scottish heritage. In total, more than 100 Scottish clans dressed in traditional tartans and playing bagpipes march through historic streets of Alexandria, along with a living history reenactment. Free. (Dec, first weekend)

BUGSY'S PIZZA

Alexandria - Just down the street from the Visitors Center is Bugsy's Pizza (111 King Street, 703-683-0313, www.bugsyspizza.com) with original beams in the building made from tobacco boats. All you can eat pizza and salad lunch buffet. Just $6.75. Many pizzas are unique combos to try (esp. at the pizza buffet). Across the street is another hometown favorite - The Scoop Ice Cream. If there's a nip in the air and you don't have a fancy for ice cream, have a helping of homemade cobbler (blueberry, apple, cherry or peach) from the pie case on the counter. Ice cream flavors run the spectrum: cherry blossom, lemon custard, peanut butter, maple nut, and new batches are made fresh every day. After all that food, walk just one block to the riverfront.

EMBASSY SUITES OLD TOWN

Alexandria - 900 Diagonal Road. Family Fun Packages all year. Your kids get a "kid-tested" pack of goodies, an indoor pool, soft play area for toddlers, and the whole family gets a wonderful cooked to order full breakfast and snacks before dinner. All rooms are suites with separate bedroom, microwave, and refrigerator from around $170.00/night. Hotel is directly across the street from the King Street Metro Station (Blue/ Yellow Line/ Amtrak/Virginia Rail Express) - (800) EMBASSY or http://embassysuites1.hilton.com

HAMPTON INN ALEXANDRIA - OLD TOWN / KING STREET

Alexandria - Old Town is at 1616 King Street, (703) 299-9900. www.hilton.com A nice choice for DC/Alexandria area lodging. They offer On the House™ hot breakfast buffet served from 6:00-10:00am each morning featuring rotating hot entrees, premium coffees and teas, fresh fruits, cereals, and freshly baked breakfast pastries and are a quick 2 block walk to the Metro or an even quicker step out the door to Old Town historic attractions. There's an outdoor pool, too. Packages and weekend rates around $119.00.

GUNSTON HALL

Alexandria (Mason Neck) - 10709 Gunston Road (I-95 or US Rte. 1 to SR 242 east) 22079. Phone: (703) 550-9220 or (800) 811-6966. www.gunstonhall.org. Hours: Daily 9:30am-4:30pm. Closed New Years, Thanksgiving, and Christmas. Admission: $10.00 general admission, $5.00 grounds pass. Online coupon. Tours: Guided house tours are offered every half hour. These tours focus on the life of George Mason and his family; they tell of the slaves, servants, and the others who worked for the Mason family; and point out the architectural features of the house. The house tour takes approximately 45 minutes. Educators: Grade appropriate Curriculum guides and videos can be reserved online.

For updates visit: www.KidsLoveTravel.com

North East Area

The colonial plantation home of George Mason, author of the Virginia Declaration of Rights and a framer of the United States Constitution, this house has elaborately carved woodwork.

Reconstructed outbuildings help to illustrate the work of domestic servants and slaves. There's a nature trail and a short orientation film presented in the Visitors Center. Special events make this even more interesting. "That all men are born equally free and independent, and have certain inherent natural Rights... among which are the Enjoyment of Life and Liberty, with the Means of acquiring and possessing Property, and pursuing and obtaining Happiness and Safety." -- George Mason. Virginia Declaration of Rights, May, 1776. Sounds familiar-yes?

PLANTATION CHRISTMAS & FAMILY HOLIDAY

Alexandria. Gunston Hall Plantation. Visitors can see how families lived and celebrated the holidays in 19th century homes, aglow in candlelight and decorated with native plant material, fruits and flowers. Cider by the fireplace, open-hearth cooking demonstrations, carriage rides. Buffet of yuletide fare available. Admission. (December, second weekend)

MOUNT VERNON, GEORGE WASHINGTON'S

Alexandria (Mount Vernon) - 3200 Mount Vernon Memorial Hwy (end of George Washington Memorial Parkway) 22121. www.mountvernon.org. Phone: (703) 780-2000. Hours: Daily 8:00am-5:00pm (April - August), 9:00am-5:00pm (March, September, October), 9:00am-4:00pm (rest of the year). Admission: $28.00 adult, $15.00 Child (6-11). Timed mansion tours are $2.00 extra. Note: Antenna Audio Tours feature lively narration of what you're seeing and include kid-friendly info. Food Court Pavilion and expanded Shops at Mount Vernon. Pathways in the historic area consist of gravel, dirt, and bricks, but

The anticipation builds as you approach the gates...

are stroller accessible. Strollers are not allowed in the Mansion. Nearby is a Working 18th-century mill (George Washington's Gristmill is 3 miles away) and features guides leading historic tours. Meet a miller and watch the water-wheel operate the stones grinding grain into flour (small additional fee). Educators: everything you could ever want to study about G.W. is on the "Education.Teachers Resources" pages including Lesson Plans and kids games & quizzes.

Explore history and get to know the "real" George Washington. Located just inside the main entrance to Mount Vernon, the Reynolds Museum & Ford Orientation Center introduces visitors to the personality and character of George Washington with a dramatic 15-minute film. When the cannons roar, the seats rumble. When you're crossing the Delaware River, the snow falls on you.

Be Washington: The newest space places you in Washington's boots. Take a seat at an interactive kiosk, and watch advisers like Thomas Jefferson, Alexander Hamilton, and James Madison appear on the screen. Choose whose counsel you wish to hear and consider their advice on real challenges in history. From there, it's your turn to act—decide your course of action and learn how Washington handled the same dilemma. Each Be Washington scenario takes an estimated 18 minutes to complete.

Another attraction is the "Mount Vernon in Miniature," an authentic, one-twelfth scale version of the Mansion. Tons of colorful dioramas take you on a personal tour of Washington's life. Now, look upon the view and take a self-guided tour featuring:

- **HANDS ON HISTORY ROOM** (Reynold Education Ctr.) - Learn how to bridle and sit on a mule; The Root Cellar - What archeological items could be found in a cellar? (answer: bottles, keys, bones from cooked food); Dress up with a wide array of Colonial clothers or play house using a scale model dollhouse, or take your picture with the Washingtons.

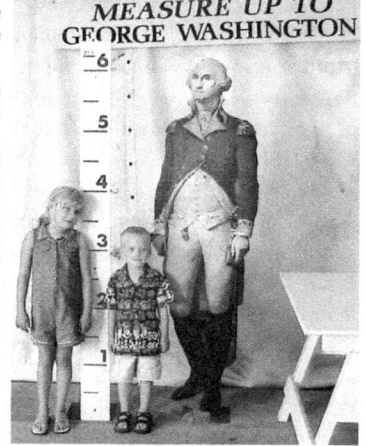

- **PIONEER FARMER** - Ever see a round barn? How about a barn where horses walk the 2nd floor? Crack corn, thresh wheat or taste a hoecake. Visit with livestock authentic to George Washington's times. A reconstructed slave cabin on the site reflects the living conditions of slaves on the Mount Vernon plantation. (open April-Oct)
- **OUTBUILDINGS** - Dung Depository (Washington was one of the first composters), coach house and stable, laundry yard, smokehouse, clerk's office and kitchen.
- **GEORGE WASHINGTON'S TOMB** - See the original site and see the actual vault where George Washington's body now lies.

Of course, the true highlight of this visit will be your HOUSE TOUR. During peak season, be prepared for a 30-90 minute wait to enter. Once inside, you'll see many authentic furnishings and learn of Washington's unique color choices for rooms (many are bright and cheerful like the giant green room where he and Martha loved to dance!) Look for the letter press (a carbon copy like machine) that General Washington used to make copies of all letters that were sent. (He wrote so many... and at that time they took so long to get delivered that sometimes you could forget what you wrote if you didn't keep a copy!). You'll also see a giant globe in his office that strangely is missing one entire continent (could it be that it wasn't discovered yet?).

GEORGE WASHINGTON'S BIRTHDAY CELEBRATION

Mount Vernon. The traditional presidential wreath-laying ceremony occurs at 10:00am, followed by patriotic music and military performances on the bowling green. Open house, Friendship Firehouse, Gadsby's Tavern Museum, and a Birthday Parade around town. There's a Revolutionary War Encampment at Fort Ward Park. Sample Washington's favorite breakfast (hoecakes & butter & honey while they last). Admission: Free. (February – President's Day weekend)

AMERICAN CELEBRATION AT MOUNT VERNON

Mount Vernon invites visitors for a day-long celebration of Independence Day. 18th-century patriotic music, a reading of the Declaration of Independence by "George Washington," the annual Red, White & Blue Concert performance by the National Concert Band of America, and FREE birthday cake (while supplies last). The First Virginia Regiment expands its encampment with military checkpoints across the estate, and guards stationed at Washington's Tomb. The Sons of the American Revolution lead a wreath laying ceremony at the tomb of our nation's first Commander-in-Chief, and visitors given a carnation to lay at the Tomb. Admission. (4th of July)

FALL HARVEST FAMILY DAYS

Mt. Vernon. Pioneer Farmer Site. Games, wagon rides, music, 18th century craft and harvest demonstrations. Make a cornhusk doll, find way through straw bale maze and meet George. Ever roast apples? Kids get to here! Slave-live interpreters and yummy open-fire cooking. This weekend, sightseeing cruises, courtesy of Spirit Cruises and Potomac Riverboat Company, available half-price. Free pumpkins. Admission fee per family. (October, third weekend)

CHRISTMAS AT MOUNT VERNON

Mt. Vernon. The Washingtons' seasonal entertaining is authentically interpreted daily. Visitors learn about holiday activities at Mount Vernon, as well tour the mansion, including the rarely-seen third floor. Christmas trees, gingerbread houses and the Christmas camel. Fresh chocolate made over an open fire. Dance the Virginia Reel. Admission fee. (Thanksgiving weekend – weekend after New Years)

Arlington

ARLINGTON NATIONAL CEMETERY

Arlington - (Ample paid parking is available to visitors, accessible from Memorial Drive) 22211. https://arlingtoncemetery.mil Phone: (703) 697-2131, (202) 554-5100 or (888) 868-7707. Hours: The Cemetery opens to the public at 8:00am every day, closing 5:00pm. Tram Tours Daily 9:00am-4:00pm, depart every 30 minutes. Admission: Walking tour is FREE. www.arlingtontours.com. Tourmobiles fare is $17.95 adult, $13.95 senior (65A+), $9.95 child (4-12) (Arlington Tours). We suggest parking at Arlington and then Tourmobiling around DC. Parking: the cost is $1.75/hour for the first three hours, and $2.00/hour thereafter. Tours: Begin at Welcome Center on Memorial Avenue starting one half hour after cemetery opens until one half hour before cemetery closes. Last tour begins 30 minutes before closing. Closed on Christmas. Note: The tourmobile is suggested for kids because the walking tour is too long.

This is the best spot to visit (especially by tourmobile), to get to the heart of Arlington. Many sites are on, or near the grounds, and some can be toured individually or as part of the tour. The tour includes the Kennedy gravesites; the Tomb of the Unknowns for the Changing of the Guard ceremony (24/7 - Look how still the guards are!); the Arlington House, The Robert E. Lee Memorial (where Lee lived for 30 years, where he chose to resign his commission in the US Army to defend Virginia in the Civil War, and where Union troops occupied it during the Civil War - Open daily, 9:30am-4:30pm, Free, 703-557-0613). Narrators on the tourmobile relate accounts of personal sacrifice and heroism as you ride past the important sites. Lots of little known facts and anecdotes. Check out the newer "Women in Military Service for America Memorial" where you'll see an emotional, patriotic film and learn many little known stories of women who served as water bearers, nurses, and POW's (the building is entirely covered in a "glass ceiling").

John F. Kennedy's gravesite burns an "Eternal Flame"

MEMORIAL DAY

Arlington & Washington DC Memorials. (800) 222-2294. Join in a formal ceremony honoring all the men and women who took up arms in defense of America and paid the ultimate price for our freedom. (May, Memorial Day)

For updates visit: www.KidsLoveTravel.com

North East Area

ASHLAND STRAWBERRY FAIRE

Ashland - Randolph Macon College. www.ashlandstrawberryfaire.com. (804) 798-8289. Guests can enjoy fresh-picked strawberries by the quart or in one of the delicious recipes cooked by the food vendors, who compete for the top honor in the "Best Strawberry Food Contest." Live entertainment. FREE. (June, mid-month Saturday)

SCOTCHTOWN, HISTORIC HOME OF PATRICK HENRY

Ashland (Beaverdam) - 16120 Chiswell Lane (I-95 exit 92B, off US 54, W. Patrick Henry Hwy. On SR 671. 11 miles NW of Ashland) 23015. Phone: (804) 227-3500 or (800) 897-1479. https://preservationvirginia.org/historic-sites/patrick-henrys-scotchtown/. Hours: Friday-Saturday 10:00am-5:00pm, Sunday 11:00am-5:00pm (March-December). Admission: $15.00 adult, $12.00 senior, $10.00 student.

Built in 1719 by Charles Chiswell, Scotchtown was the home for Patrick Henry, Virginia's first elected governor, from 1771 to 1778, and is one of the oldest plantation houses in Virginia. Scotchtown, for a short period, was also the childhood home of Dolley Madison. The Manor houses three original Henry family pieces and is unique in that all the living quarters are on one floor. Remembered best for his oratory: "Give me liberty or give me death!"

Chantilly

NATIONAL AIR AND SPACE MUSEUM / UDVAR-HAZY CENTER

Chantilly - 14390 Air and Space Museum Parkway (near Dulles International Airport at the intersection of routes 28 and 50) 20151. Phone: (202) 633-1000. https://airandspace.si.edu/visit/udvar-hazy-center Hours: Daily 10:00am-5:30pm, except Christmas. Admission: FREE. Parking Lot: Yes, public parking is $15 in Chantilly. IMAX is additional $5.00 per show. Note: A round-trip shuttle bus offers transportation between the Museum's National Mall building in Washington D.C. and the Udvar-Hazy Center in Chantilly, Virginia. Buses arrive/depart from the Jefferson Drive (north) side of the National Mall building and the Udvar-Hazy Center's main entrance. ($9.00-$12.00 per person fee). Educators: Teaching Posters & Guides are available to order or download online.

The museum is designed to memorialize and inspire wonder, quicken pulses and make spirits soar. The large Boeing Aviation Hangar has aircraft displayed on three levels. Visitors can walk among aircraft and small artifacts in display cases located on the floor, and view aircraft hanging from the arched ceiling on elevated skywalks. Many experimental flying machines are on display.

KIDS LOVE VIRGINIA

Peer inside a space capsule, get a feel of weightlessness during an IMAX film or view the hundreds of aircraft on display. The flying machines on view at the Virginia center's Aviation Hangar include the only successful supersonic airplane ever built (the Concorde), the fastest plane and the first airliner with a pressurized cabin. In the Space Hanger, you'll see the Gemini VII and Mercury 15B spacecraft and the shuttle Enterprise. In addition, the Observation Tower provides an excellent location from which visitors can watch air traffic at Dulles Airport.

If your kids get bogged down at the National Mall museums (too much history), this might be a more spacious, less rushed museum to try. Can you believe this site is just an annex to the National Mall building (they had so many extra artifacts they needed to house elsewhere)?

Colonial Beach

GEORGE WASHINGTON BIRTHPLACE NATIONAL MONUMENT

Colonial Beach - 1732 Popes Creek Road (off SR 3 south side of the Potomac River) 22443. Phone: (804) 224-1732. www.nps.gov/gewa. Hours: Daily, 9:00am-5:00pm. Closed Thanksgiving Day, Christmas and New Years Day Admission: FREE Note: Ranger talks offered on the hour 10:00am-4:00pm. Educators: Excellent Workbooks and Lesson Plans on Washington and the natural history: www.nps.gov/gewa/forteachers/classrooms/curriculummaterials.htm

George Washington was born on his father's Pope tobacco farm on February 22, 1732. When George was 3 1/2, his father took his family to live at Mount Vernon. In 1779 the home where Washington was born, burned. A Memorial House was built near the spot in 1930. Today the National Park Service operates a colonial farm where costumed interpreters recreate the sights, sounds and smells of 18th century plantation life. Daily activities include a 14-minute film at the visitor center/museum, tours of the memorial house, the colonial kitchen, spinning shop and the farm buildings. Also on the property: Some of the brick foundation of the original house where he was born, The Washington Family Cemetery: where George's father, grandfather, and great-grandfather are buried, a picnic grounds with a nature trail, and the Potomac River beach area (sunning, not swimming, is allowed). Come to see where the first President of the United States was born.

GEORGE WASHINGTON'S BIRTHDAY PARTY

Colonial Beach. Washington Birthplace. George Washington Birthplace National Monument. Visitors can celebrate George Washington's birthday with special park ranger programs commemorating the event. Gingerbread and hot cider will be served in the log house. On his actual birthday, February 22nd, Birthday cake served at 1:00 pm in the visitor center. The birth site will be illuminated by candle lanterns all day. Free. (February – President's Day weekend)

WASHINGTON CHRISTMAS

Colonial Beach. George Washington Birthplace National Monument. The Memorial House at George Washington's Birthplace is decorated for Christmas, candlelit and filled with colonial music. The plantation is busy as costumed interpreters depict holiday preparations in colonial times. Admission fee. (December, Saturday after Christmas)

SKY MEADOWS STATE PARK

Delaplane - 11012 Edmonds Lane (one mile south on SR 17 at Rte. 710 west) 20144. Phone: (540) 592-3556. www.dcr.virginia.gov/state_parks/sky.shtml. Hours: 8:00am-dusk Visitor Center 10am-4pm. Admission: $5.00 per vehicle.

This park offers a peaceful getaway on the eastern side of the Blue Ridge Mountains. Rich in history, the park has rolling pastures and woodlands, and scenic vistas. The park also has access to the Appalachian Trail and a primitive hike-in campground, as well as picnicking, hiking and riding trails, interpretive programs and a visitor center in the historic Mount Bleak House (video presentation, nature walks). The historic Mount Bleak House is furnished as a middle-class farmhouse (about 1860) and serves as the park's visitor center. It is open during the summer and on weekends in the spring and fall. Tours are offered on weekends and holidays.

Fredericksburg

FREDERICKSBURG AREA MUSEUM

Fredericksburg - 907 Princess Anne Street (corner of Princess Anne and William Streets) 22401. Phone: (540) 371-3037. https://famva.org. Hours: Thursday-Tuesday 10:00am-5:00pm. Admission: $5.00 adult, $3.00 student (7-18). Educators: Trail to Freedom Tool Kit under Teachers Resources.

Housed in the old 1816 Town Hall / Market House, the Federal building survived the destruction of the Civil War. This museum displays artifacts of the town starting with the formation of North America and proceeding to the present. Children enjoy the dinosaur footprints that were found in the area, as well as an Indian hut and Colonial fort, and period weapons used in the Revolutionary and Civil Wars. Look for the actual newspaper from 1767!

FREDERICKSBURG TROLLEY TOURS

Fredericksburg - Fredericksburg Visitors Center, 706 Caroline Street. 22401. www.fredericksburgtrolley.com. Phone: (540) 898-0737. Admission: $25.00 adult, $22.00 military, $10.00 child (6-12). Tours: Start at the Fredericksburg Visitor Center. 75 minute tours depart 2-3 times daily (every couple hours or so).

Enjoy an entertaining and informative tour of Fredericksburg aboard the trolley. Hear information about Chatham House and 50 of the 100 historic homes in town (even the oldest one). The tavern wench, the Apothecary assistant and "Mary Washington (George's mom)" will come out and wave as you pass by. See the original stonewall of the battlefield. Funny tidbits: Why were some homes built in layers? What happened if you didn't go to church at least twice a month in the Anglican Church? Why did they build narrow homes? This tour is a great way to hear the Revolutionary and Civil War history of Fredericksburg with a great overview of the museums and restaurants in town. Afterwards, you'll know which spots you want to personally visit.

HISTORIC KENMORE

Fredericksburg - 1201 Washington Avenue 22401. www.kenmore.org. Phone: (540) 373-3381. Hours: Monday-Saturday 10:00am-5:00pm, Sunday Noon-5pm (March-December). Closing at 4pm (November, December). Closed major winter holidays. Admission: $12.00 adult, $6.00 student (ages 6-17 or with student ID). Note: Summer Discovery Workshops and Colonial theatre. FREEBIES: kids stuff page has puzzles, coloring and games.

Kenmore, one of the most elegant Colonial mansions in America, lies in the heart of historic Fredericksburg. Built in 1775 by Fielding Lewis for his wife Betty, the sister of George Washington, the house is currently undergoing a major restoration. Tours focus on the building of the house and the craftsmen and artisans who worked on it. What did colonists use to start fires, make brushes, and protect toddlers from injury? What two-century-old clues are hidden behind plaster and paneling? Why are there decorative brick arches in the cellar? Does the house have a secret passage? What unusual object has been stored in the attic for over 100 years? The best time to visit is during Family Tours or special events: Parents and children (age 4 and above) learn about the lives of 18th century Virginians in family tours designed with hands-on activities. No reservations needed. Usually summer weekday mornings or year-round weekend re-enactments.

GEORGE WASHINGTON'S BIRTHDAY

Fredericksburg. Historic Kenmore Plantation & Gardens. The nation's first President was a frequent visitor to the elegant, colonial mansion of his sister, Betty Washington Lewis in Fredericksburg. Special character tour and FREE kids admission on President's Day. $5.00 adults. (February - weekday during President's week)

HUGH MERCER APOTHECARY SHOP

Fredericksburg - 1020 Caroline Street (Old Town) 22401. Phone: (540) 373-3362.

www.washingtonheritagemuseums.org. Hours: Wednesday-Saturday 11:00am-4:00pm, Monday 11:00am-4:00pm, Sunday Noon-4pm. Closed winter holidays. Admission: $7.00 adult, $3.00 student (6-18). Half price admission on President's Day. Note: Living Legacies annual September event features exhibits and demonstrations honoring the crafts of the 18th and 19th centuries.

Dr. Mercer practiced medicine for fifteen years in Fredericksburg. His patients included Mary Washington. Walk into this 18th century doctor's office and learn about all the interesting things that were used for medicines back then. While smelling the entertaining scents from unusual (mostly herbal) medicines, visitors may (or may not!) want to view utensils formerly used for draining blood, amputating, pulling teeth and performing operations. You will even see a saw that looks like it belongs in a tool box! On the way out, stop by the garden to view herbs and plants used for medicinal purposes. They've got real leeches in here! Does mom ever say – "You're driving me crazy..."? They've got the perfect medicinal cure here!

MARY WASHINGTON HOUSE

Fredericksburg - 1200 Charles Street (downtown) 22401. Phone: (540) 373-1569. www.washingtonheritagemuseums.org. Hours: Wednesday-Saturday, 11:00am-4:00pm, Monday 11:00am-4:00pm, Sunday Noon-4:00pm. Closed January 1, Thanksgiving, December 24, 25, 31. Admission: $7.00 adult, $3.00 child (6-18). Half price admission on President's Day. Note: Living Legacies annual September event features exhibits and demonstrations honoring the crafts of the 18th and 19th centuries.

Mary Ball Washington spent the last 17 years of her life in this home bought for her by her son, George Washington, in 1772. The white frame house sits on the corner of Charles and Lewis Streets and was in walking distance to Kenmore, home of Mary's daughter Betty Fielding Lewis. Some of Mary's original personal possessions, including her "best dressing glass" and the boxwood bushes she planted years ago are present. The most interesting room is the old kitchen quarters.

MOTHER'S DAY

Mary Washington House. (800) 678-4748. George Washington's sentimental farewell to his mother as he left for his presidential inauguration in 1789 is dramatically re-created every 30 minutes. Admission.

CANDLELIGHT TOUR OF THE MARY WASHINGTON HOUSE

Mary Washington House. Christmas open house that features an evening of candlelight tours and refreshments. Free. (first Sunday night in December)

RISING SUN TAVERN

Fredericksburg - 1304 Caroline Street, Old Town 22401. Phone: (540) 371-1494. www.washingtonheritagemuseums.org. Hours: Wednesday-Saturday 11:00am-4:00pm, Monday 11:00am-4:00pm, Sunday Noon-4:00pm. Admission: $7.00 adult, $3.00 student (6-18). Half price admission on President's Day. Note: Living Legacies annual September event features exhibits and demonstrations honoring the crafts of the 18th and 19th centuries.

Built by Charles Washington in 1760 as his home, this building was later operated as a tavern, the only "proper" tavern in the bustling port city of Fredericksburg. Discover popular pub phrases and terms, while learning about the life of a "tavern wench". She'll show you an early cash register, an 18th century mousetrap, and the confined sleeping quarters used then. Visitors can learn about subjects as serious as the separation of educated men from common men. There are silly things, too, like the bathing rituals of those times (they bathed completely only twice a year!). The Rising Sun was a "proper" tavern (as defined in those times)…never more than 5 to a bed!

CHRISTMAS OPEN HOUSE AT THE RISING SUN TAVERN

Rising Sun Tavern. Join them for a holiday open house featuring 18th-c. entertainment and refreshments. On this occasion the Tavern features the sights and sounds of Christmas. Free (first Friday night in December)

RIVERSIDE CENTER DINNER THEATRE

Fredericksburg - 95 Riverside Parkway 22406. Phone: (540) 370-4300 or (888) 999-8527. www.riversidedt.com.

Watch favorite American tales come to life on stage. This professionally performed musical is geared especially for children of all ages. You will be charmed by the cast as they serve a fabulous lunch to your table. Productions like: Jack and the Giant or Willy Wonka. Saturday Matinees and selected weekday matinees, year-round. Lunch and show is about $20.00 per person.

FREDERICKSBURG AND SPOTSYLVANIA CIVIL WAR BATTLEFIELDS

Fredericksburg - (I-95 south to Rte. 3 exit east. At intersection of Rte. 3 & Bus Rte. 1) 22407. Phone: (540) 373-6122. www.nps.gov/frsp. Hours: Parks open daily dawn to dusk. Visitors Centers open 9:00am-5:00pm daily except Thanksgiving, Christmas and New Years. Admission: Free. Tours: The popular History at Sunset Friday evening walking tours are from June 6 - August 15.

North East Area

The Civil War was one of America's greatest tragedies and no region suffered more than the Fredericksburg area. Four major battles were fought here. Eventually, the cost of these battles would be too much for the South to bear. Two visitors centers help interpret four battlefields. A self-guided tour of the battlefields begins at the Fredericksburg Battlefield and continues into Spotsylvania County. The battlefield parks, wayside exhibits, exhibit shelters, interpretive trails and many historic buildings help tell the story of the Civil War battles. Highlights on the map or audio (rental tape ~$3.00) tour are:

WILDERNESS BATTLEFIELD - May 5-6, 1864. This conflict introduced Union General Grant to Lee in battle. Even though the battle ended in stalemate, Grant pressed southward, "On to Richmond". (Orange, 540-373-4461, Rte 20, 1 mile west of Rte 3)

SPOTSYLVANIA BATTLEFIELD - May 8-21, 1864. On the most direct route to Richmond, warring troops engaged for 2 weeks including 20 hours on May 12 in the most intense hand-to-hand fighting of the war at the "Bloody Angle".

CHANCELLORSVILLE BATTLEFIELD - April 27-May 6, 1863. Action included a spectacular military maneuver by Lee and his most trusted subordinate, "Stonewall Jackson", but the day ended in calamity when Jackson was fatally wounded by his own troops. (I-95, Rte. 3 west)

> Stonewall Jackson died in an outbuilding on the Chandler Plantation at Guinea Station on May 10, 1863. Guinea Station was the busy Confederate supply station during the Chancellorsville Campaign.

FREDERICKSBURG BATTLEFIELD - December 11-15, 1862. Called "Lee's most one-sided victory", the battle focused on Sunken Road and the Stone Wall at Marye's Heights.

CHATHAM - across the Rappahannock River off SR218; mansion served as a Union headquarters and field hospital during the Civil War. Clara Burton and Walt Whitman provided care here to wounded soldiers. Visitors can see a new exhibit containing a replica pontoon boat, modeled after those used to cross the Rappahannock River in the Battle of Fredericksburg. A free movie depicts the impact of the Civil War on area residents. Daily 9:00am-4:30pm. FREE. (540) 371-0802.

GEORGE WASHINGTON'S FERRY FARM

Fredericksburg - 268 Kings Highway (SR 3 east, along the Rappahannock River) 22407. Phone: (540) 370-0732. www.ferryfarm.org. Hours: Daily 10:00am-4:00pm, Noon-5pm Sundays. Open later spring-fall. Closed major winter holidays & January & February. Admission: $12.00 adult, $6.00 student (ages 6-17 and anyone with a student ID). Discovery Workshops may be slightly more but include activity. Discounted Combo tickets to Ferry Farm & Kenmore. FREEBIES: Kids Stuff page has puzzles, coloring and games.

Located 38 miles south of Mount Vernon on the banks of the Rappahannock River, this is the boyhood home of the father of our country…not to mention, the reported place where the famous "cherry tree" incident (and legend) occurred. This was his father's 600 acre plantation where he grew up and later learned how to survey. The current property is under ongoing archeological excavations. After taking a look at the exhibits in the Visitors Center, folks can take a self-guided tour of the farm Washington inherited at age 11 and where he lived between the ages of 6 and 20. Only facades of one home are viewed, but new artifacts turn up all the time. We suggest Discovery Workshops for the kids in the summer. Each workshop teaches hands-on activities about Colonial life at Ferry Farm and the Fredericksburg area. Best of all, the staff here are creative and energetic about the site and interpretation.

GEORGE WASHINGTON'S BIRTHDAY

Fredericksburg. Ferry Farm. Games, crafts, storytelling, and refreshments for children. This is the place where he celebrated 14 of his childhood birthdays. Colonial re-enactors and demos, a stone toss across the Rappahannock River and, of course, birthday cake. Admission (February, President's Day)

FABULOUS 4TH AT FERRY FARM

Fredericksburg - Along the Rappahannock River. (800) 678-4748. Heritage Festival. Live music, raft race, food, children's games, fireworks. FREE. (4TH of July)

GINGERBREAD EXHIBIT

Fredericksburg - Washington's Ferry Farm. This annual Gingerbread House Contest and Exhibit features confectionery delights created by area children and adults. (first Saturday thru the end of December)

CELEBRATION OF JAMES MONROE'S ANNIVERSARY

Fredericksburg - James Monroe Museum. 908 Charles Street. (800) 678-4748, (540) 654-1043. Scottish music and dancing, colonial crafts, and an open house at the James Monroe Museum will honor the anniversary of the birth of our nation's fifth president. FREE. (April-last Saturday)

North East Area

CIVIL WAR LIVING HISTORY

Fredericksburg - Downtown Historic Fredericksburg & nearby battlefields & monuments. (800) 678-4748, Visitors can join in on the celebration of the region's rich heritage, highlighting crafts, dress, music, and merchandise from the colonial era. Re-enactments of battles. Admission for Civil War Tours. (early May for 10 days)

FREDERICKSBURG NATIONAL CEMETERY LUMINARIA

Fredericksburg - This ceremony remembers the Revolutionary and Civil War veterans who are buried in the cemetery, as well as others from Fredericksburg's past. Scouts light a candle for each of the 15,300 soldiers buried in Fredericksburg National Cemetery. Tours of the cemetery are given throughout the night, punctuated each 30 minutes by the playing of "Taps." Rain date: Memorial Day. FREE. (Memorial Day weekend)

CHILDREN'S ART EXPO

Fredericksburg - Hurkamp Park or downtown street. (800) 678-4748. Messy creative fun for children of all ages. FREE. (Late July or early August Saturday)

GREAT ADVENTURE MAIZE MAZE

Fredericksburg - Belvedere Plantation. www.belvedereplantation.com. (540) 371-8494. Cowgirls and cowboys step inside the 14 acre wild-west themed maze, ride 75 foot long zip lines, swing from ropes onto hay piles and take hayrides to the pumpkin patch. Admission (ages 4+). (September/October)

LITTLE WELSH FESTIVAL

Fredericksburg - 900 block of Charles Street. (800) 678-4748. Enjoy a day filled with Welsh and Celtic poetry, storytellers. Children's activities honor James Monroe's Welsh heritage. Admission. (September, third Saturday)

BATTLE OF FREDERICKSBURG ANNIVERSARY TOURS

Fredericksburg - Old Town. (800) 678-4748. www.hffi.org. Battle of Fredericksburg Reenactment, living history, candlelight tours of historic homes. Adm.(Dec, 2nd wkend)

CELEBRATE THE HOLIDAYS WITH THE MONROES

Fredericksburg - James Monroe Museum & Library. (800) 678-47748, (540) 654-1043. Holiday open house with period music, refreshments & costumed re-enactors. FREE. (December, first Saturday)

RAPPAHANNOCK MODEL RAILROAD CLUB CHRISTMAS TRAIN

Fredericksburg - https://www.rmrailroaders.com/ Visitors of all ages can enjoy the magic of operating toy trains. Large Scale, and O scale Layouts, some with operating accessories, are in operation. For the hobbyist, vendors representing all scales sell new and used trains, and replacement parts. Youngsters have the opportunity to see 'Thomas' trains in operation, including a 'build-your own layout', and the complete range of 'Thomas' accessories. The highlight of the show is the 'modular' railroad project. Individual members have designed, built, and 'scienced' portable modules which can be assembled almost any where to create a train layout. National Guard Armory. Admission. (second weekend In December)

WHITE OAK MUSEUM

Fredericksburg (Falmouth) - 985 White Oak Road (six miles east of Fredericksburg on Rte 218) 22405. Phone: (540) 371-4234. https://www.vafrgs.org/resource/white-oak-civil-war-museum/ Hours: Wednesday-Sunday 10:00am-5:00pm Admission: $2.00-$4.00 (age 7+).

White Oak Museum houses one of the nation's most extensive collections of Civil War artifacts, representing both Union and Confederate troops. Most items were discarded or lost by troops camping in Stafford before and after the Battles in Fredericksburg and Spotsylvania in 1862-1863. One display contains 60,000 bullets collected from soldiers discards or practice shots. A giant cannon ball shot attracts interest. Life-size replicas of soldiers huts give you an idea of how primitive and sparse shelter was throughout even the winter months. Many Civil War soldiers died of wounds and disease.

VIRGINIA RENAISSANCE FAIRE

Fredericksburg (Spotsylvania) - https://www.renfest.org/festivals/virginia-renaissance-faire. The Faire brings a unique brand of educational interactive family entertainment. Join in the revelry as the little 16th century town of Staffordshire celebrates a visit from the Queen. Feast on a turkey leg as you watch craft demonstrations and shop at village artisans. Enjoy jousting knights, coursing hounds, musicians and magicians. Participate in a game of skill, sing a song in the pub and be knighted by the Queen. Lake Anna Winery. Admission. (starts weekends, mid-May and then weekends in June)

COLVIN RUN MILL

Great Falls - 10017 Colvin Run Road (Beltway exit 47A, Rte. 7 west) 22066. Phone: (703) 759-2771. www.fairfaxcounty.gov/parks/crm/. Hours: Thursday-Sunday 11:00am-4:00pm, last tour 3:00pm. Admission: Weekend Tour: $12.00 adult, $10.00 Student, youth and seniors. Admission to park is FREE except for some special events. Tours: offered on the hour, last tour at 4:00pm.

Colvin Run Mill has an early 19th century wooden water wheel and operating gristmill. The old Miller's House features an exhibit about the process of milling and the families who operated the mill. Another exhibit in the renovated 20th century dairy barn features the history of the Great Falls community. It offers daily tours, educational programs, special events, and outdoor concerts. The mill operates on a regular basis (usually 1st & 3rd Sundays). You can picnic on the grounds, feed the ducks, play in the activity barn, and learn about America's technological roots. **COLVIN RUN MILL GENERAL STORE** - It originally served the local community and continues to function today selling penny candy, freshly ground cornmeal and wheat flour, popcorn and an array of old-fashioned goods.

North East Area

VIRGINIA INDIAN FESTIVAL

Great Falls - Riverbend Park. www.fairfaxcounty.gov/parks/riverbend. Four Virginia tribes - the Mattaponi, Pamunkey, Rappahannock and Chickahominy - demonstrate life skills including tool and canoe making, dancing, cooking and storytelling. Pottery and other native crafts for sale. Archaeology and historical exhibits. hands-on activities for children. Admission. (second Saturday in September)

Harpers Ferry

HARPERS FERRY NATIONAL HISTORICAL PARK

Harpers Ferry - 171 Shoreline Drive (off US 340, confluence of the Potomac and Shenandoah rivers in the states of West Virginia, Virginia, and Maryland) 25425. Phone: (304) 535-6029. www.nps.gov/hafe/. Hours: The Visitor Center is open every day, 9:00am-5:00pm, except Thanksgiving, Christmas, and New Year's Day. Admission: Per vehicle is $10.00 or $5.00 per individual. Tours: Ranger guided tours daily (summer) and weekend afternoons (rest of year). Educators: African Americans in the Civil War curriculum & Jeopardy game under "For Teachers". Note: To get the "feel" for this area, catch the short videos in Building #8 and #15. Hiking, fishing, canoeing and rafting are offered on the Shenandoah and Potomac rivers and Appalachian Trail. The John Brown Wax Museum is in town and open for a small additional fee.

John Brown believed he could free the slaves, and he selected Harpers Ferry as his starting point. Today John Brown's Fort and the Arsenal ruins are part of the legacy of our nation's struggle with slavery. Some say this is really where the Civil War truly began. The story of Harpers Ferry is more than one event or individual, but many. Harpers Ferry witnessed the first successful application of the Industrial Revolution, the arrival of the railroad, John Brown's attack on slavery, the largest surrender of Federal troops during the Civil War, and the education of former slaves. Two thousand acres of restored buildings and brick sidewalks share exhibits, interpretive programs and hiking trails. Shuttle buses provide transport to the Lower Town Historic District where ranger guided tours include: John Brown's Raid, Civil War, Stonewall Jackson, Camp Hill, Harpers Ferry and the C&O Canal.

A quaint, historical town that was so much fun to explore...

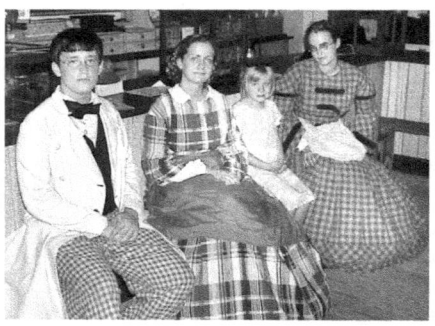

Exhibits and museums included are: the Industry Museum, the Marshal's Office, Dry Goods Store (they could get almost anything... even coconuts from the Hawaiian Islands), Wetlands museum, John Brown's Fort, Black Voices Museum (slave or free, they still had special laws), Civil War Museum and Jefferson Rock. The site interpreters do an excellent job of absorbing you into history and teaching you little known facts of the mid-to-late 1800s - all at one site!

YULETIDE 1864

Harper's Ferry Historic Town. Harper's Ferry soldiers attempted to create their own version of Christmas on the battle front. Programs and activities feature local citizens and soldiers preparing for the Yuletide, a Civil War style Santa Claus dispersing presents to the soldiers, a Victorian Cotillion, Yuletide confections, and special guided walking tours. Admission. (first weekend in December)

FRYING PAN PARK: KIDWELL FARM AND SPRING MEETING HOUSE

Herndon - 2709 West Ox Road (Beltway exit 9A or C, Rte. 66 west to Rte. 50 west exit) 20171. Phone: (703) 437-9101. www.fairfaxcounty.gov/parks/fryingpanpark/. Hours: Farm: 9:00am-5:00pm daily. Visitors Center Monday-Saturday 10:00am-4:30pm, Sunday Noon-4:30pm. Visitors center closed most holidays. Farm open except winter holidays. Admission: Except for special events and some educational programs, Frying Pan Park and the Kidwell Farm are FREE. Please call for use fees and availability of the equestrian facilities. Tours: Groups are welcome and guided tours are available by appointment. Wagon Rides: 10:00am- 4:00pm, March to November (call to confirm). Note: The Country Store, Spring House and Blacksmith Shop are open to the public during special events and programs. The Easter Bunny hops by in the spring, fall harvest activities abound in October and Santa comes to the farm in December. Indoor and outdoor horse riding arenas and bridle trails.

Kidwell Farm recreates the era from 1920 to 1940...a time of great transition in rural America. These two decades saw the advent of tractors, milking machines, mechanical bailers and other improvements in modern

> January through April is a very busy birthing time on the farm. Click on their online Birthing Schedule to see which baby animals are available to see when you visit.

agriculture. Visitors can pet the friendly farm animals, watch the farm hands at work, enjoy a picnic or take a walk through a country setting. The four-room Schoolhouse served youngsters in grades one through seven and the first two years of high school (now the hub of the park's arts and crafts, fitness, children's classes and summer camp programs). The Moffett Blacksmith Shop served local farmers from 1904 until 1955. The shop contains much of the smithy's original equipment. Today, the bellows pump, the anvil rings and the sparks fly during demonstrations. The Spring Meeting House was built in 1791. It was used for town meetings as well as for religious services. Other attractions at Frying Pan Park include hayrides, music, living history, farm life demonstrations, games and a whole lot of good old fashioned fun!

HISTORIC CHRIST CHURCH

Irvington - PO Box 24 (on Route 646, just off Route 200, between the towns of Kilmarnock and White Stone) 22480. www.christchurch1735.org. Phone: (804) 438-6855. Hours: Friday-Saturday 10:00am-4:00pm and Sunday 1:00-4:00pm (April & November), Add Mondays & Thursdays (May-October) except Thanksgiving, Christmas, and New Year's Day. Admission: $10.00 for adults (age 19 +). Free for kids and military. Tours: Guided tours of the church are available April-November, 10:00am-4:00 Monday-Saturday, and 2:00–5:00pm on Sundays.

Completed in 1735, Christ Church remains the best preserved of colonial Virginia's Anglican parish churches. The Center houses a museum on the history of Christ Church. When you visit, be sure to pick up a Museum Activity Book. It's packed with things like a museum artifact hunt, a brick making crossword puzzle, and a Carter Tombs word scramble. Each summer, the grounds come alive with hands-on activities that teach young visitors about the history of the church and life in colonial Virginia. Whether trying on colonial clothing, molding a brick like eighteenth-century craftsmen, or searching for artifacts in the museum, children and their families can make their visit a fun-filled day of history.

Worship services are held in the church, Sundays at 8:00am from Memorial Day to Labor Day.

CARTER'S CREEK PARADE OF BOATS

Irvington - (804) 438-5714. Decorated boats light up the evening scene on Carter's creek in front of the Tide's Resort. Area residents and visitors vie for prizes for the most unusual and most traditional boat decorations. (December, second Saturday)

RAPPAHANNOCK TRIBE AMERICAN INDIAN POW WOW

King & Queen County - Tribal Center. (Route 623 Indian Neck Rd.) (804) 769-0260. Dancing, history orientation, crafts foods. https://www.rappahannocktribe.org/ (October, second weekend)

CALEDON NATURAL AREA

King George - 11617 Caledon Road (Rte. 218) 22485. Phone: (540) 663-3861. www.dcr.virginia.gov/state_parks/cal.shtml. Admission: $4.00 per vehicle. Visitor Center is open weekends Noon - 4pm and Summers Wed-Sat 10am-4pm.

Summer home to one of the largest concentrations of American bald eagles on the East Coast, Caledon attracts birdwatchers galore. As many as 60 eagles have been spotted on the bluffs overlooking the Potomac River in King George County. However, limited tours of the eagle area are offered seasonally. A visitor center and picnic area with restrooms are available too.

PAMUNKEY RESERVATION

King William - 175 Lay Landing Road 23066. www.pamunkey.net. Phone: (804) 843-4792. Hours: Thursday-Saturday, 10:00am-4:00pm., Sunday, 1:00-4:00pm (June-August). Weekends only (September-November). Admission: $3.00-$5.00 Note: Can be an adventure just finding it. Here are the directions from Williamsburg. I-64 West to West Point exit (Rte. 33), after crossing over Pamunkey River into West Point, turn left at first traffic light (Rte. 30), Follow signs, turn left on Rte. 632 (Mt. Olive-Cohoke Road), At stop sign, turn left on Rte. 633 (Powhatan Trail), Turn right on Rte. 673 (Pocahontas Trail).

Get out to the rural, small town feel of this authentic 75 member Pamunkey Indian Reservation. You won't see teepees or huts, but instead trailers and small homes - even a church - most Indians were converted to Christianity during Capt. John Smith's time. On the property you'll pass Powhatan's gravesite (Pocahontas' father), cotton or corn crops and a fish hatchery. Many male tribe members work outside the reservation while most women tend to farm or make pottery. Inside the museum you might be greeted by  "Still Waters" or "Gentle Rain" as they invite you in to watch a short video about the Pamunkeys, and then you take a self-guided tour of the exhibits. Learn that Pamunkey were the most powerful of the great Powhatan tribes. Chief Powhatan and his famous daughter (Pocahontas) lived among the Pamunkey and their tribe is proud of their heritage and bravery. Kids will probably most like the cypress tree dugout canoe, the turtle shell ceremonial rattle, and the original popcorn (small corn on the cob).

BELLE ISLE STATE PARK

Lancaster - 1632 Belle Isle Road (Rte. 3 to Rte. 354 to Rte. 683) 22503. Phone: (804) 462-5030. Admission: $5.00 per car. www.dcr.virginia.gov/state-parks/belle-isle. Park open 8am-6pm.

Located in the rural Northern Neck area, Belle Isle State Park features diverse tidal and nontidal wetlands, lowland marshes, tidal coves and upland forest land. With 733 acres, seven miles of shoreline and access to Mulberry and Deep creeks, visitors can explore a wide variety of tidal wetlands interspersed with agricultural fields and upland forests. Belle Isle is open daily and features three picnic shelters, hiking and bridle trails, motor boat launch, overnight lodging at the Bel Air Guest House or Mansion, bicycle, canoe and motorboat rentals, guided canoe trips, a car top launch area, restrooms, a universal access playground, and conservation education programming and other interpretive programs.

Leesburg

LEESBURG ANIMAL PARK

Leesburg - 19270 James Monroe Highway (Rte. 7 towards Leesburg to Rte. 15 south, next to Sunshine Farms) 20175. www.leesburganimalpark.com. Phone: (703) 433-0002. Hours: Thursday-Monday 10:00am-4:00pm, Weekends til 5pm. Please call if inclement weather. Admission: $14.95-$16.95 (age 2+). Reduced winter admission. Extra $3.50-$5.00 for animal food or rides. Christmas Village in Dec.

A petting zoo that offers the opportunity to get up close and personal with some of the friendliest animals around. Pet and feed various animals including llamas, goats, sheep, miniature donkeys, deer, antelope and many others. Meet squirrel monkeys and zebra. In the spring help feed the bottle babies and meet newborn lambs, goats, and bear cubs. There is also an opportunity to visit Giant Tortoises, Lemurs, and Serval Cat. See the newest exhibit, the gibbons, or visit old favorites Libby, the miniature donkey or Nilgai, the blue cow or Indian antelope. Join in on a wagon ride or a pony ride or get up close and personal with some of the resident animals in the park at Keeper's Corner. Indoor Jungle Play Zone and Discovery crafts room.

PUMPKIN VILLAGE

Leesburg Animal Park & Pioneer Gardens. Come and enjoy all the activities: Giant slides, moon bounces, hay maze, tree swing, apples, cider and all the critters. Admission. (late September thru early November)

LOUDOUN MUSEUM

Leesburg - 16 Loudoun Street SW 20175. www.loudounmuseum.org. Phone: (703) 777-7427. Hours: Friday-Sunday 10:00am-4:00pm. Admission: FREE

The museum currently maintains displays including Native American artifacts, furniture and silver made by Loudoun County craftsmen, Civil War artifacts, letters written by freed slaves to their former masters in Loudoun, and documents signed by George Washington and James Monroe. The original 18th century county courthouse bell is a featured exhibit and its interpretation leads the visitor through Loudoun's history as the bell tolled for celebrations, announcements, and special activities. The museum's Discovery Room features a small replica of an early 19th century Quaker kitchen (complete with hearth, cookware, and utensils), activity baskets full of reproduction tools and toys, a play area, children's books, and period costumes for role playing.

Manassas

PIED PIPER THEATRE

Manassas - 9419 Battle Street 20108. https://www.virginiaartfactory.org/about-us/ Phone: (703) 330-ARTS. Performances: Fall & Spring Saturdays at 7:30pm. Sundays at 3:30pm. See schedule on website. Performances held at various locations. Admission: Varies. Usually around $16-$20.00.

Students of the theatre school perform many classics each year including plays such as Charlotte's Web, Peter Pan and Narnia.

MANASSAS NATIONAL BATTLEFIELD PARK

Manassas - 6511 Sudley Road (SR 234 - between I-66 and US 29) 20109. Phone: (703) 361-1339. www.nps.gov/mana. Hours: Daily 8:30am-5:00pm. Admission: FREE. Note: Visitor's Center has a museum and slide program (12 minutes) plus a 3D map of strategies (told from the soldier's point of view). Educators: "Baptism of Fire: Soldiers and Civilians at the First Battle of Manassas" is a curriculum based education program for 4th, 5th and 6th grades.

The 5000 acre park is the scene of two important Civil War battles. The first and Second Battles of Manassas were fought along the waters of Bull Run Creek. It was on this battleground that General Jackson was first observed standing "like a stone wall". Tour by walking (easy access to Henry Hill which has the best scenic viewpoint of the First Manassas Battle and the Stonehouse). Tour by driving (focuses more on the Second Battle of Manassas) or, tour by horse. Initially the first battle (July 21, 1861) was not taken too seriously (more like a sporting activity) as picnickers and sightseers accompanied the well equipped (but ill-trained) Union Army as it marched out of DC to fight the Confederates.

After 10 hours of deadly battle, the Union army had to retreat and the war was now taken seriously. One year later, with tattered uniforms, the Union was again gravely defeated by Confederate General Lee and his worn troops.

Start your visit at the Henry Hill Visitors Center. Check the board for daily interpretive programs. Of particular interest are the cute lights on the lighted battlefield model; the first civilian casualty (Mrs. Henry - died in her bed); the civilian picnics with Senators giving out free sandwiches; and the Stone House that started as a rest stop and turned into an aid station during the battles (many soldiers write about "Stone House" in their diaries). Walking tours of the fighting on Henry Hill during the First Battle of Manassas begin here daily at 11:00am and 2:00pm

INDEPENDENCE DAY CELEBRATION

Manassas - In town & Manassas Park. (703) 335-8872. Rides, games, entertainment, kids stage, food and fireworks.

SPLASHDOWN WATERPARK

Manassas - 7500 Ben Lomond Park Drive (Exit 44 off I-66) 20109. Phone: (703) 361-4451. www.splashdownwaterpark.com. Hours: Open from Memorial Day through Labor Day. Park opens at 11:00am and closes at 6:00-8:00pm. Open daily when school is out. Admission: Generally around $12.00-$16.25 per person. Spectators/ late afternoon entry is discounted. Note: Funbrellas & Pavillions for shade, shower and lockers, lifeguards, volleyball, tennis, lounge chairs. Café.

Fun family entertainment billed as "like being at the beach without the drive." This outdoor waterpark has Five Water Areas, 11 Acres of Fun! Includes the Zero Depth Beach Area, Boat Slide, Water Raindrops & Bubblers, 770 ft. Lazy River, Children's Area with 4 Water Slides, Two 70 ft. Tall Waterslides, Two fast Cannonball Slides, 25 Meter Lap Pool, Log Walks & Lily Pad Walk, and Two Tropical Twister Waterslides.

MASON NECK STATE PARK

Mason Neck (Lorton) - 7301 High Point Road (US 1, then east to SR 242) 22079. www.dcr.virginia.gov/state_parks/mas.shtml. Phone: (703) 339-2385 or (703) 339-2380 (visitor center). Admission: $10.00 per car. Note: Hiking trails, picnicking and Visitors Center.

The peninsula is the site of an active heron rookery. The park also attracts several other migrating and non-migrating species of birds, including whistling swans and assorted species of duck. Bald eagles also inhabit the area. The park boasts several hundred acres of hardwood forests. In addition, several wetland areas are also found along with birdwatching and guided canoe trips on the Potomac River. More than three miles of hiking trails wind through the park providing a glimpse of nature by the bay. Elevated walkways allow visitors to explore some of the marsh areas in the park. Bicycles are available for rent by the hour.

McLean

THEODORE ROOSEVELT MEMORIAL AND ISLAND

McLean - 700 George Washington Memorial Pkwy, Turkey Run Park (east of the Key Bridge on the Potomac River) 22101. www.nps.gov/this. Phone: (703) 289-2500. Note: Two-hour parking is available off the southbound side of the George Washington Parkway. The footbridge to the island is just minutes from the Rosslyn Metro Station. Access to the island is available only from the northbound lane of the George Washington Memorial Parkway. For a different experience, rent a canoe or kayak the perimeter of the island. Open year-round 6am-10pm.

Theodore Roosevelt's deep love of nature and strong commitment to conservation are reflected throughout the 88-acre island, where 2.5 miles of hiking trails pass through dense forests and marshy swamps. The memorial features a 23-foot statue of a strong, "fit-as-a-bull-moose". The terrace is surrounded by four granite tablets inscribed with the President's philosophy on nature, manhood, youth and the state. Along the island's southern end, the swamp trail passes a rare tidal freshwater marsh, filled with cattails and redwing nests. The island's drier patches attract foxes, great owls, ground hogs, raccoons and opossums. Open weekdays 7:30am-4:00pm. FREE. Visitors are reminded to carry water with them, especially during the warmer months. Bicycles are not permitted on the Island. Dogs must be on leash at all times.

NORTH ANNA NUCLEAR INFO CENTER

Mineral - 1022 Haley Drive 23117. www.dominionenergy.com/about-us/making-energy/nuclear/north-anna-power-station/visiting-north-anna. Phone: (540) 894-2029. Hours: Monday-Friday 9:00am-4:00pm (excluding holidays). Appointment only, though.

North Anna, Dominion Virginia Power's second nuclear station, generates 1,786 megawatts from its two units. This nuclear facility provides much of the electricity for Central Virginià. Dominion has established information centers to offer an in-depth look at nuclear generation and electricity production. See models of a nuclear reactor and the containment structure. Generate your own electricity using muscle power. Learn about the entire nuclear energy path, from uranium mining to electricity production.

Montpelier Station

MONTPELIER, JAMES MADISON'S

Montpelier Station - 11350 Constitution Hwy. (SR 20 SW of downtown) 22957. Phone: (540) 672-2728. www.montpelier.org. Hours: Thursday-Monday 9:00am-4:00pm. Admission: $35.00 adult, $15.00 child (6-12). Online discount. Tours: Signature tours offered every half hour from 10am-3pm. Note: Natural History Summer Day Camps. Seasonal Big Woods Walks. Café and Museum Shop. Educators: Excellent material for biography reports online on the "Student Field Trips" page.

Montpelier, nestled in the foothills of the Blue Ridge Mountains, was the lifelong home of James Madison. Madison was raised at Montpelier, lived here after his marriage to Dolley, returned here after his presidency, and died here in his study surrounded by the books and papers that marked so much of his life's work.

Learn about our fourth president and the "Father of the Constitution", as well as the effervescent Dolley, who inspired the title "First Lady". Enjoy a 15 minute video documentary about the Madison's or, while at the Visitor Center, stop by to see the Treasures of Montpelier - Madison's spyglass, a brace of pistols, snuff box, and a reproduction of Dolley's red dress.

The centerpiece of the Montpelier experience is the tour of the lifelong home of James Madison. Watch an 1820s mansion emerge from the past as some of the nation's best craftsman and artisans peel back the layers of history to convert it back to Madison's retirement years.

Nestled between the mansion and the Formal Garden in Dolley's backyard, near where she held grand summer barbeques, is the Hands-on Restoration Tent. Here you can try your hand at the building crafts of Madison's time. Make a brick, saw a log, and nail a plank the way Madison's craftsmen did. Play period games and try doing chores of the period. (Open daily April through October). Next, hike two miles of trails in the old-growth forest and stroll to the cemetery and nearby slave cemetery. Look at the place Madison called "a squirrels jump from heaven" and view the historic trees in the arboretum or watch archeologists dig.

JAMES MADISON BIRTHDAY CELEBRATION

Montpelier Station - Montpelier Estate. This date marks the anniversary of the birth of President James Madison. (March 16th)

DOLLEY MADISON'S BIRTHDAY

Montpelier Station - Montpelier Estate. Enjoy the gracious hospitality of America's first First Lady on her birthday with free cake for all, and free admission for anyone born on this date. (May 20)

MONTPELIER HUNT RACES

Montpelier Station - Montpelier Estate. Experience the thrill of steeplechase horse racing at the 74th running of the Montpelier Hunt Races on the historic grounds of James Madison's Montpelier. Jack Russell Terrier races, stick horse races, dog agility demonstrations, and other entertainment. www.montpelierraces.org. (first Sat. in Nov)

VETERANS DAY AT MONTPELIER

Montpelier Station - Montpelier Estate. Montpelier salutes all veterans with free admission for those who are serving or have served in the U.S. Armed Forces.

JAMES MADISON MUSEUM

Montpelier Station (Orange) - 129 Caroline Street 22960. Phone: (540) 672-1776. www.facebook.com/jamesmadisonmuseum. Hours: Daily 10:00am-5:00pm. Closed New Year's, Memorial Day, Independence Day, Labor Day, Thanksgiving & Christmas. Admission: $10.00 adult, $6.00 senior, military, 1st responders, $3.00 child (6-17).

The Nation's only James Madison Museum commemorates the 4th President of the U.S. and Father of the Constitution. Exhibits deal with the life and times of Madison and include furnishings from Montpelier, correspondence, fashions, and books from the Madison library. The focal point of the Madison Room is Madison's favorite chair, a campeche chair given him by his good friend, President Thomas Jefferson. Stories of truths and myths about James and Dolley are told. There is an unusual Hall of Agriculture with farm devices, machinery and tools in a partially reconstructed cube house.

WESTMORELAND STATE PARK

Montross - 1650 State Park Road (just off SR 3) 22520. Phone: (804) 493-8821. www.dcr.virginia.gov/state_parks/wes.shtml.   Admission: $7.00/vehicle, plus small swimming fee. Vehicle entrance fee is waived for overnight guests.

The park extends about one and a half miles along the Potomac River, and its 1,299 acres neighbor the former homes of both George Washington and Robert E. Lee. The park's Horsehead Cliffs provide visitors with a spectacular view of the Potomac River. Opportunities for family fun - a large swimming pool and adjacent bathhouse, launching ramp for power boats, campgrounds, climate-controlled cabins, a fishing pier and kayaking tours (no bicycle trails; no bridle trails). Seven trails, including self-guided interpretive trails, cover six miles. Hikers can observe the flora and wildlife present on the coastal plain. The park's location next to the Potomac River allows visitors to see how the changing river level affects the land. The Visitor Center exhibits include marine, bird and other wildlife displays. A collection of sharks' teeth is also on display. It's open on weekends from noon until 5:00pm. during May, September and October as well as Wednesdays through Sunday from Memorial Day through Labor Day.

NATIONAL MUSEUM OF MARINE CORPS

Quantico - (I-95 exit next to the U.S. Marine Corps Base) 22134. Phone: (212) 358-0800 or (800) 397-7585. www.usmcmuseum.com. Hours: Daily 9:00am (0900) to 5:00pm (1700) except Christmas Day. Admission: FREE. Note: It includes a gift shop, eateries, memorial park and artifact restoration. Family Days or Storytimes every weekend. Visitors bringing young children to the National Museum of the Marine Corps are encouraged to speak with a Museum Docent at the Information Desk if they are concerned that the Museum's exhibits may not be age-appropriate for their children. Educators: Gallery Recon scavenger hunts are designed for school and youth groups to complete as they move through the exhibits. Education page has gallery Guides and worksheets.

Half an hour's drive from the nation's capital, the National Museum of the Marine Corps explores Marine aviation from the dawn of flight through both world wars and Korea as well as a gallery devoted to the War on Terror. Before entering major galleries, visitors pass through an orientation theater featuring a short, introductory film about the Corps and its history.

As they exit the theater, visitors will find themselves in a replica of a recruiting station, from which they will move aboard a bus, the windows of which are television screens transmitting oral histories of Marines recounting their feelings on the verge of boot camp. If you make it through Boot Camp, immerse in realistic exhibits, examine weapons and equipment and use interactive devices to better understand how this small, elite fighting force came to make a large influence on American history. It's a clever way to immerse the kids in military history. The museum's 210-foot tilted steel mast and glass atrium with suspended aircraft features is hard to miss.

Reedville

REEDVILLE FISHERMEN'S MUSEUM

Reedville - 504 Main Street (located on Main Street, Reedville on Cockrell's Creek) 22539. Phone: (804) 453-6529. www.rfmuseum.org. Hours: Thursday-Saturday 11:00am-4:00pm, Sunday 1-4pm. Admission: $3.00-$5.00 (age 12+)

Visitors learn about the Northern Neck's menhaden fishing and watermen's heritage. The Walker House, a restored watermen's home (c.1875), allows one to glimpse at the daily life in those early years. Special exhibits highlight the museum year-round. A walking tour of Reedville is available at the museum. See the 1922 buy boat, ELVA C. and the skipjack, CLAUD W. SOMERS, built in 1911. Sailings several times each season depart at 10:00am.

TANGIER ISLAND CRUISE

Reedville - Buzzards Point Marina 22539. www.tangiercruise.com. Phone: (804) 453-2628. Tours: The Breeze leaves port every day at 10:00 am and returns about 4pm. Cruises run $30.00 adult, $15.00 child (4-12). Reservations, please.

Cruise to Tangier Island from Reedville, Va. aboard the "Chesapeake Breeze". The ship often passes fishing boats working their nets or large ocean freighters traveling between Baltimore and Norfolk, or points beyond. After a relaxing one and one half hour narrated cruise, the ship docks at Tangier where you are met by a friendly guide. During your two and one-half hour visit, you may wish to eat a family style seafood dinner at the famous Chesapeake House. Picnic area, sandwich and gift shops are also conveniently located. Walk around this quaint island, or take a tour on a mini-bus. Tangier is a quiet destination for those who would see a largely unspoiled fishing village with its quaint narrow streets, the "soft crab capital" of the nation. It is most similar to Smith Island, an island complex nearby. Although modernization has come to the Island, it still has not lost its charm.

North East Area

The people of Tangier, who speak with a lingering trace of Elizabethan accent, are warm, friendly and proud of their Island.

LAKE ANNA STATE PARK

Spotsylvania - 6800 Lawyers Road (adjacent to Route 601 off Route 208) 22553. Phone: (540) 854-5503. www.dcr.virginia.gov/state_parks/lak.shtml. Admission: $7.00 per vehicle, $2.00-$4.00 beach (per person). Park entrance fee waived for overnight guests.

The land in Lake Anna State Park used to be known as "Gold Hill" and contained the Goodwin Gold Mine. Gold was first discovered in 1829 with mining reaching its peak in the 1880's. The last gold to be found was in a zinc mine during the 1940s. The Visitor center exhibits trace the history of gold mining in the area and highlight the natural features of the park. Panning for gold and nature programs are popular activities.

While boating and fishing on the beautiful lake are major attractions, Lake Anna State Park also has more than 13 miles of hiking trails, lakeshore picnicking, a guarded swimming beach, a children's play area, a boat ramp, a food concession stand, a bathhouse and a children's and handicapped fishing pond. Also, a new campground and camping-cabins area is open.

Stratford

STRATFORD HALL PLANTATION / STRATFORD MILL

Stratford - (SR 3 to SR 214) 22558. www.stratfordhall.org. Phone: (804) 493-8038 or (804) 493-8371. Hours: Wednesday-Sunday 10:00am-4:00pm. Closed Christmas Eve, Christmas, New Years Eve and Day. Closed some weekdays in winter. Admission: $15.00 adult, $14.00 senior (60+) and $13.00 military, $9.00 child (6-13). Reduced admission in winter (children FREE). $5-$8.00 for Grounds Only/Visitors Ctr Pass. Note: A Plantation dining room in a wooded setting serves a plantation lunch daily. Potomac River beach nearby. The road to the overlook, mill and beach on the Potomac River is open to vehicular traffic from 10:00am-4:00pm. Educators: click "Educational Resources" icon.

STRATFORD HALL - On a high bluff above the Potomac River is the colonial house with its greatest distinction being the family of patriots who lived there. Thomas Lee, a prominent Virginia planter, built Stratford in the late 1730s. Using brick made on the site and timber cut from virgin forest, workers constructed the H-shaped great house, its four outbuildings and coach house and stables.

Stratford was the home of Thomas Lee's eight children. His sons Richard Henry Lee and Francis Lightfoot Lee were the only brothers to sign the Declaration of Independence. Their cousin, "Light Horse Harry" Lee, the dashing Revolutionary cavalry leader, made Stratford his home for over twenty years. Robert Edward Lee was born in the big bedroom on the upper floor of the Great House (crib still in its place). Visitors walk through meadows where the young Lees rode their horses and follow a trail to "cool, sweet spring".

STRATFORD MILL - The Gristmill grinds grain just as it has for 250 years and the flour is sold at the Plantation Store. The mill operates, when weather permits, from Noon-3:30pm on the second Saturdays (May-October).

EASTER EGG HUNT

Stratford - Join them for this fun annual event for children ages 1 to 12. The hunt begins exactly at 11am on the Oval. No rain (or snow) date. (Saturday of Easter weekend)

CHRISTMAS AT STRATFORD HALL

Stratford - Be transported back to the festive holiday times of the Lees at Stratford Hall. Enjoy the tour of the Great House, including period music and dancing. Dinner and lodging are available by reservation. (second weekend in December)

LEESYLVANIA STATE PARK

Woodbridge - 2001 Daniel Ludwig Drive (US 1 to Rte. 610 east) 22191. Phone: (703) 670-0372. www.dcr.virginia.gov/state_parks/lee.shtml. Admission: $10.00 per vehicle.

Located on the Potomac River, this park offers many land and water related activities including biking, picnicking, fishing and boating. Newer boat launching facilities, concessions area, a new visitor center and an environmental education center are available. The park offers four hiking trails and boasts many scenic overlooks of the Potomac River including one on the remains of a Civil War Confederate gun battery at Freestone Point. Leesylvania was a home of Virginia's legendary Lee Family. Once a year (in June), there is a Civil War Weekend at Leesylvania. Explore the park's rich Civil War history, tour Freestone Point Battery and Fairfax House, and view a re-enactment of historical happenings. See Civil War era weapons fired where similar guns once blazed.

Washington, DC

Chapter 2

A Quick Tour of our Hand-Picked Favorites Around...

Capital - DC Area
Washington, D.C.

To try to name favorites in D.C. is pretty nearly impossible as the entire area is one small place packed with dozens of historical attractions one must see in their lifetime to truly feel American.

Before you fill your day with museum visits, here are some tips to make the visit easier:

Overnight in nearby Virginia suburbs close to a Metro Station so once you get up in the morning - you can easily navigate the Metro into town. If you like to picnic, the National Mall and West or East Potomac Park has dozens of lawn sites to spread out a picnic blanket. You'll be dining, al fresco, by a view of **famous monuments**. As the sun started setting, we especially enjoyed walking the perimeter of the Tidal Basin in Potomac Park with a view of the FDR Memorial and The Jefferson Memorial, as they are backlit towards nightfall. Also, surrounding the White House are oodles of vendors offering the best prices in town on souvenirs and sandwiches.

How To Do Attractions - every family is different but honestly you can "do" as many as your family desires if you work the 10:00am-7:00pm full day. Maybe devote an entire day to the FREE **Smithsonian Museums** & **National Mall** buildings. DC by Foot, a walking tour company, gives FREE, kid-friendly tours infused with games, fun facts and trivia. Or, just wander from one building to the next. Be sure to go online first and print off any "Hunts" (scavenger hunts) that interest you (ways to engage, not overwhelm young guests). Play pilot in a mock cockpit at America by Air, an exhibition on permanent display at the Smithsonian **National Air and Space Museum**. Teach kids about history at the newly renovated **National Museum of American History** and get a rare look at the original "Star-Spangled Banner," the flag that inspired Francis Scott Key to write the national anthem. The museum's Spark!Lab uses fun activities to help kids and families learn about the history and process of invention through games and conducting experiments plus there's an Under 5 Zone just for pre-schoolers. Walk among the butterflies or witness a view of the blinding Hope Diamond at the **National Museum of Natural History**.

For updates visit: www.KidsLoveTravel.com

Maybe following a thread of your favorite President is the best way to tour. **Fords Theatre Museum & Tour** is a newly renovated museum using 21st century technology to transport visitors to 19th-century Washington, DC. The museum's collection of historic artifacts (including the Derringer pistol that John Wilkes Booth used to shoot Lincoln and a replica of the coat Lincoln wore the night he was shot) is supplemented with a variety of narrative devices. As you sit in the theatre for the park ranger presentation, chills run up your spine!

Sites and attractions are listed in order by City, Zip Code, and Name. Symbols indicated represent: 🍽 Restaurants   🛏 Lodging

CLYDE'S AT THE GALLERY

Washington - 707 7th St. NW (take US 50 into town. Follow Metro: Gallery Place / Chinatown) 20001. (202) 349-3700. www.clydes.com. Sit down lunch option in Washington, D.C. Clyde's at the Gallery offers a great Kids Menu for $7.99. Nine entrees to choose from with basics. Every Kids Meal is served with a toy, activity sheet & crayons, milk or soft drink, and ice cream or seasonal fruit dessert. Teens will love the Margarita Pizza...adults, be sure to try their seafood – oysters or their meaty crab cakes maybe? Reasonable for D.C. pricing!

OLD TOWN TROLLEY TOURS

Washington - 50 Massachusetts Ave NE (departs at Union Station & the Welcome Center) 20001. www.trolleytours.com/washington-dc Tours: $39.95 adult, $29.95 child (4-12). Online discounts. "Hop on - Hop off" privileges at 16 conveniently located stops. Trolleys will come by each stop at least every 30 minutes. No Reservations Required. Moonlight tours, too.

A one-of-a-kind fully narrated tour of Washington DC covering over 100 points of interest. The popular Old Town Trolley tour covers Washington's major attractions such as the Lincoln Memorial, Georgetown, Washington National Cathedral, the White House, the museums of the Smithsonian Institution, and the Vietnam Veteran's Memorial. The licensed and professional tour guides share colorful anecdotes, humorous stories and well researched historical information.

As you tour the nation's capital, you will have the opportunity to get off the trolley and visit memorials, museums, and historical points of interest; as well as opportunities for shopping and dining throughout the city. When you're ready, just re-board and it's on with the tour. Your Boarding Pass is your ticket to rejoin the tour at any designated stop.

FORD'S THEATRE

Washington - 511 10th Street, NW (between E and F Streets) 20004. Box Office: (202) 347-4833. NPS Phone: (202) 426-6924. www.fords.org or www.nps.gov/foth. Hours: for museum & tours the site is open daily from 9am-4pm. Final entry into the theatre is at 3:30pm. Visits to Ford's Theatre NHS are FREE but do require a ticket. Tickets can be reserved online for a small fee. Tours: Extend that feeling with History on Foot tours lead by an actor in costume ($18.00 per person). The Peterson House, where Lincoln died, is open for tours too. Educators: click on Education icon for Printable Resources/Educational Resources. Click on "Explore Lincoln" for background material for reports.

ACT I - Ford's Theatre museum preserves and displays over 8,000 artifacts relevant to the assassination of Abraham Lincoln. The museum uses 21st century technology to transport visitors to 19th-century Washington DC. The museum's collection of historic artifacts (including the Derringer pistol that John Wilkes Booth used to shoot Lincoln and the replica coat Lincoln wore the night he was shot) is supplemented with a variety of narrative devices. Interactive, self-guided exhibits set the stage for guests by painting a social and political picture of Washington, DC, and the United States during the 1860s.

For updates visit: www.KidsLoveTravel.com

ACT II - Visitors move into the theatre itself for a presentation—either of a one act play or a National Park Service ranger talk—that illuminates the dramatic events of April, 1865. See the Presidential Box (notice how the view from here is almost like being on stage), the inner door (notice how mangled it is) to the box, and many historical artifacts such as the evenings program (notice it announced Lincoln's attendance that was publicized as a long awaited appearance of the Commander and Chief) and the Notice of Reward for the killer. Who was supposed to be a guest in the box with the President and Mrs. Lincoln that night? Why didn't they come? As you sit in the theatre for the presentation, chills run up your spine!

ACT III - The journey will continue across the street at the Petersen House, where visitors will learn more about President Lincoln's final hours, the vigil at his deathbed and the subsequent hunt for his assassin.

INTERNATIONAL SPY MUSEUM

Washington - 800 F Street, NW (Metro: Gallery Place/ Chinatown) 20004. Phone: (202) 393-7798. www.spymuseum.org. Hours: Daily 9am-7pm. (hours vary October-March). Last Admission: 2 hours before closing. Closed major winter holidays. Admission: $27.95 adult (12-64), $24.95 senior (65+), $17.95 child (ages 7-11). Weekends a little more. Children age 6 and under FREE. All admission tickets are date and time specific and are subject to availability. Advance Tickets are highly recommended. Note: The exhibit spaces are tight (maybe for effect-spies hide in small, hidden passages). The Permanent Exhibition is most appropriate for ages 12+.

Packed with high-tech, interactive displays and activities, visitors can take on a spy's cover and test their skills of observation and surveillance, while learning about the history and the future of espionage. Examine over 200 spy gadgets, weapons, bugs, cameras, vehicles, and technologies. Look for the Bond car and a Buttonhole Camera. Learn about the earliest codes--who created them and who broke them. A spy must live a life of lies. Adopt a cover identity and learn why an operative needs one. See the credentials an agent must have to get in - or out.

DC UNDER THE STARS

Washington - White House Gifts, 701 15th Street NW (Pennsylvania Ave NW & 15th St NW & New York Ave NW) 20005 Phone: (301) 839-5261. https://signaturetoursdc.com/ Tours: Depart nightly at 7:30pm. 3 hour duration. $66.00 adult, $56.00 child

The DC The Lights Tour is the most popular and highest rated Washington DC night tour. It hits all of the major attractions in DC, but you get to see them lit up at night. Washington DC is one of the most beautiful cities in the world at night. Just like their other tours, your tour guide will hop off with you at each attraction in DC.

WHITE HOUSE

Washington - 1600 Pennsylvania Avenue, NW (Metro: Metro Center, McPherson Square) 20005. Phone: (202) 456-7041. www.whitehouse.gov and https://www.washington.org/DC-faqs-for-visitors/how-can-i-tour-white-house. Hours: Visitors Center: Daily 7:30am-4:00pm. Tours: The White House is currently open only to groups (of 10 or more) who have made arrangements through a congressional representative. These self-guided tours are available from 7:30am-11:30pm. Tuesday through Thursday and 7:30am-1:30pm Fridays & Saturdays (excluding federal holidays), and are scheduled on a first come, first served basis.

You are given a specific entry time. Educators: Life in the White House, a presentation of the rich history of the White House and West Wing video online.

WHITE HOUSE VISITOR CENTER: All visits are significantly enhanced if visitors stop by the White House Visitor Center located at the southeast corner of 15th and E Streets, before or after their walking or White House group tour. The Center features many aspects of the White House, including its architecture, furnishings, first families, social events, and relations with the press and world leaders, as well as a thirty-minute video. Allow between 20 minutes to one hour to explore the exhibits.

WHITE HOUSE TOUR: You are given a specific entry time. There are many items you can't bring onto the property. The tour is self-guided with guards and Secret Service people in every room. You aren't rushed through and they willingly answer questions. The entry has lots of interesting displays and artifacts.

America's most famous address...
1600 Pennsylvania Avenue

For updates visit: www.KidsLoveTravel.com

Washington, DC

Some of the rooms you can peak into are the East Room, Green Room, Blue Room, Red Room, State Dining Room and then out through the North Portico. It is definitely an impressive place to visit.

The guided OUTSIDE tour combined with the Visitor Center and online video presentations give you the best "feel" for the White House without actually going inside. I think they realize citizens still want to know about the President's house but can't always go through the "hoops" necessary to secure an inside visit these days. Please note that restrooms are available,food service is not.

EASTER EGG HUNT

White House - This annual tradition dates back to 1878 and President Rutherford B. Hayes. Children ages 3-6 can frolic on the South Lawn searching for over 24,000 wooden eggs that have been hidden throughout the grounds. There is also an Easter celebration at the Ellipse including entertainment, music, storytelling, the Easter Bunny, and food giveaways for the whole family to enjoy. www.whitehouse.gov/easter/. FREE. (Easter weekend)

NATIONAL ZOO

Washington - 3001 Connecticut Avenue, NW (I-395 north to exit 8B, Washington Blvd. To Arlington Bridge. Cross Bridge, veer to left. Turn right on Constitution, left on 17th. Metro: Zoo) 20008. http://nationalzoo.si.edu. Phone: (202) 633-4800. Hours: Daily 9:00am-4:00pm. Open until 6:00pm (April-October). Closed Christmas Day. Admission: FREE. Educators: Curriculum guides, Wildlife Explorer Kits and Activity Sheets are all online on the "Education" icon.

Most of you are thinking Giant Pandas at the National Zoo. See Bao Bao, the Zoo's famous panda, on the web cams. Like babies? Popular areas are: Asian elephants, Cheetah cubs, Tiger cubs or animals in the Kids' Farm. It wouldn't be the National Zoo without a Bald Eagle Refuge. While many animals are always or usually in indoor exhibits, many others, including giant pandas, bears, seals, sea lions, and great cats, are usually outdoors. The Zoo is set on hilly terrain and some paths are steep. Comfortable shoes are recommended. You can expect to see more animals early in the morning. Print off a scavenger hunt sheet before you visit (on Info for Visitors web page).

ROCK CREEK PARK AND NATURE CENTER

Washington - 5200 Glover Road, NW 20008. www.nps.gov/rocr/. Phone: (202) 426-6829. Hours: Wednesday-Sunday 9:00am-5:00pm. Closed most national holidays. FREE. Educators: click on: For Teachers and then Curriculum for lesson plans and scavenger hunts.

This 2,000-acre park provides a perfect setting for an urban escape or a family outing. Explore a woodland trail. Discover other planets. Touch live animals. Visit a historic flour mill or a 17th century colonial home (Old Stone House). The park has a golf course, tennis courts, picnic tables, bike trails, jogging trails, and horseback riding. The Rock Creek Nature Center is home to the only planetarium in the National Park system and the Discovery Room has a live beehive viewing area, visible through glass panes. Guided nature walks and curriculum based environmental education programs take place daily.

SIGNATURE TOURS DC

Washington - 20018. https://signaturetoursdc.com/top-of-the-line-tour/.

When you get on Washington Signature Tours bus you get a unique, entertaining guided tour of Washington DC that allows you to explore the fabled monuments of DC with stops that offer great photo ops so you take home great memories. You enjoy a comfortable ride in a family friendly setting at an affordable price.

SIGHTSEE DC: Washington DC has a lot to offer. With our bus tour you will be able to see all Washington DC monuments and attractions with live narrative that will captivate you. 5 or 6 hour tours leave from National Archives at 10am and include a lunch stop and seasonal boat ride. $89 adult, $79 child.

TOP OF THE LINE: At each stop, your guide will accompany you on foot to get an informative, insider's view and great photos of each special place, before conveniently boarding the bus again to the next ones. And from April to October, you will take a one-hour boat ride on the lovely and historic Potomac River to experience DC's monuments and views from the unique perspective of the water. You will also have a lunch break at either the Georgetown waterfront (April-October) or the Pentagon City Mall (October-April) where you can purchase lunch from one of several delicious locations. $99 adult, $89 child (12 & under). 6 hour tour departs at 10am. Includes tickets to tour US Capitol. **(Tours depart National Archives 800 Pennsylvania Ave NW)**

US CAPITOL & MORNING MONUMENTS: The US Capitol and Monuments tour gives you an insider's look at our US Capitol where you will get to see the hear the Capitol Tour guide give you information on how it was built and many more historical facts. 5 hour tour starts at 8am. Meet at Neptune Fountain. $74 adult, $64 child.

FREDERICK DOUGLASS NHS

Washington - 1411 W Street SE 20020. www.nps.gov/frdo/. Phone: (202) 426-5961. Admission: FREE. Hours: 9am-5:00pm. Tours: Ranger-led tours of the home are available daily at 9:00am, 12:15pm, 1:45pm, 3:00pm, and 3:30pm. Tour tickets are available by reservation ($1.50 admin fee) or on a first-come first-served basis. Tours of the home last approximately 30 minutes. Note: The historic home is set high atop a hill. There are approximately 85 steps between the Visitor Center and the house.

The Frederick Douglass National Historic Site is dedicated to preserving the legacy of the most famous 19th century African American. This restored home to a former slave is where you can begin to learn about his efforts to abolish slavery and his struggle for rights for all oppressed people. Begin with the 17-minute film "Frederick Douglass: Fighter for Freedom." Look for his original piano and documents he published.

FRANKLIN D. ROOSEVELT MEMORIAL

Washington - 900 Ohio Drive, SW (West Potomac Park at West Basin and Ohio Drive) 20024. Phone: (202) 426-6841. www.nps.gov/fdrm/. Hours: Park ranger in attendance 9:30am-10pm. Closed Christmas. Admission: FREE. Note: The memorial did not originally feature any renderings of the president in his wheelchair. FDR did not wish to be portrayed in his wheelchair, and designers honored this request. Many people with and without disabilities were angered by this omission, and a statue of FDR in his wheelchair was installed in 2001.

"The only thing we have to fear is fear itself". These are the words of our 32nd President, a man who truly knew the meaning of the word courage. Despite,

at age 39, being stricken with polio and paralyzed from the waist down, he emerged as a true leader, guiding our country through some of its darkest times: the Great Depression and World War II. The rambling FDR Memorial (it spans 7.5 acres) consists of four "rooms" arranged chronologically to represent the 32nd President's unprecedented four terms in office. A fountain in the first room flows peacefully, representing the healing effect water had on the president during his term in the Navy and while at Warm Springs, GA. The second room addresses the Great Depression and the hope FDR cultivated with his extensive social programs.

The third room represents the war years, 1940-1944 with choppy, unsettling stonework and water. In a stark contrast, the final room projects peace and optimism. Acknowledging FDR's own physical difficulties, his memorial was the first creation of its kind designed with easy access for people with disabilities.

HOLOCAUST MEMORIAL MUSEUM, UNITED STATES

Washington - *100 Raoul Wallenberg Place, SW (I-295N to I-395N exit Smithsonian, near the National Mall, just south of Independence Ave., SW, between 14th Street and Raoul Wallenberg) 20024. www.ushmm.org. Phone: (202) 488-0400 or (800) 400-9373. Hours: Daily 10:00am-5:30pm, except Yom Kippur and Christmas. Extended weekday hours in the spring/summer. Admission: FREE. Timed tickets required for permanent exhibition; available same day or in advance on their website. Usually sold out by Noon.*

Our teen-aged daughter had just studied WWII so she had interest in the Holocaust Memorial Museum. There are two "exhibit tracks" to follow: the General Exhibit and Daniel's Story (a softer version for tender hearts and kids). We'd recommend walking through Daniel's Story to everyone BEFOREHAND to prepare you for the intensity to  follow in the main exhibit. The permanent collection of the U.S. Holocaust Memorial Museum tells the moving story of the persecution of the Jewish people. The exhibition is divided into three parts: "Nazi Assault," "Final Solution," and "Last Chapter." The narrative begins with images of death and destruction as witnessed by American soldiers during the liberation of Nazi concentration camps in 1945. Most first-time visitors spend an average of two to three hours in this self-guided exhibition. Parents and pre-teens or teenagers - be prepared to be changed.

JEFFERSON MEMORIAL

Washington -*16 East Basin Drive SW (East Potomac Park, South end of 15th St., SW on the Tidal Basin) 20024. Phone: (202) 426-6822. www.nps.gov/thje/. Hours: The public may visit the Thomas Jefferson Memorial 24 hours a day. However*

Washington, DC

Rangers are on duty to answer questions from 9:30am to 10pm daily. Admission: FREE.

Easily recognizable to Jeffersonian architects, the colonnade and dome memorial reflect Jefferson's love of this architectural style. The graceful, beautiful marble design pays tribute to the third president and primary author of the Declaration of Independence. Inside, there is a large bronze statue and excerpts from his writings on the walls. Jefferson stands at the center of the temple, his gaze firmly fixed on the White House, as if to keep an eye on the institution he helped to create. A museum is located in the lower lobby of the memorial.

LINCOLN MEMORIAL

Washington - 900 Ohio Drive, S.W. (west end of Mall, 23rd St. and Constitution Ave., NW) 20024. Phone: (202) 426-6841. www.nps.gov/linc/. Hours: Visitors Center 8:00am-midnight. Park ranger in attendance 24 hours, However Rangers are on duty to answer questions from 9:30am-10pm daily. Admission: FREE. Note: New! Free Interpretive Ranger Talks via your telephone. Dial (202) 747-3420 to hear new Lincoln Memorial programs organized around more than ten themes.

The most famous of the monuments, this site was used for several of history's greatest moments. The artist opted to portray Lincoln seated, much larger than life, a symbol of mental and physical strength. Lincoln faces the US Capitol. Murals sculpted by Jules Guerin adorn the temple's inner walls. Emancipation is on the south wall and hangs above the inscription of the Gettysburg Address. Unification is on the north wall, above Lincoln's Second Inaugural Address. The view of the National Mall from this vantage point is spectacular. It gives you chills every time you visit.

NATIONAL MALL

Washington - (stretches from 3rd St., NW and the Capitol grounds to 14th St., between Independence and Constitution Aves.) 20024. Visitor Information: (202) 426-6841. www.nps.gov/nama/. Hours: Rangers on duty 9:30am-10pm.

Officially, the National Mall is green space that begins at 3rd Street and stretches to 14th Street. Visitors and locals, however, widely use the term to refer to the entire expanse of monuments and museums, from the grounds of the Capitol to the Lincoln Memorial. Pierre L'Enfant's original plans for the city called for this open space and parklands, which he envisioned as a grand boulevard to be used for remembrance, observance, and protest.

Today, it serves this purpose, hosting concerts, rallies, festivals, as well as Frisbee matches, family outings, picnics and memorials: The Presidential Memorials; Vietnam Veterans Memorial (the Wall); U.S. Navy Memorial and Naval Heritage Center (701 Pennsylvania Ave., NW); Korean War Veterans Memorial (West Potomac Park, Independence Ave., beside the Lincoln Memorial); and the National World War II Memorial (East end of the Reflecting Pool, between the Lincoln Memorial and the Washington Monument). Call a veteran from a Memorial to thank him/her for their service.

> Park resources include the 2,000 American elms which line the Mall and the 3,000 internationally-renowned Japanese cherry trees which grace the Tidal Basin.

CHERRY BLOSSOM FESTIVAL

Washington - DC's annual National Cherry Blossom Festival is a celebration of the coming of spring and commemorates the gift of 3,000 cherry trees given to the U.S. by Tokyo mayor, Yukio Ozaki in 1912. The two-week festival includes many cultural, sporting and culinary events culminating with the Festival Parade and DC's Sakura Matsuri Japanese Street Festival, presenting over 80 organizations highlighting Japanese performances, arts, crafts and food. The Parade showcases entries from across the country and around the world. And a circus, lavish floats, gigantic helium balloons, exciting international performance groups, marching bands and celebrity guests. Also, The Smithsonian Kite Festival on the grounds of the Washington Monument. www.nationalcherryblossomfestival.org. Most events are FREE. (first two weeks of April, beginning end of March)

SMITHSONIAN FOLKLIFE FESTIVAL

Washington National Mall. www.folklife.si.edu. National, even international, celebration of contemporary living traditions. The Festival typically includes daily and evening programs of music, song, dance, celebratory performance, crafts and cooking demonstrations, storytelling, illustrations of workers' culture. The Festival encourages visitors to participate - to learn, sing, dance, eat traditional foods, and converse with people presented in the Festival program. FREE. (last weekend in June, first weekend in July, Thursday-Sunday)

For updates visit: www.KidsLoveTravel.com

Washington, DC

JULY 4TH CELEBRATION

Washington, DC- Constitution Avenue. Celebrate the nation's birthday in the nation's capital. Don't miss the parade, with more then 100 marching units stepping out at noon along Constitution Avenue. When that's over, popular music groups entertain from mid-afternoon until the fireworks at Washington Monument. FREE.

BUREAU OF ENGRAVING AND PRINTING TOUR

Washington - Department of the Treasury, 14th and C Streets, S.W. 20228. www.moneyfactory.com. Phone: (202) 874-2330 (local) or (866) 874-2330. Hours: Public Tour: 9:00am-10:30am & 12:30pm-2:00pm (every 15 minutes). Extended Summer Hours (March-August): 5:00-6:00pm (every 15 minutes). Tours are about 40 minutes long. Visitors Center: Weekdays 8:30am-3:00pm and spring/summer early evenings. The Bureau is CLOSED on weekends, federal holidays and the week between Christmas and New Years. Tours: Tickets are required for all tours from the first Monday in March through the last Friday in August, on a first-come, first-served basis. The ticket booth is located on Raoul Wallenberg Place (formerly 15th Street). They offer same day tickets only. The Ticket Booth opens at 8:00am - Monday through Friday, and closes when all tickets have been distributed. Lines form early and tickets go quickly, most days' tickets are gone by 9:00am. Many are in line by 7:00am. No tickets required (September-February). Please plan accordingly. Note: Please be advised that strollers are not allowed.

You'll see millions of dollars being printed during a tour of the BEP. The tour features the various steps of currency production, beginning with large, blank sheets of paper, and ending with the paper money we use every day! The BEP designs, engraves and prints all U.S. paper currency. Did you know they also produce postage stamps and White House invitations? Established in 1862, the Bureau, at that time, used just six people to separate and seal notes by hand in the basement of the Treasury building. The Bureau moved to its present site in 1914. Though new printing, production and examining technologies have brought us into the 21st century, the Bureau's engravers continue to use the same traditional tools that have been used for over 125 years - the graver, the burnisher, and the hand-held glass. At any given time, you may see millions of dollars roll off the presses in a flash!

WASHINGTON MONUMENT

What is an Obelisk?
A tapering 4-sided stone shaft with a pyramid on top!

Washington - 15th & Jefferson Drive (National Mall area, Tourmobile stop, Metro Smithsonian stop) 20228. Phone: (202) 426-6841 or (877) 444-6777 reservations. www.nps.gov/wamo/. Hours: Washington Monument are from 9:00am-4:45pm, closed December 25 and July 4th. Admission: Free tickets are distributed for that day's visit from the kiosk on the Washington Monument grounds on a first-come first-served basis. Also online. All visitors 2 years of age or older must have a ticket to enter the Monument. Hours for the ticket kiosk are 8:45am-4:30pm, but tickets run out early. While tickets to the Washington Monument are free of charge, pre-sale callers/online orders will incur a $1.50 service charge. Note: Bookstore, restrooms and concessions on site.

Take the fast elevator ride to the top of the Monument for a panoramic view of the city. Most rides make stops to allow viewing of the commemorative stones set along the inside walls of the elevator shaft. Many folks like to start here as Washington was our first President and the view gives you a good feel for the lay of the land in D.C. The 555-foot tall obelisk is marble and is the tallest free-standing obelisk in the world. Why are there two different colors of marble used? The immense structure represents Washington's enormous contribution to the founding of our republic.

NATIONAL MUSEUM OF U.S. NAVY

Washington - 805 Kidder Breese Street, SE (Washington Navy Yard) 20374. Phone: (202) 433-6897. www.history.navy.mil/content/history/museums/nmusn.html Hours: 9:00am-5:00pm Monday-Friday, Saturday-Sunday Holidays 10am-5pm. Educators: Lesson plans & activities on the Teacher Resources icon.

Opened in 1963, the Navy Museum is housed in the former 600-foot long Breech Mechanism Shop of the old Naval Gun Factory. Exhibits offer a look at the traditions and contributions of the Navy throughout American history. Popular attractions include the fully rigged fighting top from the frigate Constitution, a submarine room with operating periscopes and a variety of large guns which can be elevated and aimed by the visitor. There is no admission charge.

For updates visit: www.KidsLoveTravel.com

Washington, DC

NATIONAL ARCHIVES

Washington - 701 Constitution Avenue, NW (Metro Archives station - The Rotunda entrance, which includes the Exhibit Hall, is on Constitution Avenue) 20408. Phone: (202) 357-5000. www.archives.gov. Hours: Daily 10:00am-5:30pm. Open later each spring and summer. Admission: FREE. Educators: Lesson Plans and great biographical writings can be used for teachers and kids' reports.

The Rotunda of the National Archives Building in downtown Washington, DC, contains the permanent exhibit of the Constitution, Bill of Rights, and the Declaration of Independence. An exhibit called the Public Vaults displays over 1,000 fascinating records (originals or reproductions) from the National Archives holdings. Often, the wait may be long, but most say worth it, to enter the Charters of Freedom.

PRESIDENT LINCOLN'S COTTAGE

Washington - 140 Rock Creek Church Rd NW, Armed Forces Retirement Home campus (Metro-Georgia Ave-Petworth. Head northeast) 20011. www.lincolncottage.org. Phone: (202) 829-0346. Hours: Visitors Center: Daily 9:30am-4:30pm, opens at 10:30am Sundays. The site is closed Thanksgiving, Christmas, and New Year's Day. Admission: $15.00 adult, $5.00 child (6-12). Tours: One hour, guided tours are offered of the Cottage and a portion of the Soldiers' Home grounds. Reservations online are highly suggested. This tour is suitable for children 6 years or older.

Located on a picturesque hilltop in Washington, DC, President Lincoln's Cottage is the most significant historic site directly associated with Lincoln's presidency aside from the White House. During the Civil War, President Lincoln and his family resided here from June to November of 1862, 1863 and 1864. In part, the Lincolns were seeking privacy to grieve after the death of 12-year-old son Willie. Until recently, little was known about the home. Much has been pieced together from diaries, letters and newspaper stories. While you may be thinking you'll get to see the chair or bed Lincoln's family sat on - this museum instead focuses on the person. "Historical" voices and images illuminate the compelling stories of Lincoln as father, husband, and Commander in Chief. In "Lincoln's Cabinet Room" (Visitors Center) visitors can participate in an innovative interactive experience exploring Lincoln's Toughest Decisions. Students can play the roles of rival cabinet secretaries and debate the emancipation. We especially like that, before touring the Cottage, visitors first gather in the theater for an introduction to the site. An interactive audio-visual presentation sets the context for the Lincolns' move here.

CAPITOL BUILDING, UNITED STATES

Washington - (east end of the National Mall) 20540. Phone: (202) 737-2300 or (800) 723-3557. www.visitthecapitol.gov Hours: Monday-Saturday 9:00am-3:30pm. Admission: FREE. Visitors must obtain free tickets for tours on a first-come, first-served basis, at the Capitol Guide Service kiosk located along the curving sidewalk southwest of the Capitol (near the intersection of First Street, SW, and Independence Avenue). Ticket distribution begins at 9:00am, daily. Tours: Guided tours of the U.S. Capitol Building are free of charge. Tours must be booked in advance and schedules can fill up quickly (particularly in spring), so it is advisable that you book your tour well in advance. Note: A limited number of free passes to the House and Senate galleries are available by contacting your representative's office, in advance or reserving a tour at the Visitors Ctr. An underground tunnel connects to the Library of Congress too.

The Capitol is one of the most widely recognized buildings in the world. It is a symbol of the American people and their government, the meeting place of the nation's legislature, an art and history museum, and a tourist attraction visited by millions every year. The bright, white-domed building was designed to be the focal point for DC, dividing the city into four sectors and organizing the street numbers. Begun in 1793, the Capitol has been built, burnt, rebuilt, extended, and restored. An 180-foot dome is adorned by the fresco Brumidi painting (took him 20 years to complete). The Rotunda, a circular ceremonial space, also serves as a gallery of paintings and sculpture depicting significant people and events in the nation's history. The Old Senate Chamber northeast of the Rotunda, which was used by the Senate until 1859, has been returned to its mid-19th century appearance. The third floor allows access to the galleries from which visitors to the Capitol may watch the proceedings of the House and the Senate when Congress is in session...learning firsthand how a bill becomes a law. The Visitors Center, an underground facility, includes an exhibitiion gallery, orientation theatres, a cafeteria, gift shops, and restrooms.

LIBRARY OF CONGRESS

Washington - 101 Independence Ave, SE (Metro: Capitol South) 20540. Phone: (202) 707-8000. www.loc.gov. Hours: Monday-Saturday 10:00am-5:30pm. Admission: FREE public tours. Tours: Docent-led scheduled public walking tours are offered Mondays through Saturdays in the Great Hall. Ask at the information desks in the Visitors' Center of the Jefferson Building (west front entrance). You may enter this building on the ground level under the staircase at the front of the building, located directly across from the U.S. Capitol. Educators: Kids and Families - Log on, play around, learn something. Teachers - 10 million primary sources online.

The world's largest library is home to much more than just books. At the Library of Congress, kids can see a perfect copy of the Gutenberg Bible, personal papers of 23 presidents, a collection of Houdini's magic tricks, the Wright Brothers' flight log books and more. Equipped with new information desks, a visitors' theater features a 12 minute award winning film about the Library and interactive information kiosks. The Visitors' Center enhances the experience of approximately one million visitors each year.

SMITHSONIAN INSTITUTION

Washington - *(I-295N to I-395N located on the National Mall exit and may be entered from many directions. Follow signs.) 20560. Phone: (202) 357-2700 or (202) 633-1000 (voice). www.smithsonian.org Hours: All museums are open from 10:00am-5:30pm, daily. Admission: FREE. Educators: Click on "For Educators" button and you'll find a wealth of exciting approaches to curriculum and related crafts or projects! Have your kids go to the For Kids pages to explore before they go - their pages are whimsical and short - meant to pique interest, not destroy it. Note: Docents are available in many popular galleries daily to answer visitor questions between 10:30am and 2:30pm, Mondays through Saturdays and Sundays from noon to 4:00pm.*

A visit to Washington, DC is not complete without experiencing at least one of the 14 Smithsonian museums. The Castle is the original building, completed in 1855, which provides an overview of the entire offering to help your family determine which museums interest you the most (you probably can't do them all). Be sure you have on your walking shoes. DC by Foot, a walking tour company, gives FREE, kid-friendly tours (gratuity recommended) infused with games, fun facts and trivia. Or, just wander from one building to the next. Be sure to go online first and print off any "Hunts" (scavenger hunts) that interest you (ways to engage, not overwhelm young guests). The following are highlights of the myriad of exhibits and activities offered especially for children. Maybe only choose two to explore each visit.

- **ON THE MALL**: Outside the National Air and Space Museum, a scale model of the solar system entitled Voyage: A Journey through our Solar System helps children grasp the magnitude of the world around them. During the summer months, a ride on the world's oldest carousel, near the Arts and Industries Building, is a sure treat.

- **AMERICAN ART MUSEUM**: (Gallery Place Metro station at 8th and F Streets N.W. Open 11:30am-7:00pm). The Smithsonian American Art Museum is dedicated exclusively to the art and artists of the United States. All regions, cultures, and traditions are represented in the museum's collections, research resources, exhibitions, and public programs. The collection features colonial portraits, nineteenth-century landscapes, American impressionism, twentieth-century realism and abstraction, There's a neat display of license plates from every state that write out the Preamble to the Constitution (clever). You may especially like the Washington and Lincoln studies (ever study Lincoln's eyes?). The Civil War space is good, too.

The original Smithsonian Museum is a great place to start your visit

- **HIRSHHORN GALLERY**: The Smithsonian's modern art museum's "Young at Art" program introduces young visitors to different artistic disciplines through hands-on activities. Participants can act in a play, create portraits in chocolate, make clay sculptures, and more. The museum also offers regularly-scheduled guided family tours.

- **NATIONAL AIR & SPACE MUSEUM**: Play pilot in a mock cockpit at America by Air. The large space provides a world-renowned collection of flying machines from the Wright Brothers' Kitty Hawk Flyer to the Apollo 11 Command Module. Kids can see a moon rock, Lindbergh's Spirit of St. Louis and a variety of special films. The museum's IMAX theatre

See the ACTUAL Wright Brother's famous airplane...WOW...

Washington, DC

provides large format and 3-D glimpses of space and beyond.(fee for IMAX shows AND Planetarium shows).Not only does the planetarium have a spectacular star field instrument, but also Sky Vision™. For the first time, you'll feel the sensation of zooming through the cosmos with a blanket of color and sound. Infinity Express: A 20-Minute Tour of the Universe; Cosmic Collisions, or Stars Tonight (free) program.

- **NATIONAL MUSEUM OF AMERICAN HISTORY**: Also known as "America's Attic," this popular museum houses such treasures as the First Ladies' inaugural gowns, Dorothy's Ruby Red Slippers, Mr. Roger's sweater, Abraham Lincoln's top hat, Lewis and Clark's compass, Custer's buckskin coat, Thomas Jefferson's bible, Edison's light bulb and the flag that inspired "The Star-Spangled Banner." Your mouth will drop when you first turn the corner and see it! The museum's Spark!Lab uses fun activities to help families learn about the history and process of invention through games and conducting experiments plus there's a Zone just for pre-schoolers. America on the Move, explores the world of transportation, including real artifacts from historic Route 66.

Early Americans hauled 25 pails of water (at 21 lbs each!) just to do a load of laundry...

- **NATIONAL MUSEUM OF NATURAL HISTORY**: Walk among the butterflies or witness a view of the blinding Hope Diamond at the National Museum of Natural History. After seeing a digitally-restored Triceratops or dining in the special dinosaur café, check out the famous Insect Zoo. Kids can learn all about these creatures and non-squeamish types are allowed to handle them for an up-close look. The renovated Mammal Hall shows some of the museum's specimens in lifelike, realistic settings. The Ocean Hall is the largest exhibit - exploring the ancient, diverse, and constantly changing nature of the ocean, the long historical connections humans have had with it, and ways in which we are impacting the ocean today.

The "priceless" Hope Diamond...

- **NATIONAL MUSEUM OF AFRICAN AMERICAN HISTORY & CULTURE**: (15th & Constitution Ave., NW) It has close to 37,000 objects in its collection related to such subjects as community, family, the arts, religion, civil rights, slavery, and segregation. Personal items such as Harriet Tubman's silk shawl. Rosa Parks dress she was sewing the day of refusal, Louis Armstrong's trumpet, James Brown's cape, Jim Crow era "Colored" signage and a segregated drinking fountain, feet and wrist shackles, Muhammad Ali's boxing headgear, and modern artifacts such as President Obama's campaign office.
- **NATIONAL MUSEUM OF THE AMERICAN INDIAN**: (4th Street & Independence) Experience culture at the National Museum of the American Indian, where FREE programming from storytelling and dance festivals to music performances by Native composers is available based on changing monthly performance schedules. The four story brilliantly lighted atrium captures your senses to explore the simple chronicle of people's courageous survival to present day accomplishments.
- **NATIONAL POSTAL MUSEUM**: Located next to Union Station, the National Postal Museum offers its young visitors insights into the interesting world of mail service. Children can create a souvenir postcard, learn about the history of the Pony Express and the legend of Owney the Postal Dog, and participate in a direct mail marketing campaign. Climb up into the cab of an Interstate Mail Truck and blow the bell and whistle. 2 Massachusetts Ave., NE. Metro: Union Station.
- **SACKLER GALLERY** @ The National Museums of Asian Art: Through the Sackler Gallery's ImaginAsia, kids visit a featured exhibition with a special guide written for children and create an art project to take home. Other special family programs include Asian dance and music lessons, storytelling, and more.

NATIONAL GALLERY OF ART

Washington - 6th Street & Constitution Avenue, NW (Metro: Archives/Navy Memorial, on the National Mall between Third and Seventh Streets) 20565. Phone: (202) 737-4215. www.nga.gov. Hours: Monday-Saturday 10:00am-5:00pm, Sunday 11:00am-6:00pm. Closed Christmas and New Years. Admission: FREE.

This fine art museum contains a collection of European and American works in chronological order with recognizable names including da Vinci, Renoir, Monet and Whistler. The new NGAkids Still Life interactive encourages young artists to explore the world around them by arranging artistic elements and everyday objects into works that mirror those of the old masters. But there are surprises in store, as some of the objects unexpectedly spring to life! Experiment with spatial arrangements, size variables, and perspective angles, then switch modes and add layers of textured "brushstrokes" to create a more

For updates visit: www.KidsLoveTravel.com

Washington, DC

abstract image. This Art Zone activity is suitable for all ages. Visitors with children can also participate in drop-in workshops, take several postcard tours of the collection using a packet of cards with pictures of objects and questions for discussion or rent a family-oriented audio tour. Ask for the "Great Picture Hunt" at the info desk which lists paintings of special interesst to kids.

WINTER SCULPTURE GARDEN ICE-SKATING RINK

Washington - The National Gallery of Art ice-skating rink in the Sculpture Garden will open for the ninth consecutive year through mid-March, weather permitting. Since it first opened in 1999, the ice-skating rink has been a popular and affordable recreational destination that attracts thousands of visitors each season. The rink's sleek, modern design creates open vistas throughout the parklike setting and offers skaters—both novice and skilled—a truly unique Washington, DC experience.

HOLIDAY HOMECOMING

Washington - Warm up your holiday season with spectacular art exhibitions and lively performances in the nation's capital. Lighting of the National Christmas Tree (White House Ellipse), Discovery Theatre children's performances (Discovery of Light), house tours, Crèche Nativity display and Christmas Pageant at National Cathedral. www.washington.org/holidayhomecoming/. Some events require fee. (December)

Chapter 3
North West

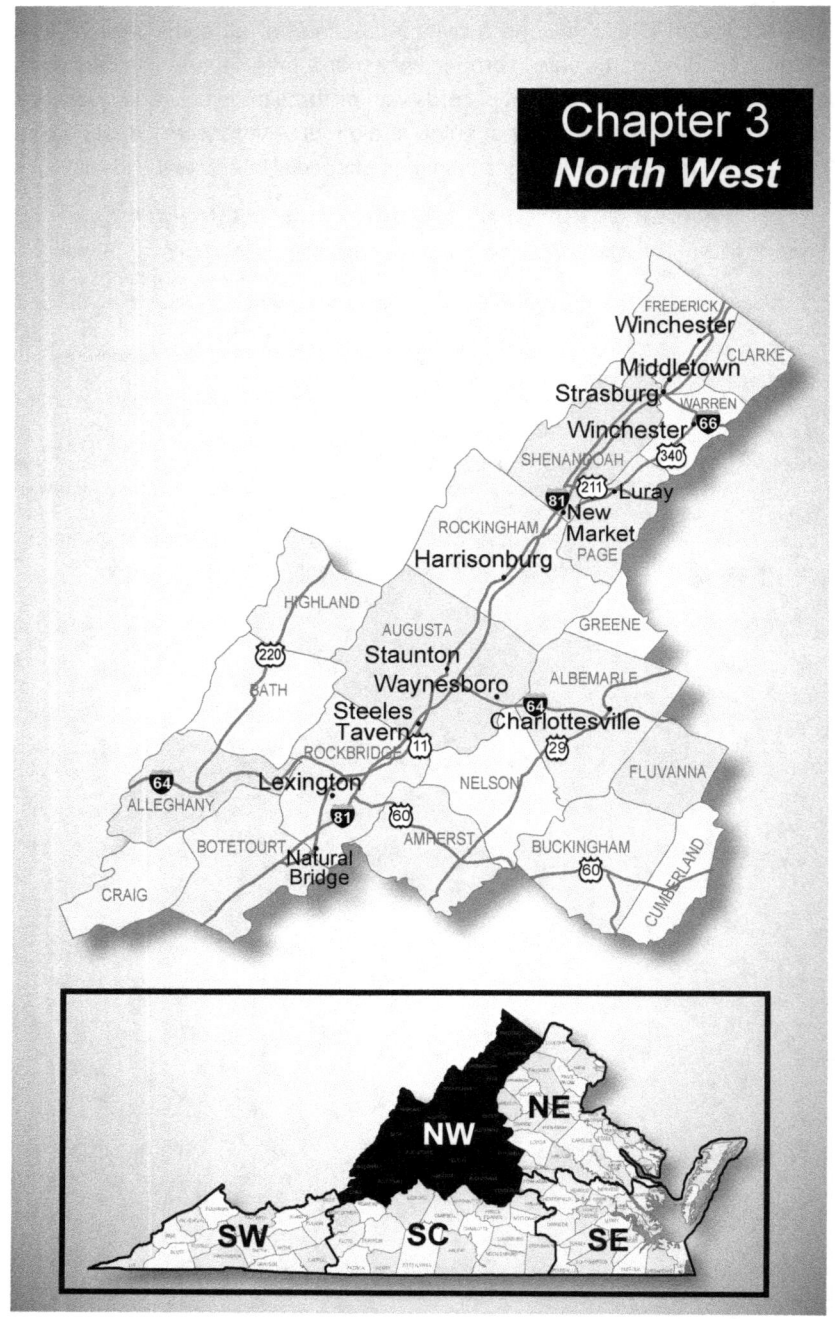

A Quick Tour of our Hand-Picked Favorites Around...

North West Virginia

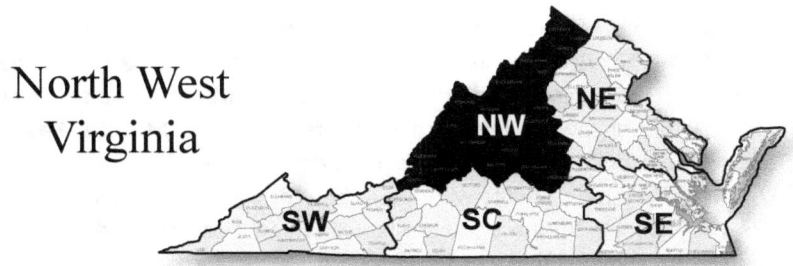

Experience the Heart of the Shenandoah Valley along a stretch of I-81. The beautiful scenery of the Valley and surrounding mountains will enhance your visit to natural wonders, historic sites, an old-fashioned homestead and a unique "parade" for a family fun excursion.

Begin in Winchester where you can see the beginnings of a president while he was still a young man and then pop into a little museum with a lot of creativity. At the **Shenandoah Valley Discovery Museum**, not only can you work at an apple factory, but also learn how to become a paleontologist. The Paleo Lab is open to stop by and watch the fossil preparation of a real dino find!

Just outside of Winchester, see **Dinosaur Land** in White Post. Every pre-historic creature — Allosaurus to Yaleasaurus — roams the land. For dino lovers, this site is a must. Corny – but oh the pictures are fun to take. There's also a Reptile Zoo at Luray Caverns complex for the big enthusiast.

And it just wouldn't be right not to stop at **Route 11 Potato Chips** in Middleton, guaranteeing delicious snacks for your ride home. See the many unique varieties being made through viewing windows, too. If you're daring try the Chesapeake Crab savory chips or the Sweet Potato dessert chips.

Explore nature's artistry at **Luray Caverns**, the most beautiful and musical caverns we've found in the Eastern United States. You won't want to leave without trying to match wits with the **Luray Garden Maze**. Hope you don't get lost! Explore nature's artistry at Shenandoah Caverns, the only Virginia cavern with an elevator. And certainly don't miss the spectacular parade floats from the Rose Parade, Presidential Inaugurals, Miss America and other big parades at **American Celebration on Parade**. Truly a one-of-a-kind museum, it is super colorful. Wait til you see the kids eyes pop when they enter!

KIDS LOVE VIRGINIA

For Civil War buffs, visit **New Market Battlefield** and learn its impact on Valley citizens at the Bushong House on the grounds. Inside, dress as soldiers. Outside, walk in the same fields where men lost their shoes – why?

Experience the life and thoughts of Thomas Jefferson where he spent much of his time…Charlottesville. We recommend the Children and Families tours of **Monticello** and its grounds. Did you know he had a business producing nails? Which side of the house is the front? Down the street from Monticello is our favorite tavern (and Jefferson's, too) – **Michie Tavern**. Take a journey of the senses as you're invited to dance the Virginia Reel, drink an 18th century punch, write with a quill pen, or play the dulcimer. This just wets your appetite for the Southern buffet served next door in the Ordinary dining room. Yum and fun!

Feeling nostalgic? The **Walton's Mountain Museum** is the birthplace of Earl Hamner Jr., who created the story behind the Waltons TV series based on his family's experiences growing up in the Depression era in the rural village of Schuyler (pronounced Sky-ler). The school building he once went to is now a showplace for scenes of John-Boy's Room, the big Kitchen, 1930s Family Room, and Godsey's Store. Ah, those simpler times. Good-night John-Boy…

Take your kids back to the 18th & 19th centuries at a living history farm, **Frontier Culture Museum,** in Staunton which recreates the farming and daily activities of a typical rural family living on a German farm, an Ulster (Scotch-Irish) farm, a house Worcestershire (English), and the American farm. Costumed staff demonstrate trades and traditions by showcasing old-time ways of living with the land. You will find this to be such a welcomed difference from typical living history farms – tying in a diversity of cultures is a wonderful way to see how our lives today are a mixture of habits from blended cultures.

This I-81 corridor could also be named "Stonewall Country." Slip back in time with a **Carriage Ride** through historic Lexington. At an easy pace, horse-drawn carriages travel the streets and guides tell stories of town history while passing the **Stonewall Jackson House** (worth stopping in afterwards to learn about his most unusual lifestyle), Lee Chapel, Washington & Lee University, catching a glimpse of VMI, and through residential historic districts.

While in the town of Natural Bridge, be sure to check out some "natural" opportunities we recommend. The most frequent stop is at the naturally formed **Natural Bridge** – one of the Seven Natural Wonders of the World! The bridge towers some 215 feet above Cedar Creek, making it 55 feet higher than Niagara Falls. Descend into the ravine and walk the trail or visit with

North West Area

Monacan Indians tribe members in their re-created village. If you plan to stay all day and night, the property also has caverns, a fabulous **Wax Museum & Factory Studio Tour** and the "**Drama of Creation**" nightly music and light performance beneath the bridge. The next day, drive your family vehicle through a zoo at **Virginia Safari Park**. With the windows or sliding doors open, your brave explorers can feed animals like elk, deer, ostrich, antelope and our favorite...zebras.

Sites and attractions are listed in order by City, Zip Code, and Name. Symbols indicated represent: |O| Restaurants   🛏 Lodging

BRYCE RESORT

Basye - PO Box 3 (11 miles west of I-81, exit #273, on Rt. 263) 22810. Phone: (540) 856-2121 or (800) 821-1444. www.bryceresort.com. Admission: Summer activities range average $5.00. Skiing rates based on time of day and rentals beginning at around $25.00. Ski packages with lift tickets and lodging are available. Note: Nearby are go carts, bowling, and roller rink fun.

Ride through rural Virginia to Bryce Resort where you can be on the links, the lake, the slopes, or the trail. Bryce has golf, skiing, hiking, dining, lodging, and great scenery. They also have 45-acre Lake Laura with a beach area, swimming, paddle boats and canoes, windsurfing, and fishing; sightseeing lift rides and grass skiing; mountain bike and in-line skate rentals; ziplining, and no-snow mountain tubing. Other activities near the Resort include miniature golf and horseback riding. Get a bird's eye view of the Shenandoah Valley from the eight ski runs at Bryce Resort. Now you can enjoy skiing, snowboarding and snow tubing from the friendly slopes. Bryce's Skiwee program for children is much acclaimed, while adults can benefit from lessons of their own. Rentals, a ski cafeteria with massive fireplace, ski boutique, and Coleman's Restaurant also await.

SHENANDOAH RIVER STATE PARK

Bentonville - 350 Daughter of Stars Drive (8 miles south of Front Royal, just off US 340) 22610. Phone: (540) 622-6840. www.dcr.virginia.gov/state_parks/and.shtml. Hours: 8:00am-dusk Admission: $10.00 per car.

Situated on the Shenandoah River with nearly 1700 acres along six miles of shoreline. A large riverside picnic area with shelters, trails, river access and a car-top launch makes this a popular destination for families, anglers and canoeists alike. 30 primitive and canoe-in campsites (individual and group) are available. With more than 15 miles of trails, the park has plenty of options for hiking, biking and horseback riding, including seasonal guided trail rides. The Indian Hollow Horse Livery operates April-October.

KIDS LOVE VIRGINIA

WADE'S MILL

Brownsburg / Raphine - 55 Kennedy-Wades Mill Loop (I-81 exit #205. Follow Rt. 606 west (Raphine Road) for 4 miles. 24472. www.wadesmill.com. Phone: (540) 348-1400 (mill). Hours: Thursday-Sunday 10:00am-5:00pm. (April-mid-December). The water wheel operates Saturdays 10am-noon and Sundays 3-5pm. Admission: FREE to visit Wade's Mill. Prices vary for specific cooking classes and special events or tours. Annual Apple Butter Fest in mid-October.

Wade's Mill is a working water-powered flour mill listed on the National Register of Historic Places. The shop features the mill's own flours, pottery, basketry and the "Cooks' Corner", with everything you need to cook and bake with their flours. Buy a homebaked treat and walk around the inside and outside of the mill, seeing and hearing its inner workings.

Charlottesville

ASHLAWN-HIGHLAND: JAMES MONROE

Charlottesville - 1000 James Monroe Pkwy (I-64 exit 121 SR 20 south to SR 53 east to CR 795 south, 2 miles beyond Monticello) 22902. Phone: (434) 293-9539. www.ashlawnhighland.org. Hours: Daily 9:00am-6:00pm (April-October). Daily 11:00am- 5:00pm (November-March). Closed New Year's Day, Thanksgiving Day & Christmas Day. Admission: $16.00 adult, $12.00 Child (6-12). Local resident & military discount. Neighborhood Pass savings. Note: Picnicking welcome. Educators: Biographies of James Monroe's life and politics are online. Even some favorite party recipes of Monroe's are there.

Tour the 535 acre estate of one home of our fifth President James Monroe. Great to visit during summer Camps or other living history festivals or events like Monroe's Workshops (hands-on soap, lantern doll making, open hearth food). His neighbor, Jefferson personally picked the site for him and this place has more of a feel of an early 1800s working plantation. Guided tours of the main house full of Monroe possessions and periodic demos of cooking and spinning plus a look at the overseers house and the slave quarters and gardens are included. Be on the lookout for "President Monroe" stopping by to chat with the youngsters.

PRESIDENT JAMES MONROE'S BIRTHDAY

Charlottesville - Ashlawn-Highland. Join as they celebrate the 250+ year anniversary of James Monroe's birth. Visit with James Monroe & other costumed re-enactors. (April 28)

CELEBRATING AMERICA'S INDEPENDENCE

Charlottesville - Ashlawn-Highland. Work and play on a 19th century plantation. Craft demonstrations, colonial games and more. Bring your picnic and lunch with us on the lawn. (July 4th)

North West Area

CHRISTMAS BY CANDLELIGHT

Charlottesville - Ashlawn-Highland. Fresh boxwood, fruits, holly and more adorn the historic home in the early 19th century style of President James and Elizabeth Monroe, with a late 19th century emphasis in the Victorian addition. Candle-light tour and re-enactment. Customs, holiday decorations, refreshments, and music. Admission fee. (December, selected days mid-month)

LEWIS AND CLARK EXPLORATORY CENTER

Charlottesville - Darden Towe Park (off Stony Point Road) 22902. Phone: (434) 979-2425. www.lewisandclarkvirginia.org. Hours: Keelboat Barn open Fridays & Saturdays 10:00am-4:00pm and Tuesday-Thursday 1:00-5:00pm (May-October). Admission: $7.00.

Inspired by the journals of Lewis and Clark, the Exploratory Center has a life-size replica of the Lewis & Clark Expedition's keelboat as its background. Activities include art and science projects, chiseling a dug out canoe, learning carpentry skills, knot tying and compassing. Visitors can also hike on beautiful trails by the Rivanna River.

MICHIE TAVERN

Charlottesville - 683 Thomas Jefferson Pkwy (I-64 exit SR 20 south to US 53 east, near Monticello) 22902. Phone: (434) 977-1234. www.michietavern.com. Hours: The Ordinary is open 11:15am-3:30pm (April-October) & 11:30am-3:00pm (November-March). Museum is open year-round. Tours are Daily 9:00am-5:00pm. Last tour: 4:20pm. Closed Christmas & New Year's Day. Admission is FREE to active military & family. $6.00 adult (12-61), $5.00 senior (60+), $2.00 child (6-11). Save on the cost of adult admission to the area's historic attractions by purchasing the "Neighborhood Pass" combo ticket or buying the Tour with Lunch. Lunch in the Ordinary: Buffet Only, $22.95 adult, $11.50 youth (12-15), $7.50 Child (6-11) child 5 and under eat FREE. (prices do not include beverage, dessert, sales tax or gratuity). Tours: Interactive tours: April-October. Self guided tours November through March. Educators: Lesson Plan - under Tours/Educational icon.

Learning to write with a quill pen...

THE TAVERN MUSEUM - Visitors experience the Tavern's past through an historical journey which recreates life when Mr. Michie operated his Inn. Guests are ushered into 18th century tavern life through a sensory experience where taste, touch, sight, smell, and sound recreate the past. Visitors are invited to dance the Virginia Reel in the Assembly Room, drink an 18th-century tavern punch (very yummy...get the recipe!), write with a quill pen, or wear a costume and play the dulcimer.

Jenny learns the "Virginia Reel"

Youth especially enjoy Mr. Michie's Treasure Hunt. Unravel the Innkeeper's clues to the past and a bag of (chocolate) gold coins rewards the successful explorers. After visiting the original Inn, the tour continues through the Tavern's dependent outbuildings, the ca. 1822 Printer's Market and the ca. 1797 Meadow Run Grist Mill. How would you make reservations at a stagecoach stop? Learn what "mind your beeswax" really means. This is a must see "Family Focused Fun".

THE TAVERN'S ORDINARY - Warm inviting smells of southern fried chicken and lively music and laughter often greets visitors shortly before they are formally welcomed to Historic Michie Tavern. The Tavern's dining rooms, the Ordinary, feature hearty fare offered by servers in period attire in a rustic Tavern setting. Their southern buffet is based on 18th century recipes. Patterned after the southern tradition, many guests choose the bountiful midday fare as their main meal of the day. The Colonial fried chicken and stewed tomatoes are the tastiest you'll find! During the colder months guests enjoy the winter menu before a roaring fire.

CANDLELIT YULETIDE TRADITIONS

Charlottesville - Michie Tavern. The original Tavern is decorated for the evenings and will offer a variety of special activities. Adults and youth will be invited to sing traditional carols with the Tavern musicians. Living history interpreters and story-tellers are available to entertain guests. Period refreshments are served from the 18th-century tap bar. Admission is free to the original Tavern during the evenings of Yuletide Traditions. Feast tickets must be ordered in advance. (second weekend evenings in December)

MONTICELLO

Charlottesville - Thomas Jefferson Pkwy. (I-64 exit SR 20 south to US 53east) 22902. Phone: (434) 984-9822. www.monticello.org. Hours: Daily 8:30am-6:00pm. Winter hours 10am-5pm. Closed Christmas Day. Admission: $32.00 adult & senior, $10.00 child (12-18). Neighborhood Pass - A combination discount ticket for touring Monticello, Ash Lawn - Highland and Michie Tavern is available at the Visitors Bureau located on Rt. 20 South. Tours: Guided tours leave approx. every 5 minutes. A shuttle bus or hike takes you to the top of the mountain where you receive a timed entrance card for the tour. Peak season waits can exceed 45 minutes. Note: Free exhibit at the Monticello Visitors Center on Rte. 20 south. Stop here first to glance over 400 objects found on the property of Monticello and

North West Area

to view the 40 minute film "Thomas Jefferson: The Pursuit of Liberty" shown daily on the hour in the summer and at 11:00am and 2:00pm the rest of the year. Tours for families featuring hands-on objects are available in the summer. Plantation Community weekends throughout the year. Educators: Monticello Classroom full of the best resources. Read a bio, scavenger hunt, build your own house, encrypt a message or ask Thomas Jefferson online.

In 1769 at the young age of 26, Thomas Jefferson began the design and construction of Monticello. Monticello is the autobiographical masterpiece of Thomas Jefferson, designed and redesigned and built and rebuilt for more than forty years. Jefferson was the third president and author of the Declaration of Independence. This was his home when he wasn't serving in public affairs.

Monticello sure looks like a President's house...

Visitors to Monticello tour the mountaintop main house, seasonal plantations and gardens and his gravesite. Much of Jefferson's diversity of interests can be found in artifacts around the house's 10 rooms of the first floor (esp. the items from Lewis and Clark's journeys). Which side is the front of the house? In fact, Jefferson never spoke of a single "front." Instead he spoke of both an "east front" and a "west front." How was the house heated? What are the holes over Jefferson's bed? The elliptical openings in the closet provided light and ventilation. Mulberry Row slave quarters and plantation industries are also on the tour. While you may have to wait a little while for your tour time, you can wander through the row and talk with the tradesmen and women who are making baskets or nails (from iron rods). You might also have a chance to see Virginia hams or chickens being cooked with period methods. The slave quarters are outlined on the grounds and the costumed slaves are pretty candid about life there. A discussion point might be: Advocating freedom for all people - but Jefferson held slaves?

ANNIVERSARY OF THOMAS JEFFERSON'S BIRTH

Charlottesville - Monticello. This outdoor ceremony is held at Jefferson's gravesite and features fife & drum corps and wreath-laying by Jefferson - affiliated groups. Admission: Free. (April 13th)

MONTICELLO INDEPENDENCE DAY CELEBRATION & NATURALIZATION CEREMONY

Charlottesville - Monticello. The one hour ceremony takes place on the West Lawn. A guest speaker will address people from countries around the world as they take the oath of U.S. citizenship at Monticello's Annual Independence Day Celebration & Naturalization Ceremony. (July 4th)

VIRGINIA DISCOVERY MUSEUM

Charlottesville - 524 E Main St (east end of downtown Pedestrian Mall) (I-64E, exit 12B North Monticello Avenue) 22902. www.vadm.org. Phone: (434) 977-1025. Hours: Monday-Saturday 9:30am-5:00pm. Closed Thanksgiving Day, Christmas Eve, Christmas Day and New Year's. Admission: $10 adults, $8.00 child (age 1+). Note: A historic carousel with six painted aluminum horses is nearby.

Young people (ages 1-10 best) and their adults explore and learn together about science, history and the arts. Permanent hands-on exhibits include walking into a construction zone; a reconstructed pioneer log cabin; a play town; Creation station; and a Jefferson exhibit. One of the most popular permanent exhibits is "See the Bees" alive in their hive. Or, meet live insects, hermit crabs or guinea pigs. Especially nice for locals and during those times of year when Monticello / Michie Tavern don't have living history family exhibits for the young.

UNIVERSITY OF VIRGINIA

Charlottesville - University Avenue, look for signs to Peabody Hall (on US 29 and US 250 Bus Routes 22903. Phone: (434) 924-3200. www.virginia.edu/academicalvillage/. Admission: FREE. Tours: Historical tours are offered daily at 10:00am, 11:00am, 2:00pm, 3:00pm and 4:00pm. No tours during holidays or exam periods. Parking is available at the Memorial Gym parking lot at Emmet Street and Ivy Road.

THE KLUGE-RUHE ABORIGINAL ART COLLECTION - one of the foremost private collections of Australian Aboriginal art in the world. 400 Peter Jefferson Place, (434) 244-0234. www.virginia.edu/kluge-ruhe/

McCORMICK OBSERVATORY - One of two observatories is open on the first and third Friday night of each month for about 2 hours. 1st and 3rd Fridays, 9:00pm-11:00pm, April-October; 8:00 pm-10:00pm, November-March. (434) 924-7494. www.astro.virginia.edu/pubnite.

UNIVERSITY OF VIRGINIA ART MUSEUM - Rugby Road, (434) 924-3592 or www.virginia.edu/artmuseum/. Fine arts museum of the University of Virginia, exhibits art from around the world dating from ancient times to the present day, with an emphasis on art produced during Jefferson's time.

UNIVERSITY OF VIRGINIA ROTUNDA & CENTRAL GROUNDS - Thomas Jefferson wished to be remembered as the "Father" of the University which embodied his vision as an educator and his passion for architecture.

North West Area

UNIVERSITY OF VIRGINIA CAVALIERS BASKETBALL-www.johnpauljonesarena.com

VIRGINIA FESTIVAL OF THE BOOK

Charlottesville - (434) 924-3296. www.vabook.org. This annual public festival features authors and book-related professionals in more than 150 programs. Events held throughout the city and county. Most events are FREE. (late March, long wkend)

APPLE HARVEST FESTIVAL

Charlottesville - 1435 Carters Mountain Trail. www.CarterMountainOrchard.com. (434) 977-1833. Celebrate harvest season in the mountains! Pick your own apples, enjoy a hayride, and spread a blanket to listen to the bluegrass music, all while enjoying the gorgeous views of the Blue Ridge Mountains, the Piedmont, and Charlottesville. Visit craft and food vendors, sip fresh apple cider, and browse the country store. (monthlong in September)

JEFFERSONIAN THANKSGIVING FESTIVAL

Charlottesville - Historic Court Square & Downtown Mall. www.jeffersonthanksgiving.org. (434) 978-4466. More than 50 activities are scheduled at seven different venues to let visitors experience what the community was like during the American Revolution. Events include colonial folk music and dancing, lite fare & special kids activities at the Ball, children's games, a kickoff parade, horse-drawn carriage rides, dramatic play, the "little militia" at the soldier encampment, demonstrations and lectures on history and culture. (November, second weekend)

DOUBLE TREE HOTEL

Charlottesville - 990 Hilton Heights Road (off Rte. 29, near airport). 22901. (434) 973-2121 or https://www.hilton.com/en/hotels/choshdt-doubletree-charlottesville/. The Doubletree Hotel Charlottesville overlooks the Rivanna River in the heart of Virginia's Blue Ridge Mountains. Nice spacious rooms w/ coffee maker and hair dryers and really comfy beds (plus tables to play or eat on). Warm chocolate chip cookie at check-in. Restaurant with buffets and kid pricing. Many fast food, casual restaurants down street (for frozen custard, go to Kohr's Brothers just a few blocks away). Nice family packages that include nearby site ticket packages. Indoor pool with cute-shaped steps for entry. From $129/night.

___

ANNIVERSARY OF THE BATTLE OF POINT OF FORK

Columbia - On the south bank of the James River. (434) 842-2277. Re-enactment of the Battle of Point of Fork, which occurred on June 5, 1781 between British Colonel Simcoe and American General Steuben. The Revolutionary War era event will feature period music, merchants, military encampment, battle reenactment and batteau rides. www.lynchburg.net./gaskins/PointofFork. FREE. (June, first weekend)

BEAR CREEK LAKE STATE PARK

Cumberland - 929 Oak Hill Road (from US 60, go north on Rte. 622 and then west on Rte. 629) 23040. www.dcr.virginia.gov/state_parks/bea.shtml. Phone: (804) 492-4410. Admission: $7.00 per car. Swimming $2.00-$5.00 per person (includes paddle or canoe boat rental).

Nestled in the heart of Cumberland State Forest in central Virginia is a park with activities center on a 40 acre lake with a boat launch, fishing pier, boat rentals and swimming beach, as well as lake-side camping, archery picnicking, bike rentals, a playground, hiking and a 14 mile multi-use trail.

CUMBERLAND STATE FOREST

Cumberland - 751 Oak Hill Road (north of State Route 60, west of State Route 45) 23040. Phone: (804) 492-4121. www.dof.virginia.gov/stateforest/list/cumberland.htm.

The 16,233 acre Cumberland State Forest is located in the piedmont of Virginia. Bear Creek Lake State Park is located within the Forest offering: camping, picnicking, swimming, boating, and hiking. Permanent campsites are installed inside the Park. Trails: A 16 mile Willis River Hiking Trail; and the Cumberland Multi-Use Trail (Hike, Bike, Horse). Fishing: There are five lakes located within the Forest. (Bear Creek Lake, Oak Hill Lake located off of Route 629, Winston Lake located off of Route 629, Arrowhead Lake located off of Route 629 and Bonbrook Lake located off of Route 626.). Archery Course: Consisting of a 3-D range and a practice range.

BELLE BOYD COTTAGE

Front Royal - 101 Chester St. (off US 340) 22630. https://warrenheritagesociety.org/belle-boyd-cottage/. Phone: (540) 636-1446. Hours: Tuesday-Saturday 10:00am-4:00pm (April-October). Admission: FREE and self guided.

This cottage was the home of the famous Confederate spy, Belle Boyd, when she visited the area during the Civil War. Guided tours feature Belle's story as a spy and a glimpse of life during the 1860's. Another, more thorough, site for a peek into Belle Boyd's life history is near Harper's Ferry, WV. Ask the folks at Harper's Ferry for directions.

SKYLINE CAVERNS

Front Royal - 10344 Stonewall Jackson Hwy (I-81 to I-66 to Rte. 340 south) 22630. Phone: (540) 635-4545 or (800) 296-4545. www.skylinecaverns.com. Hours: Open daily 9:00am. Closes at 6:00pm (mid June-Labor Day). Closes at 5:00pm (mid March - mid June & Labor Day - mid November). Wintertime closes at 4:00pm. Admission: $28.00 adult, $14.00 child (6-12). See website for discount coupons. Note: The Skyline Arrow is a ten minute ride on a one-fifth scale miniature train that carries you around Horseshoe curve, across apache Flats, by Kissing Rock and Sinkhole Overlook, and thru Boothill tunnel. Admission is $7.00 (age 2+). Mirror Maze is $7.00 per person.

North West Area

The cavern is one of the only places in the world that features unique formations known as Anthodites, "orchids of the mineral kingdom". Anthodites seem to defy gravity. Their delicate white spikes spread in all directions, including upwards, from their position on the cave ceiling. Their growth rate is estimated to be only one inch every seven thousand years. Other features include: the Capitol Dome, The Wishing Well, Cathedral Hall, and Rainbow Falls, which plunges over 37 feet from one of three underground streams that flow through the caverns.

JAMES RIVER STATE PARK

Gladstone - Rte. 1, Box 787 (from Rte. 60 west turn right on Rte. 605 at the J. River Bridge, left on Rte. 606) 24553. www.dcr.virginia.gov/state_parks/jam.shtml. Phone: (434) 933-4355. Admission: $5.00 per car. Note: Picnicking, boat launches, primitive campgrounds, equestrian camping and fishing. New Outdoor Adventure Livery Service - canoeing, kayaking, tubing and biking rentals.

The park features almost 1500 acres of rolling farm meadows, quiet forest and beautiful mountain vistas. Visitors can canoe, fish or camp along the banks of the historic James River or around scenic Branch pond. The park has nearly 20 miles of multiuse trails for hiking, biking and bridle use. Green Hill Trail and the fishing pier are wheelchair accessible. The Nature Center has live native reptiles and amphibians on display, as well as replicas of birds and other wildlife of the area. Also, there are hands-on exhibits, wildlife field guides and activity books. The center hosts several interpretive programs including Creature Features and crafts programs.

GRAND CAVERNS

Grottoes - 5 Grand Caverns Drive (I-81 exit 235 east to SR 256) 24441. Phone: (540) 249-5705 or (888) 430-CAVE. www.grandcaverns.com. Hours: Daily 9:00am-5:00pm (April-October). 10am-4pm rest of year. Admission: $13.50-$23.00 (age 6+) Tours: Guided one hour tours begin every 30 minutes. Note: Hiking and biking trails, picnic shelters, swimming pool, miniature golf, tennis courts and a gift shop. Annual bluegrass festival early September.

This is America's oldest show cave. The panorama of subterranean beauty has been open to the public since 1806. Cathedral Hall, 280 feet long and over 70 feet high, is one of the largest rooms of any cavern in the East. Rare "shield" formations create a variety of formations like the famous "Bridal Veil, Stonewall Jackson's Horse and Dante's Inferno". The walls point out signatures of Civil War soldiers. General Stonewall Jackson even quartered his troops at Grand Caverns. The 5000 square foot Grand Ballroom was the scene of many early 19th century dances.

Harrisonburg

EXPLORE MORE DISCOVERY MUSEUM

Harrisonburg - 150 South Main Street 22801. www.iexploremore.com Phone: (540) 442-8900. Hours: Tuesday-Saturday 10:00am-5:00pm. First Fridays of the month 4:00-7:00pm (free admission). Admission: $8.50 per person (age 1+).

Exhibits include a theater (complete with stage, lighting, costumes and sets), farmer's market (dig for vegetables, select produce at the farmer's market or even go apple picking), medical center, construction and building, science, art, down on the farm, a pretend mechanics garage, and many workshops throughout the year. Ages 3 & under can wander in Over in the Meadow.

JAMES MADISON UNIVERSITY CAMPUS

Harrisonburg - Main Street (near downtown) 22802. www.jmu.edu. Phone: (434) 568-6211. Hours: Open school days, some closed summers. Admission: FREE.

JMU Permanent Attractions include:

EDITH J. CARRIER ARBORETUM - Open daily dawn to dusk, off University Boulevard; Contains a wide variety of trees and plants native to Virginia; call (434) 568-3194 for tours.

MINERALOGY MUSEUM - Open daily, second floor, Miller Hall; Features mineral specimens from around the world as well as a collection of Virginia specimens; call (434) 568-6421 for tours.

ANCIENT GREEK AND ROMAN COIN DISPLAY - Open daily, Carrier Library lobby; Showcases 71 silver, bronze and gold coins from the JMU Foundation's Fine Art Collection.

MASSANUTTEN RESORT

Harrisonburg (McGaheysville) - Rte. 644, 1822 Resort Drive (1-81N to Rt.33E at Harrisonburg. 10 miles to Rt.644 & entrance on left) 22840. Phone: (540) 289-9441 or (800) 207-MASS. www.massresort.com. Admission: Activity cards are available. Many activities are covered under lodging pricing. Golf and boat and ski rentals and fees are extra. $29.00-$40.00 for Waterpark Day Pass. Note: Shenandoah River for a half day of fishing or just relaxing while canoeing, kayaking or river tubing. Many accommodations available from hotel rooms to condos to timeshare rentals.

At Massanutten Resort in WINTERtime expect days filled with snow, whether it be on the slopes, at the tubing park, or boarding at one of the region's only snowboard parks. Experience the 1,100-foot vertical drop. Ski down the 3,300- foot Diamond Jim or the 4,100-foot Para-dice. The terrain park is for riders, skiboarders, and twin tip skiers. At night, all of the slopes are lit.

North West Area

SUMMER outdoor activities include Peaked Mountain Express - an Italian-made system of waterless tubing on special mats that create the sensation of snow tubing - without the snow! And, Mist Island Amusements offers kid-friendly, fun-filled amusements, including Finding Nemo Bounce, Island Adventure Play Land, Water Tag, a seven-station Obstacle Course, Zipline, Canopy Tours, Gem Mining and Airbrush Tattoos.

WATERPARK: This year-round mountain resort takes to the great indoors with its 42,000 square foot indoor waterpark. With an 800 gallon tipping bucket that dumps water down over the structure every few minutes as its centerpiece, guests can also climb the tower to ride one of 6 tube slides. Other indoor water activities include water cannons and a lazy river. Smaller kids have their own area with smaller slides and interactive play features. Surfers will enjoy the "Flow Ryder" which simulates surfing a wave. The indoor building itself is a pyramid-shaped structure, wood framed with a transparent roofing material and glass walls, which allows sunlight in and guests a scenic view of the Shenandoah Valley and Blue Ridge Mountains.

Activities at the year-round resort include: Basketball, Canoe/Kayak, Fishing, Golf, Hiking, Horseback Riding, Mini-golf, Mountain Biking, Skate Boarding, Skiing, Snowboarding, Swimming, Tennis, Volleyball, Crafts, Karaoke Night and Music Shows. Kids Programs include: Child Care Services, Finger-painting, Kids Night Out Slope Sliders, Weekend Programs. There is a general store, lodging, dining including a slopeside cafeteria.

HOMESTEAD RESORT

Hot Springs - 7696 Sam Snead Highway (I-64 west to exit 16 (first Covington exit), follow the signs for U.S. 220 north) 24445. Phone: (540) 839-1766 or (800) 838-1766. www.thehomestead.com. Hours: The KidsClub is open Monday through Saturday 9:00-4:00pm, and Sunday 9:00am-1:00pm. Each Saturday evening dinners are held from 6:30-9:30pm. Admission: Guest rooms vary in price and most rates include breakfast and dinner daily. Packages are available. Almost all activities require separate fees, especially golfing and skiing.

Nine slopes here with kids ski school, snowboarding and lodging/dining at restaurants, cafes and grilles. KidsClub is the club for KIDS ONLY! Headquartered in its own Clubhouse, located on Cottage Row, KidsClub features three main areas of activity: The Children's Literary Center with a library of regional folklore. A resident storyteller and, on special occasions, a children's author may visit to read excerpts from his or her book. On International Day, kids may read and learn about life in other cultures.

KIDS LOVE VIRGINIA

There's an Art & Design Center and The Science & Biology Center. There are also many other fun activities available around the resort for kids: pole fishing at the Children's Fish Pond, tennis on the mini-courts, hiking and mountain biking, hand-led horseback rides, falconry demonstrations with exotic birds, bowling, winter sports such as skiing, ice skating, snowboarding and snow tubing, swimming, nightly movies, video games, etc. A qualified babysitting service is available too.

Lexington

HULL'S DRIVE IN THEATRE

Lexington - 2367 N Lee Highway (Rte. 11 four miles north of Lexington) 24450. Phone: (540) 463-2621. www.hullsdrivein.com. Hours: Friday-Saturday (April-October). Wednesday paper lists shows playing. Gates open one hour before and movies start 20 minutes after sunset. Admission: $7.00 adult, $3.00 child (5-11).

A blast from the past, Hull's is an authentic 1950's drive-in movie theater. The drive-in has the distinction of being the only community operated drive-in in the U.S. and the only one with status as a non-profit organization. The prices are low and the food reasonable. Mostly G and PG movies are shown.

LEE CHAPEL AND MUSEUM

Lexington - Washington and Lee University (US 11 Business to University) 24450. Phone: (540) 463-8768. https://www.vmi.edu/museums-and-archives/vmi-museum/ Hours: Daily 9:00am-5:00pm. Wednesday-Friday 11:00am-6:00pm, Saturday 10:00am-5:00pm (winter). Closed for school breaks. Admission: Suggested donation $5.00 adult, $3.00 child.

Lee attended daily worship services here with students and the lower level housed his office, the treasurer's office and the YMCA headquarters (student center). Lee's office is preserved much as he left it for the last time on September 28, 1870. The rest of the lower level is a museum exhibiting items once owned by the Lee and Washington families, an exhibition tracing the history and heritage of Washington and Lee University and a museum shop. The building houses the memorial sculpture of the recumbent Lee by Edward Valentine and includes a family crypt in the lower level where the general's remains were buried. His wife, mother, father ("Light-Horse Harry" Lee), all of his children and other relatives are now buried in the crypt as well. The remains of his beloved horse, Traveler, rest in a plot outside the museum entrance.

North West Area

LEXINGTON CARRIAGE COMPANY

Lexington - 106 East Washington Street (downtown, across from the Visitor Center) 24450. www.lexcarriage.com. Phone: (540) 463-3777 (Visitor's Center) or (540) 463-5647. Hours: Daily including holidays (weather permitting) 11:00am-5:00pm (April-October). Summer months have slightly longer hours. Admission: $20.00 adult, $18.00 senior (65+), $15.00 County residents and Active military $10.00 youth (4-13). Tours: Normally 2-3 eight passenger carriages operate each day. Last tour at 1:00pm if temperature is 92 degrees or more. Narrated tour lasts 40-45 minutes.

This very educational and kid-friendly tour offers an intriguing way to tour the unique 19th century college town of Lexington. At an easy pace, horse drawn carriages travel the streets and tell stories of town history while passing Stonewall Jackson House, historic downtown, past Lee Chapel, by Washington and Lee University and thru residential historic districts. Finally, pass by the Stonewall Jackson Memorial Cemetery where the guide points out the tomb of Stonewall Jackson. The streets of town were much higher in the 1700s - note the houses' doors and balconies. Pass the Livery Inn that was once a "hotel for horses", now for people. The Lee House has the stable open to view where Traveler (Lee's famous horse) lived. Kids like the name of the house called "Skinny". This tour is worth the price for the "inside" stories alone!

STONEWALL JACKSON HOUSE

Lexington - 8 East Washington Street (US 11 Bus or US 60 into downtown, just past Visitors Center) 24450. https://www.vmi.edu/museums-and-archives/jackson-house-museum/ Phone: (540) 463-2552. Hours: Tuesday-Saturday 9:00 am-5:00pm. Special Guided tours are offered at 9:00am and again at 4:00pm. Visitors can experience self-guided tours of the house between 10:00am and 4:00pm. Closed winter holidays, January & February. Admission: $10.00 adult, $7.00 youth (ages 6-17). VMI cadets/faculty/staff/alumni FREE. Discounts for active military and veterans.

Thomas Jonathan Jackson is known to the world as "Stonewall" Jackson. In Lexington, where Jackson lived and taught for ten years before the Civil War, he was known simply as Major Thomas Jackson, a professor at Virginia Military Institute. The Stonewall Jackson House is the only home that Thomas Jackson ever owned. Jackson and his wife, Mary Anna, shared two years there before he rode off to war on April 21, 1861, never to return alive.

The kids receive a chalkboard with items to circle as they are seen on the tour.

Jackson was a health food fanatic (loved fruits and veggies, kids!) and only liked bottled water from Western Virginia. Look for the rug that was cloth and painted with layers of paint (a kind of early vinyl flooring). He collected fossils, loved kids, took cold bathes every day, exercised regularly and slept sitting up. Your guide weaves comedy into the tales of this eccentric man, "Stonewall Jackson". An excellent, fun way to study a famous historical soldier, teacher, and leader.

"Let your words be as few as will express the sense you wish to convey and above all let what you say be true."
Thomas Jackson

APPLE DAY

Lexington - Stonewall Jackson House. Apple cider pressing, music making, storytelling, and crafts activities for children. (mid-October Saturday)

CHRISTMAS REMEMBERED

Lexington - Stonewall Jackson House. Free tours, seasonal music and decorations, refreshments and crafts for children. (first Saturday in December)

VIRGINIA HORSE CENTER

Lexington - 487 Maury River Road, Rte. 39 (I-64 west to exit 55) 24450. Phone: (540) 464-2950. www.horsecenter.org. Hours: Monday-Friday 9:00am-5:00pm and anytime the Coliseum is open. Admission: FREE. Some special events and tours available to the public for a small fee. Note: They do not have horses here for lessons or trail riding. They are strictly an events facility.

The Virginia Horse Center is set in a panoramic mountain setting and boasts 600 acres, six barns, and a coliseum that seats 4000. The Center is host to over 95 events every year (see the show schedule on their website) that provide a showcase for state, national and international horse competition. The Work Horse Museum is in the Anderson Coliseum and has a collection of over 30 farm implements used by farmers in the era before motor vehicles.

North West Area

VMI, VIRGINIA MILITARY INSTITUTE

Lexington - (VMI Parade Grounds: Off US11 and Jefferson, I-81, exit 195) 24450. www.vmi.edu/vmi_museum/. Phone: (540) 464-7334. Hours: Daily, 9:00am-5:00pm. Closed Winter break Admission: Donations. Tours: Free tours of the VMI campus are conducted by cadets at Noon daily. Note: Dress parades are normally held throughout the school year on Fridays at 4:35pm, weather permitting.

The nation's oldest state military college is home to a museum which chronicles the school's history and honors VMI educated leaders and heroes. In the VMI Museum, kids can take the "Slightly More Than 20 Questions" worksheet with them as they look for Stonewall Jackson's bullet-torn raincoat, an "air" gun, a sample cadet barracks, and George S. Patton's cadet uniform. Print one off the website "For Teachers" page. The brightest and biggest exhibit is Stonewall Jackson's beloved Civil War horse.

FOURTH OF JULY BALLOON RALLY

VMI Parade Grounds. www.sunriserotarylexva.org Hot air balloon flights, tethered balloon rides, a balloon glow, children's activities, live music, great food and a fantastic FIREWORKS display! (July 4th and 5th)

Luray

LURAY CAVERNS

Luray - 970 US 211 West. 101 Cave Hill Rd (gps) (I-81 exit 264, Follow Signs) 22835. Phone: (540) 743-6551. www.luraycaverns.com. Hours: Daily, 9:00am-6:00pm (mid-March to mid-June), 9:00am-7:00pm (mid-June to Labor Day), 9:00am-6:00pm (Labor Day to end of Oct), Weekdays 9:00am-4:00pm (November to March). Admission: $32.00 adult, $29.00 senior (62+), $16.00 child (age 6-12) (Under 6 FREE with an adult). Includes tour of cavern and Museums. Discounts at local supermarkets. Rope Adventure ropes course $7-10.00. Garden Maze, $6-$10. Tours: Guided, one hour tours leave every 10-20 minutes. Note: Hiking trails, Skyline Drive nearby. Caverns are a cool 54 degrees with sloped, paved walkways. Steps at the entrance only. Paths are very easy. You can use strollers.

In 1878, cold air rushing out of a limestone sinkhole atop a big hill, blew out a candle held by Andrew Campbell, the town tinsmith. They dug away loose rock, and candle in hand, found themselves in the largest caverns in the East. Highlights of the property include:

GREAT STALACPIPE ORGAN - invented in 1954 by Mr. Sprinkle, a mathematician and electronic scientist at the Pentagon. It took three years of searching the vast chambers of the caverns, tapping potential formations with a tuning fork. Stalactites were selected to precisely match a musical scale in order to become part of what would eventually be known as the world's largest musical instrument! To listen to and sometimes, see, the rubber-tipped plunger strike a column when a key is depressed is like watching a giant child's music box. This is something to write home about! The coolest, most interesting caverns ever.

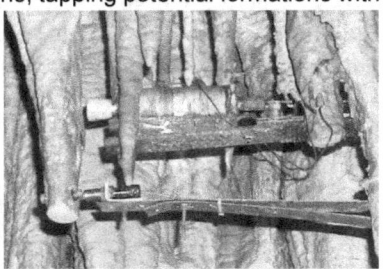

A rubber-tipped plunger stikes a tuned rock and makes beatiful music...wow!

FAVORITE FORMATIONS: the parted drapery canopy/tent; Dream Lake reflections of stalactites in the pool (you must see this to believe the optical illusion); Wishing Well of blue/green water where your coins are given to charity (the most productive wishing well in the world); and near the end of the tour the world famous fried eggs. Use your imagination to discover names for many other formations. We named one... "Shaggy Dog", another the "Giant Turtle".

Dream Lake....

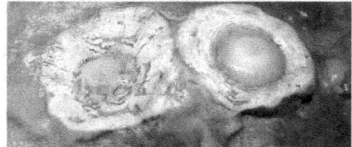

the Famous "Fried Egg" formation

CAR & CARRIAGE CARAVAN MUSEUM: 140 item exhibit relating to history of transportation, including cars, carriages, coaches and costumes dating from 1725. The prize in the collection is a 1892 Benz - oldest operating car in America. (included with Caverns admission)

THE GARDEN MAZE: A very large maze covering one acre of ornamental gardens. The 1500 trees create a ½ mile pathway of disarray, illogical rhythm and a family project to solve the puzzle (great, fun development of math skills, mom and dad). It is so-o-o- fun! Clues: Look for clues near the cave, near the fountain, and elsewhere. Watch out for those cute dead end signs. Our favorite maze ever!

For updates visit: www.KidsLoveTravel.com

LURAY ZOO

Luray - 1087 US 211W 22835. Phone: (540) 743-4113. www.lurayzoo.com. Hours: Open daily 10:00am-5:00pm. Winter hours vary weekends only. Rain or shine. Admission: $12.00 adult, $6.00 child (3-12) Note: Nature shop.

Luray Zoo is a true rescue zoo. The zoo specializes in providing a home for unwanted, abused and confiscated exotic animals. Over 87 different species are exhibited with pygmy goats, tame deer, geckos, donkeys, llamas, exotic wild animals and Virginia's largest reptile collection. Here you will find most every type of venomous snake that resides in the United States. Mammoth pythons, king cobras, and some very interesting lizards and turtle species are also on exhibit. In the outdoor section of the center, one can roam with tame animals in the petting zoo. The loose animals in the petting area love to be hand fed and loved on. African pygmy goats are the star attraction, small, cute, animated, and friendly. Also in the petting zoo are Fallow deer from Europe, Sicilian donkeys, llamas and sheep. Food for the animals may be purchased at on site feeding stations.

SHENANDOAH NATIONAL PARK & SKYLINE DRIVE

Luray - Hdqtrs. 3655 US Hwy. 211 East (Skyline Drive entrances are: Front Royal/US 340; Thornton Gap/US 211; Swift Run Gap/US 33; Rockfish Gap/US 250&I-64) 22835. Phone: (540) 999-3500. www.nps.gov/shen. Admission: Some areas (visitors centers) require $30.00 per vehicle fee for entrance (valid for 7 days). Skyline drive is FREE. Note: Junior Ranger Nature programs, camping, fishing, hiking, lodging, picnicking and restaurants (most seasonal). National Park Info Centers are: Dickey Ridge, mile 4.6; Byrd, mile 51; and Loft Mt., mile 79.5. Speed limit is 35 mph. Educators: Download lesson plans specific to topic and grade online under "For Teachers."

Shenandoah National Park lies astride a beautiful section of the Blue Ridge Mountains, which form the eastern rampart of the Appalachian Mountains between Pennsylvania and Georgia. The Shenandoah River flows through the valley to the west, with Massanutten Mountain, 40 miles long, standing between the river's north and south forks. The rolling Piedmont country lies to the east of the park. In addition to the eastern brook trout, 35 other fish species live within Shenandoah National Park's streams - so the fishing is varied. The historic 105-mile Skyline Drive, a National Scenic Byway, traverses Shenandoah National Park.

> 101 miles of the Appalachian Trail are within this park.

The Park varies in width from less than one mile to about thirteen miles, so that views from peaks and overlooks include not only the Blue Ridge itself, but also the patchwork of woods, farmlands and orchards on either side.

SKYLINE DRIVE - A long road that winds along the crest of the mountains (highest point is near Front Royal, elevation 3680 feet) through the length of the park, provides many scenic stop areas to view vistas of the spectacular landscape to east and west. Skyline Drive holds more than 500 miles of trails, including 101 miles of the Appalachian Trail. Trails may follow a ridge crest, or they may lead to high places with panoramic views or to waterfalls in deep canyons (Thornton Gap area 610 foot tunnel through solid granodiorite of Mary's Rock). Many animals, including deer, black bears, and wild turkeys, flourish among the rich growth of an oak-hickory forest. In season, bushes and wildflowers bloom along the Drive and trails.

Middletown

CEDAR CREEK & BELLE GROVE NATIONAL HISTORICAL PARK

Middletown - PO Box 229, 8437 Valley Pike (Interstate 81 to Strasburg exit #298, North on Route 11) 22645. www.nps.gov/cebe Phone: (540) 869-2064 or (888) 628-1864. Welcome Center Hours: Monday-Saturday 10:00am-4:00pm, Sunday 1:00-5:00pm (mid-March-October). Admission: FREE. Tours: Guided tours every hour are $12.00 adult, $6.00 student (6-16).

The Cedar Creek Visitors Center is the site of a well stocked bookstore, and an interpretive exhibit on the 1864 Valley Campaign and Battle of Cedar Creek. Admission includes viewing the historic video film shown throughout the day. Belle Grove, an 18th-century plantation house is on the premises and open for tours. During the Civil War, Belle Grove was at the center of the decisive Battle of Belle Grove or Cedar Creek. Today, the plantation includes the main house and gardens, original outbuildings, a classic 1918 barn, an overseer's house, the slave cemetery, a heritage apple orchard, fields and meadows, and scenic mountain views.

EASTER EGG HUNT

Middletown - Belle Grove Plantation. Easter egg hunts which include the Easter Bunny, refreshments and other activities: (Easter Saturday)

CEDAR CREEK LIVING HISTORY & RE-ENACTMENT WEEKEND

Middletown - Battlefield & Belle Grove Plantation. www.bellegrove.org. (540) 869-2028. Tour the historic Manor House, see re-enactors interpret civilian life and watch battle re-creations. Food and Civil War merchants. (October, second or third weekend)

CHRISTMAS CANDLELIGHT TOURS AT BELLE GROVE
Middletown - Belle Grove Plantation. Open House. Call for more information. Admission fee. (December weekends until Christmas)

ROUTE 11 POTATO CHIPS
Mount Jackson - 11 Edwards Way (I-81 to Middletown exit 269, turn West, then right on Caverns Road) 22842. Phone: (540) 477-9664. www.rt11.com. Hours: Monday-Saturday 9:00am-5:00pm. All varieties out for sampling along with Rte. 11 dips (best sampling on weekends). Admission: FREE. Note: Take your favorite crabcake recipe; substitute crushed Mama Zuma Habanero chips for breading, and pan or deep fry. Mmm! Taro Root are a great substitute for tortilla chips. Route 11 Dill Pickle chips were named Best Chip To Eat with a Burger.

Not too long ago, with lots of potatoes, good oil, salt, serendipity, and a little luck, Route 11 Potato Chips sprouted in an old feed store in Middletown, Virginia. Come watch the spudmasters at work through the observation window and sample the chips. The best time to see any frying action is morning or early afternoon on Fridays and Saturdays (sample warm chips right off the line!). Look for the bucket peeler and slicer (both automatic) that peels, slices and then drops chips into hot oil. Some of their specialties include fried potatoes using a blend of peanut and sunflower oil, with no preservatives. The  basic are lightly salted but they have a wide variety of flavors like barbeque, salt 'n vinegar, sour cream 'n chive, Chesapeake crab, and sweet potato chips (salted or dill pickle chips!). Interesting observation tour for all ages!

DOUTHAT STATE PARK
Millboro - Rte. 1, Box 212 (I-64 exit 27 to SR 629 north) 24460. Phone: (540) 862-8100. www.dcr.virginia.gov/state_parks/dou.shtml. Admission: $7.00 per vehicle.

Amid mountain scenery, visitors can enjoy a 50 acre lake stocked with trout, a restaurant overlooking the water, a sandy swimming beach, bathhouse, cabins, picnic areas and tent/trailer campgrounds. The park also features two completely furnished lodges that accommodate 15-17 guests.

EASTER EGG HUNT

Millwood - Historic Long Branch. (888) 558-5567 or www.historiclongbranch.com. Sunrise Services or Easter egg hunts which include the Easter Bunny, refreshments and other activities: (Easter weekend)

NATURAL CHIMNEYS NAT'L JOUSTING TOURNAMENT

Mt. Solon - Natural Chimneys Regional Park. www.nationaljousting.com. (540) 350-2510. The exciting sport of Ring Jousting requires horseback riders to spear, on a lance, a series of small metal rings suspended from a wire, as they gallop steadily past the spectators. Admission fee. (most held June and August)

Natural Bridge

NATURAL BRIDGE STATE PARK

Natural Bridge - 15 Appledore Lane (I-81 exit 175 and 180, on US 11 at jct. SR 130) 24578. Phone: (800) 533-1410. www.dcr.virginia.gov/state-parks/natural-bridge. Hours: 10:00am-6:00pm. Admission: $9.00 adult, $6.00 child (6-12). Note: Take a break for lunch and shopping: Summerhouse Cafe on Cedar Creek; Cafe and Deli in the Gift Shop; Ice cream & fudge at the Candy Counter. Chairlift $5.00 round trip.

Known by the Monacan Indians as "The Bridge of God", it started as a site of worship. In 1774, Thomas Jefferson purchased from King George III this awe inspiring "rock bridge" to preserve it as a mountain retreat. Geologists now feel that this was once a cave that collapsed to form a bridge. Today, it is considered one of the "Seven Natural Wonders of the World!"

The bridge was much, much bigger than we imagined...

BRIDGE, CEDAR CREEK TRAIL & MONACAN INDIAN VILLAGE - The bridge towers some 215 feet above the Cedar Creek, making it 55 feet higher than Niagara Falls. The span between the walls is 90 feet long, and about 100 feet wide. Descend into the ravine to Cedar Creek and pass underneath it. Visit the Monacan Indians as you stroll to Lace Falls (look for blue heron along the way). Journey back 300 years as you walk and sit amongst Monacans as you learn about and assist with canoe building, shelter construction, hide tanning, mat and rope weaving, fishing, tool making, gardening, harvesting, preparing meals, making pots and bowls or making baskets. Try to have the kids think of one or two questions to ask the Monacans - they are wonderful storytellers, you know. Daily activities change with the seasons.

CAVERNS - a 45 minute guided journey into the east coast's deepest commercial cave, 34 stories into the earth. Complete with the usual stalagmites and stalactites, but also, hanging gardens, underground streams and waterfalls. Tours depart every 20 minutes. Caverns open 10:00am-5:00pm (March-November). $18 adult, $12 child (7-17).

NATURAL BRIDGE HOTEL

Natural Bridge - US 11. (800) 533-1410 or www.naturalbridgeva.com. Inn and cottages with dining room and cafes, gift shop. We recommend staying on the property at this hotel so you can easily walk to the many sites in the complex. Lodging runs about $65.00-$150.00 per night. The dining room is nice for breakfast but a little "stuffy" for active kids for dinner. Seasonal snack shops and delis are nearby.

NATURAL BRIDGE ZOO

Natural Bridge - 5784 S Lee Hwy (Interstate 81 between exits 180 and 175) 24578. Phone: (540) 291-2420. www.naturalbridgezoo.com. Hours: Daily 10:00am-6:00pm. Open until 7:00pm weekends. (mid March - early September). Closed one hour earlier (September-November). Admission: $20.00 adult, $18.00 senior, $14.00 Child (3-12) Under age 3 are FREE. Note: Largest animal petting area in Virginia. Safari Shop. Picnic grounds.

Most are attracted here to visit the baby giraffes, bottle raised bear cubs, dozens of fuzzy miniature donkey colts, getting nuzzled by a llama, hugging a baby dromedary camel, or gazing into the eyes of a huge white tiger. Also, you can watch the only breeding colony of flamingos in Virginia, building their nests and rearing their young. Maybe try an elephant ride on weekends (additional fee).

VIRGINIA SAFARI PARK

Natural Bridge - 229 Safari Lane (Off I-81 exits 180/180B - cross over US 11 to the KOA) 24578. Phone: (540) 291-3205. www.virginiasafaripark.com. Hours: 9:00am-5:30pm, the last car admitted at 4pm. Open later on weekends. Closed sooner in March and November. Closed winters. Admission: $26.95 adult, $24.95 senior (65+), $18.95 child (2-12). Buckets of food $4.00. Admission now includes their 16-page, full color Safari Guidebook. Tours: Guided wagon tours at 1:00pm and 3:00pm on weekends for $4.00 additional per person (includes bucket of animal feed). Note: new exhibits including Tiger Territory, Giraffe Feeding, Budgie Aviary.

Virginia Safari Park is a drive-thru zoo located on 180 acres of hills and valleys, pasture and woods, where hundreds of exotic animals from all over the world roam free while you remain in your car. With the windows open, your brave explorers can feed live animals! It's truly a one-of-a-kind experience as you hand feed H-U-G-E elk, ostrich (they were so greedy and mean!), reindeer, antelope, camels, deer, and our favorite...the zebras (they were so kind and well-mannered, not pushy, and took their turns!). If you really have the courage (we're told it's OK) you can hand-feed bison and long (very long) horn cattle. We chickened out, but most folks just wait till they get close and throw the feed on the ground. Save at least one bucket of food for the camels - they'll eat everything you give them! It was interesting to watch the matriarch of the zebra herds establish her leadership role. Other herd members will fear her and let her get most of the food. Cameras are most welcome and your "drive" admission includes a visit to the free-flight bird aviary, a petting zoo with monkeys, kangaroos and tortoises; plus a giraffe feeding station. Climb up and feed the giraffes - on their level! Wagon rides (additional fee) are also available. What a day!

APPLE HARVEST & APPLE BUTTER FESTIVALS, NELSON CTY

Nelson County - Each weekend a different orchard (off 56 West or US 29) hosts an event. Call (800) 282-8223 to request a fact sheet on orchards, maps for scenic driving tours and festival dates and times. Hayrides to orchard and pumpkin patches. Cider, ham, music and apple butter making. www.nelsoncounty.com. (September / October)

New Market

ENDLESS CAVERNS

New Market - PO Box 859 (I-81 exit 264, US 11 south) 22844. Phone: (540) 896-2283. https://endlesscaverns.com/. Hours: Daily Open at 10:00am-4pm (April-October). Admission: $20.00 adult, $9.00 child (4-12). Note: Campground and mountain spring water sold at gift shop.

Through the years there have been many expeditions into the Endless Caverns to try and find an end to the complex network of underground passageways. Over five miles of cave passage are mapped and no end is in sight. During the one hour fifteen minute guided tour, you will see stunning displays of calcite formations. Your guide will explain the geology, history and explorations stories of the cavern. The caverns are presented with white lighting only, allowing you to see the natural effect.

VIRGINIA MUSEUM OF THE CIVIL WAR NEW MARKET BATTLEFIELD

New Market - 8895 Collins Drive (I-81 exit 264, US211 West, follow signs) 22844. Phone: (540) 740-3101. http://vmi.edu/museums-and-archives/virginia-museum-of-the-civil-war/. Hours: Daily 9:00am-5:00pm. Closed New Year's, Christmas and Thanksgiving. Admission: $7.00 adult, $4.00 child (6-12). Tours.: Begin your New Market Battlefield experience with a tour of the battlefield. Note: Picnicking, walking (1 mile) or driving tours (small loop) of the battlefield. Emmy-winning film "Field of Lost Shoes" shown daily on the hour. Educators: online pre- and post-visit Activities sheets posted under For Teachers icon.

This is where 257 cadets (college students) from the Virginia Military Institute aided veteran Confederate troops in victory over Union forces in 1864. The Hall of Valor - commemorates the cadets (with a 45 minute video) and highlights every major campaign in Virginia during the four years of the Civil War. In the lobby, you can pick up a scavenger hunt and try on Civil War clothing. Many of the displays are push button with interesting facts (like how the uniforms changed during the war - better, or worse?). On the grounds outside, the Farm complex is open to tour. It is an early 1800's farm where the Bushong family took refuge in the basement of the, still standing, house during the battle raging outside in his wheat fields and apple orchards. After the battle, the house would serve as a field hospital for a week, leaving permanent blood stains in the Parlor. The orchard just behind the house is where the fiercest fighting occurred. Why was it called the "Field of Lost Shoes"?

BATTLE OF NEW MARKET REENACTMENT

New Market - New Market Battlefield. This ceremony and parade honors the cadets that fought and died during the Civil War at the Battle of New Market. In the 19th century sutlers traditionally followed the armies to sell items not available to the soldiers that were not government issue, such as coffee, yard goods, paper and writing instruments, sweet treats, tobacco, patent medicines, reading materials, buttons, accoutrements, etc. This tradition continues today at reenactments. Admission. (mid-May weekend)

KIDS LOVE VIRGINIA

AMERICAN CELEBRATION ON PARADE

New Market (Shenandoah Caverns) - 397 Caverns Road (Shenandoah Caverns, I-81exit 269, 4 miles north to New Market) 22847. Phone: (540) 477-4300. www.shenandoahcaverns.com. Hours: American Celebration is open seasonally, mostly weekends and summers. Combo rates allow you to see the Caverns, Streets of Yesteryear, The Yellow Barn, and American Celebration on Parade for one price (see caverns pricing).

Mr. Hargrove and his father founded a business building parade floats, "After building so many parade floats, I felt it was sad that these huge pieces of celebration art were often discarded after one appearance," he said. His passion has become a reality for all to view. Walk thru exhibits of animated, moving figures and displays showing the pageantry and the art of parade floats and

In the driver's seat...

Americana - up close! 50 years of parades all under one roof (and a large roof it is - some of the floats top 25 feet tall and measure 60 feet long!). Most floats have appeared in events such as The Tournament of Roses Parade and Presidential inaugurals. Most floats still have their natural coverings. Learn the tricks like hidden entrances for drivers, special handles to keep people from toppling off and how they keep a float balanced. Throughout the museum, you get to climb on many floats and at the end you get to sit in the drivers seat and operate the float's animation.

SHENANDOAH CAVERNS

New Market (Shenandoah Caverns) - 261 Caverns Road (I-81 exit 269, follow signs) 28847. Phone: (540) 477-3115. www.shenandoahcaverns.com. Hours: Daily opening at 9:00am. Last Tour 5:00pm (mid March to mid June & the Day after Labor Day thru October). Last tour 6:00pm (mid June to Labor Day). Last tour 4:00pm (November to mid-April). Admission: $31.00 adult, $28.00 senior, $15.00 Child (6-12). Combo rates allow you to see the Caverns, Streets of Yesteryear, The Yellow Barn, and American Celebration on Parade for one price. General public single site pricing is not available. Note: Only caverns with an elevator so accessible to handicapped and strollers for 80% of tour. Wide, level pathways provide easy walking - but wear comfortable shoes for your 60-minute tour. The temperature in the caverns is a constant 56 degrees. Many visitors like to wear a jacket or sweater. Nice, clean picnic areas in many spots. Gift shop.

Your tour of Shenandoah Caverns begins with a ride on the only elevator in a Virginia cavern as it descends into Entrance Hall. The caverns look very much as they did when they were discovered in 1884. You'll view the famous Bacon formations featured in National Geographic (look just like fried bacon) as well as beautiful flowstone and drapery formations. In Cascade Hall you'll be dazzled by the Diamond Cascade, one of the very beautiful calcite crystal formations in the world. One of the largest stalagmites in the caverns, known as Cardross Castle, resembles that castle in Scotland. Rainbow Lake and the Oriental Garden are colorful and different. Learn some tips on taking pictures in caverns from your guide (photos welcome). Your admission to the caverns includes a stroll down Main Street of Yesteryear to enjoy a collection of antique department store window displays (From Cinderella at the Ball to the lively Circus Parade). Also, admission to The Yellow Barn, with restored antique farm wagons, indoor beehive, carriages, and vehicles. And, finally, the awesome American Celebration on Parade is included in the admission (see separate listing).

Schuyler

WALTON'S MOUNTAIN MUSEUM

Schuyler - 6484 Rockfish River Road (I-64 to Rte 29 south to Route 617 southeast and Route 800) 22969. www.walton-museum.org. Phone: (434) 831-2000. Hours: Daily 10:00am-3:30pm Weekends only March April and November. Closed December thru February. Admission: $10.00 general (age 6+). Note: Helpful to stream some of the Waltons TV series before you go.

Earl Hamner, Jr. created the story behind the Waltons TV series based on his own family's experiences growing up during the Depression era in this rural village of Schuyler. The school building he, his brothers, and sisters attended has been converted to a museum which contains nostalgic memorabilia and replicas of the sets created for the TV series. A 30 minute audiovisual presentation (with insightful interviews from the stars) precedes a self-guided tour of the museum. The show "grounded people away from the confusion of the 60's and 70's". Look For:

THE WALTON'S KITCHEN - Features a long table and benches at which the family had dinner, an old wood cook stove, period cabinet work, an antique hutch and a wooden icebox and butter churn.

JOHN-BOY'S BEDROOM - Furnished to look like the bedroom where John-Boy retreated to write. This room has 1930's-period furniture and an old Underwood typewriter that Earl Hamner, Jr. actually used when he began writing. Good Night John Boy!

THE WALTON'S LIVING ROOM - A 1930's-style family room with fireplace, sofa, piano, old Atwater Kent radio (remember they used to gather around it in the evening for programs), overstuffed chairs and other period furnishings.

> In Ike's General Store purchase a postcard and mail it from there. It will be stamped "Walton's Mountain".

IKE GODSEY'S STORE - This is a favorite for many visitors. You can have your picture taken, using own camera, with an Ike and Cora Beth cutout inside of the post office. Re-live the warmth of an old country store complete with drink box, scales, penny candy and other merchandise not found in stores today. This room doubles as a gift shop with locally produced craft items for sale.

WALTON'S MOUNTAIN MUSEUM ANNIVERSARY

Schuyler - Walton's Mountain Country Store and Walton's Mountain Museum. Stroll amid creative work against the backdrop of the Blue Ridge Mountains and mingle with fans of The Walton's. Other events include hayrides ($1.00 each), face painting, dinners, hamburgers, hotdogs, drinks, apple cider pressing, antique car & truck display, live music, local crafters and Virginia politicians. FREE. (October, third weekend)

LOVINGSTON VILLAGE INN

Schuyler (Lovingston)- 8010 Thomas Nelson Hwy. 22949. Painted Bavarian motif outside, local hand-painted murals inside each clean, simple room. Rates under $60.00. (US 29 434-263-5068). *Lovingston Cafe* - 165 Front St. 22949 (Bus 29. 434-263-8000, www.lovingstoncafe.com). Their kids menu is presented in the front cover of a children's book you can read while you wait on your food. Most kids Menu items are under $4.00 and adult entrees average $11.00. Their outdoor shaded patio is adorable.

HATTON FERRY

Scottsville - 10082 Hatton Ferry Road (Rte. 625) 24590. Phone: (434) 296-1492. www.thehattonferry.org. Hours: Saturday 9am-5pm, Sunday Noon-5pm. (mid-April through October). Admission: Donations of $5 per person and $10 per vehicle.

Hatton Ferry is the only poled ferries still operating in the United States. A ride on the ferry is a unique opportunity to experience times past. Ferries served

Albemarle County from the mid-eighteenth century to the mid-nineteenth century, and provided a means by which European settlers could communicate with other settlers and establish commercial ventures. A small exhibit explores the history of the ferry.

BATTEAU NIGHT IN SCOTTSVILLE

Scottsville - James River. www.facebook.com/batteaumusicfestival The annual James River Batteau Festival visits the Historic River Town of Scottsville. Two dozen bateaux will land in late afternoon, and their crews will be dressed in period costume. Other events include music, food, vendors and a period encampment. (June, third Wednesday)

Staunton

FRONTIER CULTURE MUSEUM

Staunton - 1290 Richmond Road (I-81, Exit 222, Route 250 West, first left after light) 24401. Phone: (540) 332-7850. www.frontiermuseum.org. Hours: Daily, 9:00am-5:00pm. Winter Hours: 10:00am-4:00pm (December 1 to mid-March). Closed on Thanksgiving Day, Christmas Day, certain days in January, and during severe weather. Admission: $12.00 adult, $9.00 senior, $11.00 student (age 13-college), $7.00 child (6-12). Winter season is pay what you like. Tours: Most families opt for the self-guided tour (approximately 2-3 hours). Group (15+) guided tours are available. Note: Visitor Center offers displays and a short film about the development of the museum. Learn also the whys and how these European people immigrated here and what they brought with them. Holiday events and outdoor movies. Food Trucks available during events. Snacks and drinks available at Museum Store. Picnic tables are available.

The Frontier Culture Museum offers an international living history experience. The museum's costumed staff demonstrate 17th, 18th, and 19th century trades and traditions in four authentic, historic farms and a blacksmith forge. Rare breed livestock, heirloom gardens, agricultural crops, and period furnishings help costumed interpreters showcase old-time ways of daily life and living with the land. Walk through Europe and the Americas in one day:

WEST AFRICAN: Exhibit is an example of the compound of an Igbo farmer in the mid-1700s.

GERMAN HERITAGE: The museum's German farm originally stood in the small farming village of Hordt. The farm is interpreted during the first half of the 18th century (1700-1750), the period of heaviest German emigration from this region. Kids love the "punk rock" chickens -treated like domestic pets and their unique furnace.

SCOTCH-IRISH HERITAGE: The Scotch-Irish (Ulster) farm buildings show a traditional architectural form... the thatched one-story stone farmhouse. The farm's time period is the early-1700s. School was emphasized only for boys. The farmhouse walls are 2 feet thick, ceilings 20 inches thick - never gets too cold or damp.

ENGLISH HERITAGE: The English exhibits time period is 1675-1700 England. An 18th century cattle shed and a house Worcestershire. Watch them make cheese just once a week or other basics as the women frantically cook for the midday feast daily.

AMERICAN HERITAGE: On the American site, there are 11 buildings all original to a farm from a local county (circa mid-1800s). The museum interprets the farm by showing the lifestyle of the Shenandoah Valley farmer. The Bowman house is a recreation early pioneer home. A little of every culture's influences (esp. techniques) are brought together in this farm area. A great way to show kids how the U.S. has incorporated customs of so many into one big melting pot (literally!).

You will find this to be such a welcomed difference from typical living history museums - tying in a diversity of cultures is a wonderful way to see how our lives today are a mixture of habits from many cultures.

INDEPENDENCE DAY CELEBRATION

Staunton. Frontier Culture Museum. A traditional early 19th century Independence Day celebration on the Bowman farm. Free admission all day. Live music, dance, food, fireworks and parade at Gypsy Hill Park nearby. (July 4th)

OKTOBERFEST

Staunton. Frontier Culture Museum. Visitors can enjoy musical programs that share German culture, short plays, and special living history presentations at the German historic farm. Dancing, music and contests. Admission. (first Saturday in October)

HOLIDAY LANTERN TOURS / CAROLING TOURS

Staunton. Frontier Culture Museum. Tours leave every 30 minutes to experience holidays in history complete with warm fires, candlelight and holiday cheer. Travel to four historic farms to see family vignettes about the holiday heritage of Christmas in 1720 Germany; 1730 Northern Ireland; 1690 England; and the 1850 Shenandoah Valley. A fifth play in the visitor center ties Christmas past in the present and offers light refreshments. Admission fee. Advance tickets required. (December, second & third weekend)

WOODROW WILSON BIRTHPLACE MUSEUM

Staunton - 18-24 North Coalter and Frederick Streets (Route 11 north; stay in the middle lane and follow North Coalter Street. The Woodrow Wilson Presidential Library will be on your left) 24402. www.woodrowwilson.org. Phone: (540) 885-0897. Hours: Monday-Saturday 9:00am-5:00pm, Sunday Noon-5:00pm (March thru October). Open until only 4:00pm (rest of year). Closed New Years, Christmas and Thanksgiving. Tours: six times a day. Admission: $15.00 adult, $14.00 senior (65+), $10.00 student (college), $8.00 child (6-17). Note: While in the downtown area, head over to the Historic Staunton Station and the Pullman Restaurant (540) 885-6612 or the Depot Grill (540) 885-7332.

Woodrow Wilson's first home offers an authentic picture of family life in the pre-Civil War Shenandoah Valley. Such children's activities as scavenger hunts and trying on pre-Civil War clothing are offered. Your visit to the Woodrow

Wilson Presidential Library is in two parts. The museum building is self guided where guests may explore President Wilson's life through seven galleries. The second part of your visit includes a guided tour of Wilson's birthplace, the Presbyterian Manse, the home provided by the church for the Reverend Joseph Ruggles Wilson and his family. Interpreters will take you back to 1856 when Wilson was born and discuss his family and upbringing and the lifestyle of that period. Tours are approximately 30 to 40 minutes in length and leave from the museum every 45 minutes.

As part of your own scavenger hunt, be sure to look for the limousine, his White House telephone, and the desk he used at Princeton. The Museum offers a look into Wilson's public life, from his Princeton study to his historic World War I peace efforts. Serving from 1913 to 1921 as the 28th President of the United States, Woodrow Wilson is considered one of the greatest Presidents for his pursuit of world peace and security.

CELEBRATE WOODROW WILSON'S BIRTHDAY

Staunton. Woodrow Wilson Birthplace Museum. Everyone is invited to celebrate President Wilson's birthday during the annual open house of the Presbyterian Manse and Museum. Enjoy birthday cake in the Wilson Museum, listen to live music and find out what's new at the Birthplace. There will also be special activities for kids. Free. (December, last Saturday)

AFRICAN-AMERICAN HERITAGE FESTIVAL

Staunton - Gypsy Hill Park. (540) 332-3972. www.ci.staunton.va.us. This annual African-American Heritage Festival is a celebration of the contributions that African-Americans made to our culture. The event features live music and dance performances, arts and crafts, historic exhibits, ethnic foods and children's activities. (September, third weekend)

Steeles Tavern

CYRUS MCCORMICK'S FARM

Steeles Tavern - 128 McCormick's Farm Circle (I-81 or US 11 exit 205/ SR 606 - Raphine Road, heading east) 24476. Phone: (540) 377-2255. www.arec.vaes.vt.edu/shenandoah-valley.html Hours: Open daily 8:30am-5:00pm. Closed winter weekends. Call for guided tours. Admission: FREE. Note: Farm part of the Shenandoah Valley Agricultural Research and Extension Center.

Twenty minutes north of downtown Lexington is the farm and workshop of Cyrus McCormick and his father, where he invented and marketed the first mechanized grain reaper that sparked the industrial revolution. Visitors are welcome to tour the blacksmith shop, gristmill, museum and scenic site at the McCormick farm.

On a hot July day in 1831, to a crowd of neighbors and on-lookers, 22 year old Cyrus demonstrated the world's first successful mechanical reaper in fields near his farm, Walnut Grove. The reaper and other farm machines came from the McCormick Company and the later company, International Harvester. For centuries, grain had been harvested with strong arms and backs and some form of long knife like a sickle. The Reaper harvested five times faster than any previous method, with minimal physical effort. McCormick also was a pioneer in business techniques: easy credit to enable farmers to pay for machines from increased harvests; written performance guarantees; and advertising. Each year on the first Saturday in October, they hold an annual MIll Day with vendors on hand and tours of the farm and research conducted.

A reproduction of the first mechanical reaper

MONTEBELLO STATE FISH HATCHERY

Steeles Tavern (Montebello) - 359 Fish Hatchery Lane (off Blue Ridge Pkwy to Campbell Mtn. Rd exit) 24464. Phone: (540) 377-2418. Hours: Daily 8:00am-3:30pm (April-October). Rest of year, closes weekends at 11am. FREE. www.nelsoncounty-va.gov/Organization/montebello-fish-hatchery/

If you've ever wondered what a hatchery is, or what a baby trout looks like, this is a wonderful place to explore. Staff is available to answer questions and guide your visit as you see thousands of fish being raised for eventual release to the wild. Each year approximately 170,000 newly-hatched brook, brown and rainbow trout are nurtured to maturity at the Fish Hatchery then released to stock all trout waters east of the Blue Ridge Parkway.

Families with young kids will want to visit the *Montebello General Store* (SR 56, 540-377-2650). Not only will you find snacks and old-fashioned goodies (like sassafras candies), but you can trout fish in their pond across the street at the Camping Resort. You only pay for what you catch. Bring your own equipment or purchase some there. Every child is pretty much guaranteed to get a catch in season (early spring or late fall is best).

HUPP'S HILL CIVIL WAR PARK

Strasburg - 33229 Old Valley Pike (I-81 exit 298, south on US 11) 22657. Phone: (540) 465-5884. https://home.nps.gov/places/hupps-hill-park-museum.htm. Hours: Thursday-Tuesday 9:00am-5:00pm. Admission: $5.00 adult (ages 11+).

Part of the 10-acre site where the Battle of Cedar Creek took place in 1864. Visitors see original trenches built by troops. Inside the museum is the story of Jackson's brilliant defense of the Shenandoah Valley (one of the most famous military campaigns in history, studied the world over) brought to life with a collection of artifacts from the Valley along with interpretive text. You will not only understand the campaign, but will get a vivid impression of what life was like for the soldiers who fought. Children have their own place in the museum where they can try on period costumes, ride wooden horses complete with authentic cavalry saddles and bridles, or climb into a soldier's tent. "Discovery Boxes" offer kids a chance to explore an historic topic through games, puzzles and touching artifacts.

Waynesboro

P. BUCKLEY MOSS MUSEUM

Waynesboro - 150 P. Buckley Moss Drive (I-64 exit 94, south on US 340) 22980. Phone: (540) 949-6473. www.pbuckleymoss.com. Hours: Daily 10:00am-5:00pm, Sundays Noon-4:00pm. Admission: FREE.

Art from "The People's Artist" is showcased here. The works of local artist P. Buckley Moss focus mostly on subjects from the Shenandoah Valley scenery and the Amish and Mennonite people of the area - really, basic human and Christian values. Her style is now referred to as "Moss Valley" and you'll see the Shenandoah Valley all through it. Did you know Ms. Moss had a learning disability and one teacher in class noticed her artist ability and encouraged it? A Children's Art area upstairs promotes artistic techniques. A dollhouse downstairs is like a painting that came to life. Look for the 30 little mice throughout the house. All paintings on the dollhouse walls are P. Buckley Moss originals. Follow the bird - the bird was the symbol of human soul - he opens his mouth and sings his own song...What's your song?

SOAP BOX DERBY

Waynesboro - www.brsoapbox.com. One of the largest soap box derby events in the United States. (May, last Saturday)

FALL FOLIAGE ART FESTIVAL

Waynesboro - Main Street. www.waynesboro.va.us. This event features arts and crafts by national and regional artists. Apple days-apple butter making, fresh cider, homemade apple dumplings, clowns, entertainment. Open house-tours of the Plumb House, Heritage Museum, & Fishburne Museum. (October, first two weekends)

DINOSAUR LAND

White Post - 3848 Stonewall Jackson Highway (US 522 south) (US 522, 340 & 277) 22663. Phone: (540) 869-2222. www.dinosaurland.com. Hours: Opens daily at 9:30am. Closing around 5:00 or 5:30pm (except Memorial Day-Labor Day) when they close at 6:00pm. Closed January and February. Closed Thursdays (Oct-Dec) Admission: $8.00 adult, $6.00 child (2-10). Note: Giant gift shop with every dinosaur toy and book imaginable.

Even the building was "scary"

Step into a world of the prehistoric past where dinosaurs were the only creatures that roamed the earth. See awesome meat eaters like Giganotosaurus, Megalosaurus, and also the sauropiods, armored and duckbill dinosaurs. Come face to face with the awesome Tyrannosaurus or look into the gentle face of Apatosaurus. 50 life-size reproductions of dinos and one 20 foot King Kong - have your picture taken in his hand! A 60' shark with an open mouth is also a great photo op! So, what is a dinosaur anyway? The word dinosaur means "Terrible Lizard" in Greek. Of 15 large reptilian groups including dinosaurs, only lizards, snakes, turtles and crocodiles survive at all today. You'll be surprised at how many dinosaurs look like modern reptiles (just on a larger scale).

Winchester

GEORGE WASHINGTON'S OFFICE MUSEUM

Winchester - 32 West Cork Street, US 11 (Corner of Braddock & Cork Streets) 22601. http://winchesterhistory.org/george_washington.htm. Phone: (540) 662-4412. Hours: Monday-Saturday 10:00am-4:00pm, Sunday Noon-4:00pm. (April-October) Admission: $6.00 adult, $5.000 senior and $3.00 student.

The center room of George Washington's Office Museum was used by Colonel George Washington, commander of the Virginia Regiment, as an office between September, 1755 and December, 1756 while he was building Fort Loudoun. The fort was being built to protect the colony of Virginia from Indian raids during the French and Indian War. George Washington first arrived in Winchester in 1748 as a surveyor's assistant at the age of sixteen.

For updates visit: www.KidsLoveTravel.com

This visit began a 10-year odyssey in the Virginia Backcountry which transformed Washington from an inexperienced teenager into a seasoned businessman, soldier, and politician. Kids will like the vast array of unusual looking instruments used for surveying back then and the real blood-stained floor when the building was used as a hospital during the Civil War.

MUSEUM OF THE SHENANDOAH VALLEY

Winchester - 901 Amherst Street 22601. www.themsv.org. Phone: (540) 662-1473. Hours: Tuesday-Sunday 10:00am-5:00pm. Decreased hours winters. Closed Mondays and major holidays. Admission: $15.00 adult, $10.00 senior (60+) and child (13-18).

The site includes five exhibit galleries, a tea room, reception hall, learning center and museum store. The story begins with an explanation of the Valley's geography and natural resources and the earliest Indians who lived here, and concludes with an overview of Valley highlights today. Multi-media presentations in each section bring the sights and sounds of the Valley alive. The Miniature House gallery presents five houses, four rooms, and the work of more than seventy miniatures artisans.

SHENANDOAH VALLEY DISCOVERY MUSEUM

Winchester - 19 West Cork Street (Old Town, downtown pedestrian mall) 22601. Phone: (540) 722-2020. www.discoverymuseum.net. Hours: Wednesday-Saturday 9:30am-3:30pm. Admission: $9.00 general (age 2+). Note: Museum store. Discovery Story Theater, Stories Alive and Summer Camps.

A delightful place for energetic kids wanting to explore science in a fun way! Have you ever wondered where insects come from, heard your heart beat or caught twinkles in the night sky? Some of the things we found unique to this museum included: Picking and crating apples using a large conveyor belt (lots and lots of realistic pulleys and levers here) to move them along the processing line. Kids can have fun working in teams here and it's amazing to see how fast some become the "job foreman". Learn physics with water in Watershed; touch the soft fur of forest animals in the American Indian Longhouse; or pretend you're in a Medical Center and ambulance (with a real gurney).

STONEWALL JACKSON'S HEADQUARTERS MUSEUM

Winchester - 415 North Braddock Street 22601. Phone: (540) 667-3242. http://winchesterhistory.org/stonewall_jackson.htm. Hours: Monday - Saturday 10:00am-4:00pm, Sunday Noon-4:00pm (April-October). Weekends only (Friday-Sunday) (rest of year). Admission: $10.00 adult, $8.00 senior and student, $4.00 student.

The Gothic style house built in 1854 served as General Jackson's headquarters while planning the Valley Campaign. General Jackson's office is essentially the same as when he used it, so it does preserve the essence of his surroundings at that time.

SHENANDOAH APPLE BLOSSOM FESTIVAL

Winchester - Downtown Winchester and Jim Barnett Park. www.thebloom.com. The festival celebrates the advent of spring in the Shenandoah Valley and the blooming of apple trees. More than 30 events include dances, two parades, band competitions, Circus, coronation of Queen Shenandoah and various firefighters' events. (early May)

PEACH FESTIVAL

Winchester - Enjoy fresh peaches, peach cobbler, peach sundaes and more. And it just wouldn't be Virginia without country ham sandwiches, which will also be available. The children will have fun with the barrel train and wagon rides, and there's music and more for the whole family. (540) 662-1391 www.markermillerorchards.com. (August, second Saturday)

APPLE HARVEST FESTIVAL

Winchester - Jim Barnett Park. (800) 662-1360. www.visitwinchesterva.com. Join the fun in this acclaimed annual festival featuring hundreds of arts and crafts booths, great food, live entertainment and Shenandoah Valley apples. Hayrides, pony rides, petting zoo. Virginia State Apple Butter Making Championship and the regional apple pie baking contest that decides who makes the year's best apple butter and pie. Follow the Apple Trail driving tour which takes you through scenic and historic ports of the city using an audiotape as your guide. Stop at the Visitors Center at 1360 South Pleasant Valley Road. Admission fee. (September, third week)

PUMPKIN PATCH, HILL HIGH FARMS

Winchester - Hill High Farm, 933 Barley Lane. www.thepumpkin-patch.net. (540) 667-7377. Pick your own apples, hay rides to pumpkin patch to pick your own, straw maze and farm animals. Fall treats to purchase. Admission. (Labor Day weekend thru October)

NORTH-SOUTH – FALL SKIRMISH

Winchester - Frederick County Visitor Center. (800) 662-1360. The North-South Skirmish Association will be hosting the fall skirmish, featuring competitive target shooting using Civil War firearms. Other activities include period dress competition and large sutler area. www.n-ssa.org. (October, first weekend)

WINTERGREEN RESORT

Wintergreen - (Route 664, between Blue Ridge Parkway mileposts 13 and 14, or access from Route 151) 22958. www.wintergreenresort.com. Phone: (800) 266-2444. Rates: Lodging packages for each season (Endless Fun Package or value season/midweek rates are best value - around $200 per night with all the regular property amenities available to use without additional charge- Skiing or planned excursion packages - Uniquely Wintergreen, are per person). Check out the Adventure Dome . It features gaming and theatre areas for pre-teens and above.

Thinking about heading to the mountains? Wintergreen Resort is located high atop the Blue Ridge Mountains. At Wintergreen Resort, you will find golf, 18 ski slopes (kiddie tube slopes too!) and trails (kids learn to ski lessons), 24 tennis courts, 30 miles of marked hiking trails, five swimming pools and a 20-acre lake (paddleboats, canoes, kayaks, inner tubes, fishing equipment rentals), horseback riding. Whatever you do, don't miss their sunsets (to-o-o nice) and deer families prancing around (particularly early evening). This resort offers a lot for families - We especially liked their well-organized, daily children's programs (in the Treehouse with planned crafts, games, stories, explorations of area, kids campouts and babysitting services); festivals and special events. Resort shops, restaurants, gameroom and recreational facilities are open to the public. Almost every guest room, condo or house has an efficiency or full-size kitchen - if you're watching your budget, cook your favorite meals or order a pizza from the Black Rock Market. A great mountain retreat that's close to lots of historical attractions.

WINTERGREEN NATURE FOUNDATION - A year-round nature program is offered from Trillium House (www.twnf.org). "WILD!" Activities for children (fee required) - weekday and weekend programs of outdoor fun for ages 6-12 on subjects like Inspector Wild, slippery slimies, Wild Adventurers, river ecology, insects and cave exploring.

JULY JUBILEE AT WINTERGREEN

Celebrate the red, white and blue at Wintergreen Resort! The holiday weekend is packed with fun-filled activities, including chairlift rides, live music, a family movie under the stars, and the annual Arts & Crafts Show. See fireworks light up the mountain sky on July 4 and July 5. (July 4th -6th)

FALL FOLIAGE FESTIVAL

Come one, come all to the Fall Foliage Festival at the Trillium House. The craft fair is open from 10:00am-4:00pm Saturday and Sunday. There will be hikes, face painting, pumpkins and more. The craft fair is free; other activities may involve a nominal charge. (mid-October weekend)

BLUE RIDGE MOUNTAIN CHRISTMAS

Wintergreen Resort. (434) 325-8180. Annual Gingerbread House, contests, family concerts, theatrical presentations, holiday crafts workshops, Santa on the slopes, Christmas Eve and Day dinners, and New Year's Eve celebrations. (December, third Friday-New Year's Eve)

Chapter 4
South Central

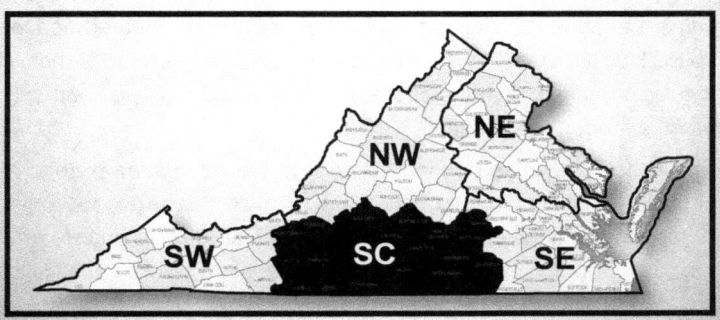

A Quick Tour of our Hand-Picked Favorites Around...

South Central Virginia

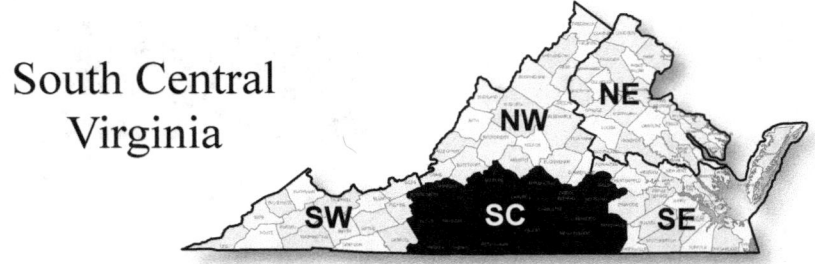

Here you will find the gold that spills from the sunsets over Smith Mountain Lake, the glory of the Peaks of Otter at dawn, and the solitude of relaxing drives along the **Blue Ridge Parkway**. South Central Virginia is a harvest festival, fine museums, glorious apples, rugged trails and breath taking overlooks.

The Indians wandering between the parallel ridges of the Allegheny Mountains named the 200-mile-long valley Shenandoah, "daughter of the stars." At the southern end of the Shenandoah Valley lies Roanoke with the world's largest neon star beckoning visitors to the "Star City of the South." The 100-foot-high illuminated structure atop **Roanoke's Star** serves as a landmark for night-time aviators.

Illuminating the Roanoke Valley culturally are many of our favorite interactive museums. The fun-filled space of **ArtVenture** has got to be our favorite hands-on interactive art gallery ever! Taking inspiration from the Art Museum's permanent collection, this organization has created spaces that absorb the kids INTO art. Your family can make prints, tell some stories, create sound from a painting, join the circus, make velcro chairs, play with clay and then paint a modern self-image!

The Valley boasts its railroad heritage at the remodeled historic N & W freight station housing the **Virginia Museum of Transportation**. Come face to face with vintage electric locomotives, classic diesels and steam giants (the No. 611 is mighty!). Climb aboard a caboose, a railway post office car, and a No. 17, 1934 Dodge school bus.

Because it's hard to understand historical slavery – especially enslaved kids – you might want to make it a little more interesting by visiting the **Booker T. Washington National Monument** in Hardy, Virginia (just southeast of

South Central Area

Roanoke and west of Smith Mountain Lake). Born into slavery on this tobacco plantation in 1856, Washington rose to prominence as an educator, orator, and later founder of the Tuskegee Institute in Alabama. Most of the historical site is outside along a quarter-mile Plantation Trail so the kids can run around freely exploring the slave cabin, barns, crops and live animals. We love places like this that give you a glimpse of the life (and humble beginnings) of an everyday American hero.

The small town of Bedford lies between Roanoke and Lynchburg on US 460. Thomas Jefferson, architect of The University of Virginia, author of The Declaration of Independence and President of the United States, chose to build a home in Bedford - **Poplar Forest**, which Jefferson designed as his personal retreat...especially to be with his grand kids. Want to pretend you're an archeologist for the day? Well, this place has digging and touching galore - enough for every family member to enjoy. Because the home is still being renovated and the grounds explored, guided tours get you involved in the "detective work". For instance, can you tell which room has "Grandpa's chair"?

Lynchburg is nestled into the foothills of the Blue Ridge Mountains and is bordered on one side by the historic James River. **Amazement Square Children's Museum** downtown is the big draw for kids. Amazement Tower, a meandering tangle of pathways, tunnels, illuminating stairs and glass elevator, connects all the Museums exhibitions, and is the tallest indoor, interactive climbing structure in the United States. Why do we like it so much? The exhibit spaces take on different approaches from most other children's museums. One promise...in order to participate here, you will make new friends – and, learn interesting approaches to common objects you see every day.

Just east of Lynchburg lies a village that sits as it was in 1865, when Robert E. Lee surrendered to Ulysses S. Grant – **Appomattox Court House**. Learn more about each of these characters, as well as, the McLean family who ironically wanted to be removed from the war, so they moved here. A sweet story about Lula McLean's Rag Doll appears online and tells the story of an unusual surrender from a child's point of view.

When most folks think of Martinsville, Virginia, they think of racing. But, we've found a museum there that gets better with age. The state museum of natural history for Virginia, the **Virginia Museum of Natural History** opened its brand-new, world-class facility in March 2007. An Allosaurus skeleton and a prehistoric whale greet visitors upon entering The Great Hall, which includes windows looking into REAL scientific labs.

104 KIDS LOVE VIRGINIA

The Lab is where VMNH researchers prepare whales, dinosaurs and other vertebrate fossils from excavations and they love when you ask questions.

Looking for a surprise just off the Blue Ridge Parkway? Well, many already know about Mabry Mill – a scenic stop serving yummy pancakes and corn cakes made from the mill ground corn meal - but, follow US 58 and SR 57 to a quaint town called Stuart, where there sits the mysterious **Fairy Stone State Park**. This is the home of the lucky fairy stones (staurolites). Their Story: After saddened Fairies (or angels) heard news that Christ had died, their tears fell onto the rocks and formed crosses made from stones. Stop by the park office to purchase fairystones (just a couple of dollars) or look for the Hunt Site to find your own as a keepsake. If you come during the summer, the water playground has wonderful, soft-sided floating logs, lily pads, frogs and turtles that kids can slide and climb on.

Sites and attractions are listed in order by City, Zip Code, and Name. Symbols indicated represent: 🍽 Restaurants   🛏 Lodging

Appomattox

APPOMATTOX COURT HOUSE NATIONAL HISTORICAL PARK

Appomattox - (VA 24, 2 miles northeast of the town of Appomattox) 24522. Phone: (434) 352-8987. www.nps.gov/apco/index.htm. Hours: Daily 9:00am-5:00pm. Closed on Federal Holidays. Admission: FREE. Note: Gift store in the tavern kitchen. It is best to walk along with ranger guided tours or during the Anniversary weekend (2nd week of April). Living History programs are offered every day during the summer months, and occasionally on weekends in the spring and fall. Actors portray historical figures from the 1860s. Please allow at least 3 - 4 hours to visit the historical village on guided tours. Educators: Teacher History Packet: www.nps.gov/apco/forteachers/curriculummaterials.htm

See the McLean House where the surrender meeting was held...

This village sits as it was in 1865, when Robert E. Lee surrendered to Ulysses S. Grant. Lee's surrender signaled the end of the Southern States attempt to create a separate nation. Learn more about each of these characters, as well as, the McLean family who ironically wanted to be removed from the war, so

For updates visit: www.KidsLoveTravel.com

they moved here. There are 27 historic structures in the village, most importantly the Tavern (where parole papers were printed quickly) and the McLean House where the surrender terms were written. There are two 15 minute slide shows you can watch or listen to audio stations along the way. The map you receive will steer you with advice on touring the village, one of them being that there is a lot of walking.

Generals Lee and Grant discuss details

It is suggested families with younger children explore the buildings surrounding the Courthouse/Visitors Center. The village buildings all represent various trades during that time period so it is also a history lesson on that time period. The Stacking of Arms story that occurred a few days later is interesting too. Learn why there were no papers signed here between General Grant and General Lee, what Lee's final request was the next day, and why they met at a home instead of the Courthouse.

APPOMATTOX-BUCKINGHAM STATE FOREST / HOLLIDAY LAKE STATE PARK

Appomattox - Route 2, Box 622 (Holliday Lake trailhead) (Rte. 636, forest. State Park Access via State Route 24 between Appomattox and U.S. 60 and from Routes 626, 640 and 692) 24522. www.dof.virginia.gov/stateforest/list/absf.htm Phone: (434) 983-2175. Admission: $1.00 per vehicle weekdays, $2.00 per vehicle on weekends and holidays (Forest). Holliday Lake $7.00 per vehicle.

HOLLIDAY LAKE STATE PARK

Located within the Forest, offering: camping, picnicking, swimming, boating, and hiking. Permanent campsites are installed inside the Park. Two shelters are available on the Forest. (Locations: Woolridge Wayside on the west end of Route 640 and Lee Wayside on Richmond Forest Road). Trails: There is one mapped trail, Carter Taylor Hike, Bike, Horse Trail. The Forest has various gated trails and Forest Roads that can be also be used. Fishing: There are two lakes located within the Forest. (Holliday Lake located at Holliday Lake State Park, and Slate River Watershed located off of Route 640 in Buckingham County.) Whether you hike on foot, ride a bike, or travel on horseback, the Carter Taylor Trail is a great place to explore. Wildlife abounds in the ever-changing oak-hickory and pine forest. Deer, turkey, and even black bear make their homes in these woods. The Sunfish Aquatic Trail is a self-guided water adventure that requires a boat and free trail brochure. A brochure map and numbered stop's provide information about the lake and environment as you paddle or peddle around its edges.

CLOVER HILL VILLAGE

Appomattox - 5747 River Ridge Road (US 460 east to Rte. 24, right on Rte. 627) 24522. Phone: (434) 352-0321. www.appomattoxhistorical.org. Hours: Grounds open daily 9:00am-dusk, Guided building tours Friday-Sunday from 10:00am-4:00pm (April-October). Closed all holidays. Admission: $2.00-$3.00 (over age 5).

Tour a 6 acre rural village where the history and heritage of Appomattox County come to life. Enjoy an educational glimpse into daily life in the past (1840 - 1920) as you browse through the general store, an extensive collection of farm equipment, and a blacksmith shop. Go back to school in a one-room schoolhouse, relax for a moment in the quiet little chapel, then stroll over to a cozy log cabin and the farm area.

LAUREL HILL - J.E.B. STUART BIRTHPLACE

Ararat - 1091 Ararat Highway (SR 773, just over the border from NC) 24053. Phone: (276) 251-1833. www.jebstuart.org. Hours: Daylight hours Admission: FREE except for special events.

Home of the Stuart family and birthplace of the famous Confederate Cavalry General J.E.B. Stuart, the "eyes" of Robert E. Lee's Army of Northern Virginia. Visitors can walk the trails where young "Jeb" learned to ride, see the swimming hole where the Stuart children played, and take in the splendor of the 80-acre core of what once was one of the largest family farms around. As the Stuart family would say, "You are most welcome to visit and picnic on our lawn".

ENCAMPMENT AT LAUREL HILL

Ararat - J.E.B. Birthplace. See the birthplace of Confederate J.E.B. Stuart. Event features a self-guided walking tour of the property & hosts a Civil War re-enactment. (October, first weekend)

Bedford

NATIONAL D-DAY MEMORIAL

Bedford - (I-460 east to Rte 122 north exit. Left off the exit and left on Tiger Trail to Overlord Circle) 24523. Phone: (540) 587-3619. www.dday.org. Hours: The Memorial is currently just an outdoor facility, subject to closing for inclement weather. Daily 10:00am-5:00pm. Closed on Christmas Day, New Year's Day, and Thanksgiving Day and winter Mondays. Admission: $12.00 adult, $8.00 veteran and child (6-18). Future plans: In addition to an auditorium and theater, the education center will house computer and video stations, exhibition space for permanent and traveling exhibits, and three galleries for displays. The Education Center's thematic galleries will draw particular attention to the clergy, medicine, and cartooning in the context of D-Day and the broader context of World War II.

South Central Area

The centerpiece of the 88-acre site is the massive Overlord arch rising above Victory Plaza. Visitors can stroll the grounds with site-brochures that offer information on the architecture and various representations of the memorial. Guided tours are also available weather permitting. Departing regularly throughout the day, these one hour programs provide more information about the events of June 6, 1944 and the symbolism of the Memorial itself. The storytelling and anecdotes are so vivid, kids understand more of the passion and history of this important day.

REMEMBERING THEIR SACRIFICE

Bedford - National D-Day Memorial. To observe Memorial Day, the Memorial has a wreath-laying ceremony to pay tribute to those who have given their lives in service to our nation. The ceremony includes music and special speakers. Free admission from 10:00am until noon. (Memorial Day in May)

ANNIVERSARY OF D-DAY

Bedford - National D-Day Memorial. Spend the anniversary of D-Day at the National D-Day Memorial where valor, fidelity, and sacrifice are honored everyday. Pay tribute to those soldiers who made the ultimate sacrifice in Normandy 64 years ago and honor those veterans who lived to fight another day. There is a ceremony at the site and tours throughout the day. (June 6th)

VETERANS DAY CEREMONY

Bedford - National D-Day Memorial. Take time to honor all who have served in the US Armed Forces during this special event. The program includes music, guest speakers, and recognition of all veterans. Admission fees suspended from 10:00am until noon. (Veterans Day in November)

HOLIDAY LIGHTS DISPLAY

Bedford - Liberty Lake Park, Rte. 122. (540) 587-6061. 30 acres of drive-thru holiday lights. Makes Bedford the Christmas Capital of Virginia. FREE. (Thanksgiving weekend thru mid-January)

POPLAR FOREST, THOMAS JEFFERSON'S

Lynchburg (Forest) - 1776 Poplar Forest Pkwy (off US 460, north on SR 811, then east on SR661) 24502. Phone: (434) 525-1806. www.poplarforest.org. Hours: Daily 10:00am-4:00pm (mid-March-December). Admission: $16.00 adult, $14.00 senior (65+), $8.00 youth (12-18) & students, $4.00 child (6-11). Tours: House tours last approximately 40 minutes. Self-guided grounds tours are available. Walk the grounds guided by brochures that describe the landscape and plantation community. Examine exhibits at the restoration workshop, archaeology laboratory, slave quarter site, and in the lower level of the house. View a 15-minute film on the restoration work and archaeological excavations in the lower level of the house. Note: Pets are welcome on the grounds at Poplar Forest. Strollers are permitted on grounds but not in the house. Picnic tables are available on site.

Visitors may purchase a small assortment of snacks in the Museum Shop. Educators: Extensive lesson plans, children's puzzles, activity sheets, Jefferson bios and themed education kits, online.

Not as big as Monticello, but you sure can tell it was designed by Thomas Jefferson...

Want to pretend you're an archeologist for the day? Well, this place has digging and touching galore - enough for every family member to enjoy. Poplar Forest (the first octagonal home in America) was the plantation and retreat Thomas Jefferson owned 90 miles from Monticello. What's unique about your visit here is that the house is open as a museum while, not after, restoration and archaeology continue on the grounds! Guided tours get you involved in the "detective work". For instance, can you tell where the "alcove bed" would have been, or which room has "Grandpa's chair"? You'll hear excerpts from Jefferson's grand daughter's letters when you explore the guest bedroom.

Seasonal Excavation stations: The space gives children a chance to literally put their "hands-on-history" as they make bricks (from area clay...it's kinda like "mixing and baking a cake" - says mom)! Spin wool; lie down on a slave bed (a wedding gift from the masters, along with a pot for cooking); trying on period clothes; making a bucket or a basket; or playing marbles with reproduction red clay marbles like those found on the property. Kids can make copies of a note using a reproduction polygraph.

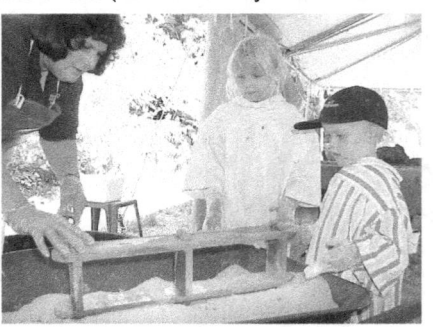

Learning how to make bricks...

JEFFERSON'S BIRTHDAY

Bedford - Poplar Forest. Celebrate the anniversary of Jefferson's birth at his retreat home with cake served noon-2:00pm. American Chestnut Foundation ceremonial planting of chestnut trees. Free. Admission Charge for House Tour. (April 13)

LIBERTYFEST

Bedford - Poplar Forest. Centertown, D-Day Memorial. (540) 586-2148. Living history actors, hands-on history, reading of Declaration of Independence, food, clowns, fireworks at Liberty Lake Park.

For updates visit: www.KidsLoveTravel.com

Blacksburg

HISTORIC SMITHFIELD

Blacksburg - 1000 Smithfield Plantation Road (at the edge of VA Tech Campus, take rte. 314 off US 460 bypass) 24060. https://www.historicsmithfield.org/. Phone: (540) 231-3947. Hours: Thursday-Saturday 10:00am-3:00pm (April to First weekend in December) Admission: $8.00 adult, $5.00 student (13-college), $3.00 child (5-12).

Take a one hour interpreted tour of a colonial frontier home built in 1775 by Colonel William Preston. Smithfield was the birthplace of two Virginia governors and the brief home of a third. The Colonel was a leader of westward expansion and a Revolutionary War Patriot. In a land of log cabins and hardship, this homestead provided a haven of aristocratic elegances. Costumed interpreters show period furnished rooms, a colonial winter kitchen, museum, smokehouse and gardens and adjacent cabin. You'll learn how they faced threats of illness (and the odd treatments used), the Shawnee and their Tory neighbors. Notice the 14 foot high stockade fence.

JUNETEENTH CELEBRATION

Blacksburg - Historic Smithfield Plantation hosts a commemorative event on "Juneteenth" to honor the lives of the African American slaves who lived and worked at Smithfield. The event features stories and music that uplift the lives of the enslaved population at Smithfield. (June 19th)

FOURTH OF JULY CELEBRATION

Blacksburg - Celebrate where Revolutionary War patriots trod. Bring a picnic, family and friends to the grounds of Historic Smithfield Plantation, the circa 1774 home. Music, dancing, Revolutionary re-enactments, children's crafts and games, walks through the magnificent plantation home. Free of charge. Ice cream and drinks for sale. (July 4th)

HOLIDAYS AT SMITHFIELD

Blacksburg - The Holidays at Smithfield are an 18th century holiday celebration. Come tour the house decorated for the holidays in Colonial style, and have a leisurely cup of tea in Susanna's Tea Room. Traditional musical entertainment, children's craft table, and holiday greenery sale. (first Sunday in December)

RED HILL-PATRICK HENRY NATIONAL MEMORIAL

Brookneal - 1250 Red Hill Rd (SR 40 east) 24528. www.redhill.org. Phone: (434) 376-2044. Hours: Daily 9:00am-5:00pm, Sunday 1:00-5:00pm (April-October). Daily closing at 4:00pm (November-March). Admission: $8.00 adult, $4.00 student (6-17).

Red Hill is the last home and resting place of Patrick Henry. Begin your tour with an orientation videotape. The museum houses the largest collection of Patrick Henry memorabilia in the world. Patrick Henry called Red Hill "one of the garden spots of the world". Of his many homes, this was said to be his favorite, with many of his 17 children being born and married here. Henry's grave, law office, coachman's cabin, stable, kitchen and gardens can be seen.

4TH OF JULY AT RED HILL

Brookneal - Red Hill, Patrick Henry's Home. www.redhill.org. Celebrate 4th of July at Red Hill, Patrick Henry's last home and burial place. Patrick Henry was Virginia's first governor and the "Voice of the Revolution." Take a guided tour with costumed docents and participate in Revolutionary drills. Other attractions include Patrick Henry and his stories, live music, arts and crafts, kids' games and a magnificent fireworks display at dusk. Admission per vehicle. (July 4th)

RED HILL CHRISTMAS BY CANDLELIGHT OPEN HOUSE

Brookneal - Visit Red Hill between 3:00 and 6:00pm and enjoy the sights and sounds of a traditional Christmas. Carolers will be on hand to entertain visitors. Partake of Brunswick stew, holiday cookies, and hot mulled cider, all compliments of the Patrick Henry Auxiliary. No admission charge. (first weekend in December)

OCCONEECHEE STATE PARK

Clarksville - 1192 Occoneechee Park Road (US 58 east near the US 15 intersection) 23927. Phone: (434) 374-2210. www.dcr.virginia.gov/state_parks/occ.shtml. Admission: $7.00 per vehicle. Note: Campsites, picnicking, an amphitheater and boat launching ramps.

Named for Native Americans who lived in the area for hundreds of years, Occoneechee is located on the Kerr Reservoir, better known as Buggs Island Lake. The visitor center introduces you to Native American culture and the indigenous Occoneechee people. The highlight exhibit is a life-size living hut once used. A one-mile interpretive trail takes visitors to the terraced gardens of the Old Plantation grounds. The park also features a 15-mile multi-purpose trail for hiking, biking and horseback riding.

Danville

DANVILLE SCIENCE CENTER

Danville - 677 Craghead Street (Crossing of the Dan) 24541. Phone: (434) 791-5160. www.dsc.smv.org. Hours: Tuesday-Saturday, 9:30am-5:00pm, Sunday from 11:30am-5:00pm. Open select holiday Mondays. Closed Thanksgiving and Christmas. Admission: $9.00 adult, $8.00 student, senior (60+) and child (ages 4-12). Digital Dome extra. Note: Visit Sproutsville, a small-scale town featuring building blocks, a stage and puppet play area, a loft, magnetic shapes, lighthouse, and light and color areas is here especially for young scientists ages 1-8.

The Science Center is loaded with hands-on exhibits that encourage you and your family to unlock the secrets of how things work. Push a button to make sparks fly. Build a crystal. Enjoy interactive exhibits in Light and Vision, Earth Science and more. The Natural History Collection is where you can meet live creatures in "Critter Corner", identify furs, go safari with large animal mounts or play with "Fossil Finds" rocks and such. In the spring, they have a seasonal Butterfly Station. See the Butterflies and look for cocoons, mix nectar and map a Monarch's migration.

VIRGINIA INTERNATIONAL RACEWAY

Danville (Alton) - 1245 Pine Tree Road 24520. www.virclub.com. Phone: (434) 822-7700. Hours: Wednesday-Sunday 9:00am-7:00pm (early January - mid-December). Weather pending, only run go karts on 75% dry tracks. Admission: Karting $35.00 half hour rental. $5.00 license fee.

Virginia International Raceway's 3.27-mile natural terrain road course, rich in history, has become the premier motorsports facility of its type in America. Each season brings at least a dozen exciting spectator events featuring vintage and modern sports cars and motorcycles. The VIR Motorsport Country Club features a restaurant and pub, meeting rooms and swimming pool. There is a 27-room trackside hotel and an 18-unit pitside Paddock Suites and Garage complex. VIR's world-class Plantation Valley Kart Track offers four-wheeled fun for all ages. Hone your racing skills on a state-of-the-art 5/8-mile, 24-foot-wide, paved karting circuit. Karts are available for rent, or you can bring your own. (age 12+ only) Did you know almost every successful professional racing driver in the world today got their start in karting?

SANTA CLAUS TRAIN

Dillwyn - www.buckinghambranch.com. Buckingham Branch Railroad Station, US 15. (800) 451-6318. Don't miss this opportunity to join Santa Claus for a special Christmas time train ride! As the train journeys through the Buckingham County countryside, Santa will pass through the seasonally decorated train and visit with the children. All tickets ~$15.00. (many excursions the first two Saturdays in December)

BLUE RIDGE INSTITUTE & FARM MUSEUM

Ferrum - 20 Museum Drive, Rte. 40 (off Rte. 220 to Rte. 40) 24088. Phone: (540) 365-4416. www.blueridgeinstitute.org. Hours: Galleries open daily during regular hours. Farm Museum: Walk-in visitors Saturdays 10:00am-5:00pm and Sundays 1:00-5:00pm, (mid-May to mid-August) Group tours are available by reservation any day April-October. Gallery open year-round. Admission: $8.00 adult, $5.00 senior (60+) and child (6-14). Gallery is FREE.

The Blue Ridge Farm Museum reflects the day-to-day lifestyle of prosperous German-American farmsteaders in the Blue Ridge in the year 1800. Visitors may find costumed interpreters preparing meals over the open hearth, baking bread in an outdoor bake oven, blacksmithing, or carrying out other household and farm chores of the period. Walk around the gardens and the farm buildings, see heirloom vegetables and historic breeds of sheep, chicken, horses, pigs, and cattle. Ask them about their special participatory programs when visitors can don Institute costumes and take part in farm activities or try their hands at vintage crafts. In the gallery, see changing exhibits of traditional life, such as old-time musical instrument making, folk toys and carvings.

BLUE RIDGE FOLKLIFE FESTIVAL

The festival brings together musicians and moonshiners, craftspeople and cooks, hot rodders and horse handlers—in short, a host of folk artists and artisans in a celebration of Blue Ridge heritage. Coon Dog contest, Steam and Engine show, storytelling, old-time Blue Ridge food and old-fashioned children's picnic games. Admission. (last Saturday in October)

Green Bay

SAILOR'S CREEK BATTLEFIELD HISTORIC STATE PARK

Green Bay - Rte. 2, Box 70 (SR 307 north to Rte. 617 north) 23942. Phone: (434) 392-3435. www.dcr.virginia.gov/parks/sailorcr.htm. Visitors Ctr open Monday-Saturday 10am-5pm, Sunday Noon-5pm. Admission: FREE. Note: Sailor's Creek Battlefield State Park is a great place to stop for lunch as it lies approximately midway between Petersburg and Appomattox Court House. Charcoal grills and picnic tables are available at the Overton-Hillsman House and the nearby Confederate overlook. No water is available. There is a restroom for use during daylight hours.

During "Black Thursday of the Confederacy", nearly a quarter of Lee's army (more than 7,700 men) were killed, wounded or captured (even eight generals) including one of Lee's sons. Lee surrendered his army three days later at Appomattox Court House. Costumed volunteers re-enact this battle near the historic Hillsman House, which served as a field hospital for northern and southern soldiers (summertime). Various interpretive programs are held throughout the year. Anniversary of Battle in April. Christmas in December.

TWIN LAKES STATE PARK

Green Bay - Rte. 2, Box 70 (US 360 west to SR 613) 23942. Phone: (434) 392-3435. www.dcr.virginia.gov/state_parks/twi.shtml. Admission: $7.00 per car. Fee waived for overnight guests. CONCESSIONS: "The Spot," a

1950s theme snack bar featuring premium hand-dipped ice cream. Also a gift shop.

This historical park offers a full array of cultural, environmental and recreational activities. Through historic photographs and interpretive signs, visitors to the can learn of the park's history. You'll find a full service campground, group camping facilities and climate controlled cabins. Enjoy swimming, fishing and lakefront picnicking at Goodwin Lake. Hikers, mountain bikers and equestrians can take advantage of a multi-use trail developed in conjunction with Prince Edward State Forest.

BOOKER T. WASHINGTON NATIONAL MONUMENT

Hardy - 12130 Booker T. Washington Highway (US 220 south to Rocky Mount, then north on SR 122) 24101. Phone: (540) 721-2094. www.nps.gov/bowa. Hours: Year-round daily from 9:00am-5:00pm except New Years, Christmas, and Thanksgiving. Admission: FREE. Tours: Ranger guided walking tours of the historic area of the park are offered daily during the summer and on Saturdays and Sundays during the school year, as weather and staff availability permit. The tour times are 11:00am and 2:00pm. These tours generally last 30 minutes to 1 hour.

Note: In addition to the Plantation Trail, the monument provides an opportunity for a 1½ mile meandering walk through fields and forests on the Jack-O-Lantern Branch Trail. Trail guides are available at the visitor center. A picnic area in a wooded setting is available.

The monument commemorates Booker T. Washington's first 9 years of childhood slavery. Born into slavery on this tobacco plantation in 1856, Washington rose to prominence as an educator, orator, and founder of the Tuskegee Institute in Alabama. Begin your self-guided tour with the audio-visual program titled "Longing to Learn" (a slide show about Mr. Washington's life with old time slave, gospel songs woven throughout the show). Here, you will learn that Mr. Washington left the Burroughs farm in 1865 at age 9, as a poor and uneducated newly freed slave. When he returned for a visit in 1908, he was a college president and influential political figure. Outside, follow the Plantation Trail through the reconstructed farm buildings, crops and animals. Demonstrations of farm life in Civil War Virginia help bring to life the setting of Washington's childhood as a slave valued at $400. Kids notice that the cabin he lived in didn't have a floor (only earth) and no glass in the windows. He ate cornbread and pork mostly. Getting into school (one day) would be like "getting into heaven." "Education and work must go hand in hand" he said. We love places like this that give you a glimpse of the life (and humble beginnings) of an everyday American hero.

JUNETEENTH

Hardy - Booker T. National Monument. This event celebrates emancipation. With the Civil War ending in 1865, approximately four million people of African descent, held in the bonds of slavery, discovered freedom. Admission fee. (June, third Saturday)

CHRISTMAS IN OLD VIRGINIA

Hardy - Booker T. Washington National Monument. (540) 721-2094. Visitors are invited to enjoy a candlelight tour of the plantation where famous educator Booker T. Washington celebrated Christmas as a slave child. Learn about his memories of Christmas while enjoying music, children's activities and refreshments. Each evening's activities include candlelight tours to the plantation kitchen cabin, incorporating living history vignettes about how Christmas was celebrated in the 1850's and 1860's, children's games and story time, and a special reading of Booker T. Washington's "Christmas Days in Old Virginia." (December, first weekend)

SMITH MOUNTAIN LAKE STATE PARK

Huddleston - 1235 State Park Road (North shore of the lake in Bedford Cty. US 460 to SR 122 south to Rte. 608 east to Rte. 626 south) 24104. Phone: (434) 297-6066. www.dcr.virginia.gov/state_parks/smi.shtml. Hours: Daily 8:00am-Dusk Admission: $7.00 per vehicle. Fee waived for overnight guests. Tours: VA Dare Paddlewheeler sightseeing cruises (540) 297-7100. Note: The Smith Mountain Dam Visitor Center is open daily 10:00am-6:00pm.

Located on the second-largest freshwater body in the state, this park is not just for water enthusiasts. In addition to water-related activities including swimming, paddle boat rentals, a boat ramp and a universally accessible fishing pier, families can also enjoy miles of hiking trails, picnicking, a visitor center, amphitheater and many special programs (Night hikes, hay rides, canoe trips, twilight programs, Junior Rangers). The park's visitor center features exhibits on the history and folklore of the area and the lake's aquatic environment. There are 13 hiking trails, each less than two miles long, which meander through the park's varied features including hardwood forests, pine forests, secluded coves and picturesque vistas. The Chestnut Ridge and Turtle Island trails are open year-round; all others are open when the visitor center is open. Primitive camping is available and they also have one three-bedroom cabin and 19 two-bedroom cabins. Both campsites and cabins have been upgraded with modern improvements.

Lynchburg

AMAZEMENT SQUARE, THE RIGHTMIRE CHILDREN'S MUSEUM

Lynchburg - 27 Ninth Street (corner of Jefferson & Ninth Streets along the riverfront, downtown) 24504. Phone: (434) 845 - 1888. www.amazementsquare.org. Hours: Wednesday-Saturday 10:00am-4:00pm. Admission: $10.00 (age 1+). Note: Big Red Barn's - farmland environment for preschoolers. Great gift shop out front.

The central exhibit of the museum is a meandering three-story interactive tangle of pathways, tunnels, stairs and a glass elevator called the Amazement Tower. Here's some of the best exhibit areas: On The James - Take the helm and row a virtual tour boat "bateaux"; work locks and dams; create a rainstorm or watch the river flood. Once Upon a Building - sit in the "Architects Office" and design a dream home or explore architecture using a computer drafting program (Jefferson influences); work as a team by manipulating a hydraulic crane to create a building or house. Indian Island - explore a Monacan Hogan and ancient village; excavate for artifacts; League of Healthy Heroes - explore electricity by making circuits and learn about gravity, walk-thru a heart or push a lung; virtual sports will test your physical fitness. Kaleidoscope - families can step inside a see-through room and paint it (The Paint Box - take off your shoes and enter the box...you won't believe the end result!) or jam with friends in the soundproof studio with electric and rhythm instruments from around the world; act out stories in the theater or make art projects to take home in imagination studio. One promise...in order to participate here, you will make new friends. Most of these exhibits are unique from most other children's museums that we've seen. Well done!

LYNCHBURG SYMPHONY ORCHESTRA

Lynchburg - 621 Court Street 24504. https://www.lynchburgsymphony.org/. Phone: (434) 845-6604.

Classical music during the seven concert season, including two for young people and a free outdoor concert with fireworks for the community.

LYNCHBURG BATTEAU FESTIVAL

Lynchburg - Riverfront Festival Park. https://vacanals.org/batteau/. Starting in Lynchburg, this eight-day event features authentic replicas of late 18th century merchant boats. Crews pole down the James from Lynchburg to Richmond, camping each night along the way. Music, camps, food vendors and exhibits. Additions to this event are a Civil War re-enactment, American Indian and African-American histories. Admission varies by event. (June, mid-month for 8 days)

CHRISTMAS AT POINT OF HONOR

Lynchburg - Point of Honor. (434) 847-1459. The annual Christmas Open House re-creates a Federal-style Christmas. The house is arranged for an early 19th century plantation party. Refreshments of mulled-cider and cookies are served. Point of Honor was built in 1815 by the Cabell family and is among the most elegant examples of Federal architecture in Piedmont Virginia. FREE. (December, first Sunday)

Martinsville

PIEDMONT ARTS ASSOCIATION

Martinsville - 215 Starling Avenue 24112. www.piedmontarts.org. Phone: (276) 632-3221. Hours: Monday-Friday 10:00am-5:00pm, Saturdays 10:00am-3:00pm. Admission: FREE.

Here's the spot for The Arts in Henry County…artistic performers, visiting artists and a rotating exhibitions gallery. The kids will gravitate to the Discovery Room where young visitors can create all types of art, inspired by the art in the museum around them. To engage your kids in the gallery pieces, be sure to ask for the Treasure Hunt page when you arrive. Look for Palette the Discovery Dog's paw print for clues. Great way to keep the kids interested, having fun, but also learning about art.

VIRGINIA MUSEUM OF NATURAL HISTORY

Martinsville - 21 Starling Avenue (corner of Rte. 220/58) 24112. Phone: (276) 666-8600. www.vmnh.net. Hours: Tuesday-Saturday 10:00am-4:00pm. Closed Thanksgiving, Christmas, New Years. Admission: $10.00 adult, $5.00 senior & college students, youth (3-17) Note: Paleo café.

An Allosaurus skeleton and a prehistoric whale greet visitors entering the Hall of Ancient Life, which includes windows looking into scientific labs. The Vertebrate Paleontology Lab is where VMNH researchers prepare whales, dinosaurs and other vertebrate fossils, including over 700 dinosaur bones stored in the

Here's our friend...Clawd, the GIANT Sloth...trying to scare us....

Museum's collections from excavations in Wyoming. If you ask good questions of a roaming scientist, they might really spend some time giving you an insider's peak at their working lab and show you current projects. Next, experience the state-of-the-art permanent exhibit galleries "Uncovering Virginia", "How Nature Works: Rocks" and "How Nature Works: Life", along with the Discovery Reef, featuring high-definition nature films. At each exhibit, there is: a recreation of the site as it is today; a lab experience where visitors can examine fossil or archaeological evidence and use the same tools as scientists to interpret that evidence; and video animation that brings to life the animals and plants that were alive at that time and in at that place. Meet "Clawd" the giant sloth (half bear... half something else). This area allows lots of hands-on looks and touches of rocks from Virginia and around the world. How do we use rocks in everyday life today? (hint: jewelry or concrete?). Where do geodes come from? See the regionally famous Fairy Stones!

MARTINSVILLE SPEEDWAY

Martinsville - 340 Speedway Road (One mile north of the intersection of the U.S. 220/58 Bypass and U.S. 220 Business) 24148. Phone: (276) 956-3151 or (877) 722-3849. www.martinsvillespeedway.com. Admission: To watch time trials is $15.00 adult and FREE for child under 12. NASCAR Cup Series tickets for Youth 12 and younger are $10, and are $25 for Youth 13 - 17.

Martinsville Speedway, founded by H. Clay Earles a year before NASCAR was formed, was one of the earliest tracks in America that's still part of the Winston Cup series. In those days, the track was a red dirt oval, with seating for a scant 6,000 folks. Now the Speedway is one of the most popular spots on the Winston Cup tour, with the 86,000-seat track sold out for two Cup races every year. Sponsors four major NASCAR races each year. Discover fun games, learn about the history of NASCAR and stay up-to-date with your favorite drivers through the NASCAR Kids Club.

Meadows of Dan

MABRY MILL

Meadows of Dan - Blue Ridge Parkway, MP 176 (US 58 and Blue Ridge Pkwy) or 266 Mabry Mill SE, 24120. Phone: (276) 952-2947 or www.mabrymillrestaurant.com. Hours: Gristmill area open 7:30am-5:00pm (May-October). Admission: FREE. Note: The Mill Restaurant serves breakfast all day plus yummy sandwiches and desserts. Please try the pancakes or corn cakes made from the mill ground corn meal.

Operated by E.B. Mabry from 1910 to 1935, this mill is one of the most photographed and artistically painted sites around the world. A trail takes you to the gristmill, sawmill, and blacksmith shop where old-time skills are demonstrated in the summer. Friday-Sunday special shows and "good ole time music" on Sunday.

NANCY'S CANDY COMPANY

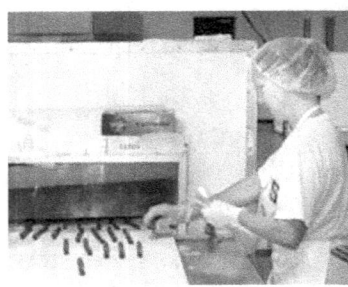

Fresh off the line...so tasty!

Meadows of Dan - 2684 Jeb Stuart Highway (off Parkway to Milepost 177.1. Exit US58, Stuart. Turn right and Nancy's is 0.25 mile on the right) 24120. Phone: (276) 952-2112. www.nancyscandycompany.com. Hours: Generally Monday-Saturday 10am-5pm, Sunday Noon-5pm.

Come see a chocolate and fudge factory in operation through viewing windows. Taste why people come from all over Virginia to eat their fudge. Everyday they have at least 40 different flavors of fudge and 60 varieties of chocolates on display, ready for you to sample. The employees leave fudge out on the counter and allow customers to taste. Flavors change with the seasons. The key lime and pumpkin fudge are examples of some unusual flavors you might try. After several tastes of fudge, it might be a good idea to try out one of the many trails at nearby Rock Castle Gorge or Fairystone State Park. Maybe bring a sack of chocolate covered pretzels to munch on. We highly recommend you call ahead and request a "chocolate talk" and candy making video presentation.

For updates visit: www.KidsLoveTravel.com

South Central Area 119

STAUNTON RIVER BATTLEFIELD STATE PARK

Randolph - 1035 Fort Hill Trail (Rte. 92 to Clover to Rte. 600, turn left, and then turn right on Rte. 855) 23962. www.dcr.virginia.gov/state_parks/stb.shtml. Phone: (434) 454-4312. Hours: The Visitor Center Saturday and Sunday 10:00am-4:00pm. The battlefield and self-guided trails are open daily from 8:00 am to Dusk. Admission: FREE.

Staunton River Battlefield State Park was named for Capt. Henry Staunton, who protected early settlers from Indian attacks. The river was important for transporting goods, especially tobacco, from the plantations in the area. This park is a 300-acre Civil War historic site on which a rag tag group of Confederate old men and young boys beat the odds...and held off an assault by 5000 Union calvary on a bridge of strategic importance to General Lee's army (that under siege in Petersburg). The visitor center displays the history of the area as well as on electric energy. It also has a ¾ mile nature walking trail and two wildlife observation towers overlooking a wetland enhancement project built for waterfowl and other wildlife.

BATTLE OF STAUNTON RIVER BRIDGE COMMEMORATION CEREMONY

Randolph - This day-long event includes a commemoration of the Battle of the Staunton River Bridge, confederate encampments, cannon firing, music, a United Daughter of the Confederacy medal presentation, interpretive programs, wagon rides, guest speakers and more. It's free. (third Saturday in June)

Roanoke

ART VENTURE

Roanoke - 110 Salem Avenue SE 24011. www.taubmanmuseum.org/programs/art-venture. Phone: (540) 342-5760. Hours: Thursday-Saturday 10am-4pm, Sunday Noon-4:00pm. Admission: ArtVenture center is $5.00 per person (age 3+).

The hands-on, interactive gallery is designed especially for kids to have a personal experience with art and fun. The following descriptions of different areas will also give you an idea of what's displayed in the main part of the art museum: Make An Impression - in a Japanese shrine, visitors will make 3-color relief prints by pressing three stamps into a template (just like Japanese, large block stamp art). History in the Making - Pocahontas storytelling and individual interpretation. Visual Vibes - connects auditory sensations with the visual world by creating vibration-musical sounds out of a famous painting (draw what you hear - what does it sound like?). Puppetry and dress up.

Please Have a Seat - inspired by the "oops!" chair, visitors complete chair puzzles and create their own designs on a velcro wall. Vital Symbols - with modeling clay, you are invited to create your own personalized clay animals, drawing ideas from West African headpieces. Familiar Faces - self-image is transformed to Expressionistic, Cubistic or Impressionistic styles. Look at Me - see through glass easels allow artists to paint an expressive portrait of a partner that may be turned into take-home  prints...this was our favorite spot for the whole family! The exhibits in the main museum showcase significant works of art from cultures around the world with a special emphasis on American art and the artistic expressions of the Blue Ridge Mountains. Wow, what fun and learning can be had here! Please include it in your family plans as often as possible.

HISTORY MUSEUM OF WESTERN VIRGINIA

Roanoke - 101 Shenandoah Ave NE 24016. Phone: (540) 342-5770. www.vahistorymuseum.org. Hours: Tuesday-Saturday 10:00am-5:00pm. Open summer Mondays. Admission: $6.00 adult, $5.00 child (3-12). Educators: The Museum's Study Guides (online) and programs are well-organized visits including hands-on activities.

The museum spans the 10,000 year history of Western Virginia with an exhibit entitled "A Crossroads of History" that traces the history of mankind in the area from prehistoric to recent times. Did you know that during the time of Lewis and Clark's expedition, the counties were larger, some extending all the way to the Mississippi? Here's a sampling of what you can find: a wigwam aside Indian pottery and beads (Rawrenoke: meant "string of shell beads" - very valuable for trading); a pioneer cabin; a 1781 land grant deed signed by Jefferson; Civil War surgical implements and walking sticks; the Victorian Boom Age late 1800's buggy and parlor room and an area where you can try you hand at making the best sailor's knots.

MILL MOUNTAIN THEATRE

Roanoke - One Market Square 24011. Phone: (540) 342-5740 or (800) 317-6455. www.millmountain.org. Performances: Wednesday-Saturday evenings at 7:30pm. Saturday & Sunday Matinees at 2:00pm. Admission: Tickets: Between $15.00-$25.00 for young audience productions.

Regional professional live year-round theatre offering dramas, musicals, children's plays, comedies, and family productions like "Miss Nelson is Missing", "Charlotte's Web" or "A Wonderful Life".

DICKENS OF A CHRISTMAS

Roanoke - A Christmas is a Victorian Christmas celebration including community caroling, story telling, a parade, and horse drawn carriage rides throughout the streets of downtown Roanoke. Area retailers offer free cider, hot chocolate and roasted chestnuts to shoppers. (first three weekends in December)

SCIENCE MUSEUM OF WESTERN VIRGINIA

Roanoke-One Market Square, downtown (4th & 5th floors near City Market) 24011. Phone: (540) 342-5718. www.smwv.org. Hours: Tuesday-Saturday 10:00am-5:00pm. Sunday 1:00-5:00pm. Closed winter holidays. Admission: $15.50 adult, $14.00 senior (60+) & youth (6-17), $8.00 child (3-5). Includes Butterfly Garden & special exhibits. Butterflies only is half price.

Their mission is to offer hands-on activities that encourage touching, twisting, spinning, pulling and turning. In How It Works, explore light, color and sound by interacting with games (make lightning come to you, create color from gas like neon). At WonderLab, view the eye

Learn about the heart with a big, kid-friendly, scientific model...

of the hurricane or a tornado! Get personal - Healthy Bodies focuses on the science behind medicine (see how blood flows, muscles connect, and the senses react). This is the best example of plaque and hardening of the arteries you'll find...you can even see a real healthy (and hardened) artery. The Living Collections Zone has many unique creatures to touch (pet a horseshoe crab, sea star or sea urchin). Moms, Dads & Grandparents will explore this right along with the kids - so much to do (not just see). Very, very well done.

VIRGINIA'S EXPLORE PARK VISITORS CENTER (BRPKWY)

Roanoke - Blue Ridge Parkway, Milepost 115 (accessible from Rutrough Road) 24014. Phone: (540) 427-1800 or https://www.virginia.org/listing/explore-park-visitor-center/15795/. Visitor Center Hours: 9am-6pm daily (May-October). Note: Mountain biking and hiking trails, fishing, canoeing and kayaking in the Roanoke River. Gift Shop.

The visitor center has many exhibits throughout the year and there is no charge for admittance into the gallery or exhibits of the visitor center. The Outdoor Living History village is currently closed, awaiting potential future re-opening with expanded programs.

VIRGINIA MUSEUM OF TRANSPORTATION

Roanoke - 303 Norfolk Avenue (I-581 exit 5, located in restored railway station next to Norfolk Southern mainline, downtown) 24016. Phone: (540) 342-5670. www.vmt.org. Hours: Tuesday-Saturday 10:00am-5:00pm, Sunday 1:00-5:00pm. Closed major holidays. Admission: $10.00 adult, $8.00 senior (60+) & students, $6.00 child (3-12). Note: A great gift shop with many Thomas the Tank Engine items.

The Valley boasts its railroad heritage at the remodeled historic N & W freight station housing the Virginia Museum of Transportation. Come face to face with vintage electric locomotives, classic diesels and steam giants (the No. 611 is mighty!). Climb aboard a caboose, a railway post office car, and a No. 17, 1934 Dodge school bus. On Main Street, view early autos, freight trucks, fire engines, carriages and air travel. Learn basic principles of the development of transportation through hands-on exhibits that kids can touch, turn, drive, spin, and climb on. Kids might also like the multi-level O-gauge model train layout (see who can spot the train first) or the model circus display or the giant Jupiter Rocket parked outside the museum. But mostly, the museum is about the American worker who built

the roads, laid the track and built the trains, cars and carriages...the people behind transportation. Meet some of them personally in the railyard (where they are restoring other trains). Pretend you're in a modern coal mine shaft seeing mineshaft transport machines at work.

GEORGE WASHINGTON & JEFFERSON NATIONAL FORESTS

Roanoke - 5162 Valleypointe Parkway 24019. Phone: (540) 265-5100 or www. fs.fed.us/r8/gwj/. Hours: 24 hours a day. Admission: FREE. Beaches are $3.00-$8.00 per car. Note: Metal detection is generally permitted on national forest. Collection of any archeological or historical object is illegal. Digging, disturbing, or otherwise altering the ground is prohibited.

These two forests stretch from one end of Virginia to the other, as well as extending into West Virginia, along the ruggedly beautiful Appalachians. Virtually every type of outdoor recreation activity you can imagine is available. Of course hiking, fishing, mountain bicycling and camping lead the way, but don't forget hawk watching, cross-country skiing, horseback riding, nature photography, and orienteering. Highlights include:

Falls of Little Stony, Clinch Ranger District, Wise (540-328-2931). Trail, trout stream, the Gorge (steep sides with large rock outcrops and rock ledges often towering hundreds of feet overhead), and the Views of three waterfalls.

Elizabeth Furnace (log cabin center/Edinburg 540-984-4101). Massanutten Storybook Trail; Bark Camp Lake Recreation Area (Wise 540-328-2981); Guest River Gorge Trail, High Knob Recreation Area (tower observation). Bear Tree Recreation Area; The Virginia Creeper Trail; Mount Rogers Scenic Byway, highest point in state with trail to the top. Also trails thru pine forests, 60 mile segment of Appalachian trail, cross- skiing, Virginia Highlands Horse Trail. (Marion 540-783-5196); Stony Fork (Wytheville 540-228-5551); Cascades Recreation Area (66 foot cascades waterfall/Blacksburg 540-552-4641); Dragon's Truth (spires of quartzite on top of mountain, looks like teeth/New Castle 540-864-5195); Fenwick Mines (old miner town); Roaring Run Furnace; Highlands Scenic Tour (20 mile scenic auto loop including Falling Spring Waterfall and Humpback Bridge - the nation's only surviving arched single-span covered bridge, Covington); Lake Moomaw; Hidden Valley (Hot Springs); Apple Orchard Falls (200 foot falls/Natural Bridge); Crabtree Falls - hike two miles to the top of the highest waterfall east of the Mississippi River, Sherando Lake. Augusta Springs Wetlands Trail (Staunton); Confederate Breastworks; Brandywine Lake (Bridgewater).

MILL MOUNTAIN ZOO

Roanoke - J.P. Fishburne Parkway and Prospect Road (on top of Mill Mtn., off the Blue Ridge Parkway and next to the famous Roanoke Star) 24034. Phone: (540) 343-3241. www.mmzoo.org. Hours: Daily 10:00am-5:00pm. Closed Christmas. Admission: $10.00 adult, $8.00 child (3-11). ZooChoo Rides are $2.00. Note: Many special events and educational programs throughout the year. Picnic facilities, a wildflower garden, ZooChoo train rides, outdoor concession/café and gift shop.

On top of Roanoke's Mill Mountain, off the Blue Ridge Parkway and alongside the famous Roanoke Star, is an AZA accredited 3 1/2-acre zoo. This zoo has exhibits of 55 or more species of mammals, birds and reptiles. Animals found here include a Siberian Tiger, Snow Leopards, Red Pandas, Japanese Macaques, Bald Eagles, Fishing Cat, Clouded Leopard and Porcupine.

ROANOKE STAR

Roanoke - 2198 Mill Mountain Spur. J. P. Fishburne Parkway and Prospect Road (on top of Mill Mountain, next to the zoo. Follow signs from downtown or off BR Pkwy Milepost 120) 24034. www.playroanoke.com/parks-and-greenways/mill-mountain-park-2/roanoke-star/. Phone: (800) 635-5535.

This attraction is sure to make the kids' mouths drop wide open. Indians wandering the parallel ridges of the Allegheny Mountains named their great valley, Shenandoah, "daughter of the stars." See the world's largest man-made star! Erected in 1949 as a symbol of the progressive spirit of Roanoke, it towers nearly 100' high above Mill Mountain. This huge structure can be seen at night for over 60 miles.

ST. PATRICK'S DAY PARADE & SHAMROCK FEST

Roanoke - Downtown. (540) 853-2889 or www.facebook.com/StPatricksDayParadeAndShamrockFestival. This is the largest St. Patrick's Day celebration in western Virginia. The parade features ten marching and bagpipe bands and many colorful entries. Celtic Festival in the Historic Market includes Celtic bands, dancers & Celtic vendors. (March 17th or weekend before)

ROANOKE FESTIVAL IN THE PARK

Roanoke - (540) 342-2640. www.roanokefestival.com The annual parade is part of the anniversary 10-day celebration of Roanoke Festival in the Park. Huge Macy-style balloons and costumed characters will be featured. Backyard circus, kids arts & crafts, storytelling, games and puppet parade. (May, Memorial Day weekend)

For updates visit: www.KidsLoveTravel.com

South Central Area

COMMONWEALTH GAMES OF VIRGINIA

Roanoke - www.commonwealthgames.org or call for locations and times. (540) 343-0987. This multi-sport festival is the event's anniversary and is recognized by the United States Olympic Committee and the National Congress of State Games. Olympic style amateur sports festival for male and female athletes of all ages & abilities. 40+ sports offered. Admission. (July, third weekend)

LAYMAN FAMILY FARM

Roanoke (Montvale) - Layman Family Farm. 615 Mt. View Church Road. (540) 966-3056 or www.laymanfamilyfarm.com. Visit the country, ride a cow train, get lost in a 10-acre corn maze and ride the hay wagon to the pumpkin patch. Admission. (Friday evenings and weekend days in September thru early November)

DIXIE CAVERNS

Roanoke (Salem) - 5753 West Main Street (I-81 exit 132) 24153. Phone: (540) 380-2085. www.dixiecaverns.com. Hours: Daily 9:30am-5:00pm. Admission: $14 adult, $6 child (5-12)

Would you believe a dog was the first one in the hole at the top of the hill... followed by several inquisitive farm boys - that was in 1920. There have been many changes over the years in lighting and passageways, but the natural wonder of this cavern remains. Experienced guides take you "up" into the mountain and then "down" underground - look for formations shaped like a wedding bell, turkey wings or a magic mirror.

South Boston

SOUTH BOSTON SPEEDWAY

South Boston - 1188 James Hagood Hwy. 24592. Phone: (434) 572-4947 or (877) 440-1540 tickets. www.southbostonspeedway.com. Season: Saturday night racing opens every March. Admission: ~$10.00 (age 10+). Pit tours are $15.00 each. Special events around $20.00.

During its history, the speedway has been the site of a number of NASCAR events, with the likes of Richard Petty taking Grand National wins at the oval. Known as America's Hometown Track, South Boston Speedway puts on a great show, with competitions among some of the best Late Model Stock car drivers around.

HARVEST FESTIVAL

South Boston - Downtown. (434) 575-4209. www.soboharvestfest.com. A day of entertainment, food, crafts, people and fun await visitors to this festival. Activities feature four continuous entertainment stages, a scarecrow-making workshop, karate demonstrations, magic shows, pumpkin decorating and tons of fair food. (September, last Saturday)

STAUNTON RIVER STATE PARK

South Boston (Scottsburg) - 1170 Staunton Trail (US 360 to Rte. 344) 24589. Phone: (434) 572-4623. www.dcr.virginia.gov/state_parks/sta.shtml. Admission: $5.00 per vehicle. Fee waived for overnight guests.

With woods by the acres, broad meadows and a lengthy shoreline on Buggs Island Lake (800-524-4347) there is much to offer. Freshwater fishing plus swimming and wading pools, camping and cabins, tennis courts, a children's playground, a boat launch, riverfront picnicking in shelters, miles of hiking trails, a multi-use trails open to hikers, bikers and equestrian riders are all well used. Buggs Island Lake and the connecting Lake Gaston are famous for the number and size of fish found there. Six wooded trails provide miles of hiking along the Dan and Staunton rivers as well as Buggs Island Lake. Some of the landscapes are little changed from the times when generals from the Revolutionary and Civil wars camped with their troops.

South Hill

SOUTH HILL MODEL RAILROAD MUSEUM

South Hill - 201 S. Mecklenburg Avenue (South Hill Chamber offices) 23970. Phone: (434) 447-4547 or (800) 524-4347. www.southhillva.org/visitor-information/museums-attractions Hours: Daily 9:00am-4:00pm Admission: FREE.

The Museum is located in the renovated railroad depot downtown and features two operating HO Scale model railroad displays. The WBA (Wiggle Bump & Agony) is a "just for fun" railroad and features four tracks traveling through tunnels and over and under bridges in the imaginary towns along the track. The museum scale layout features buildings and scenes meticulously recreated as they looked during the 1950's.

Stuart

FAIRY STONE STATE PARK

A real Fairystone... (about the size of a dime)

Stuart - Route 2 Box 723, 907 Fairystone Lake Drive (Rte. 57 from Bassett or from Blue Ridge Pkwy. via Rte. 58, 8 or 57) 24171. Phone: (276) 930-2424 or (800) 933-PARK. www.dcr.virginia.gov/state_parks/fai.shtml. Hours: VISITOR CENTER, GIFT SHOP: Features exhibits on local history, mountain culture, indigenous plants and animals, and fairy stones. It is open 9:00am - 4:00pm in the summer and sporadically during spring and fall. There's a gift shop in the park office; the shop's hours are seasonal. Admission: $7.00 per vehicle. Parking fee

South Central Area

is waived for overnight guests. Additional swimming fee for day use (summer). Note: 168 acre lake, climate controlled cabins, campgrounds, hiking trails, beach swimming and concessions, row boats, canoes, paddle boats, hydro bikes, picnicking and two playgrounds (including one in the water!), with weekend bluegrass concerts, and daily planned talks, walks, or tours.

Fairy Stone State Park, the largest of Virginia's six original state parks, is home to its namesake "fairy stones." These rare mineral crosses and the park's scenic beauty, rich history and ample recreational opportunities make it a local and regional favorite. Here's the Story: Fairies (or angels) danced playfully around springs until they heard news that Jesus Christ had died. The saddened fairy tears fell onto the rocks and formed crosses made from stones. Many famous people have visited the park (including Presidents) and have made a stone into earrings, bracelets or pocket pieces, carried or worn for luck or blessings. Don't forget to stop by the park office to purchase fairystones (just a couple of dollars) or look for the Hunt Site (next to the gas station - look for signs - 3 miles southeast of the park entrance on Rte 57). We actually found some - what a "nature's" blessing!

If you stay overnight, the cabins are charmingly rustic with electric but with no telephone or TV. Bring along board games and good books to read for evening entertainment by the fire (wood available on site for a small fee), or out on the back porch. Also, be sure to bring a flashlight...it sure gets dark out at night in the woods!

If you come during the summer, the water playground has wonderful, soft-sided floating logs, lily pads, frogs and turtles that kids can slide and climb on. A very family friendly park.

WOOD BROTHERS RACING

Stuart - 21 Performance Drive, Industrial Park (US 58, 30 minutes from Martinsville Speedway) 24171. Phone: (276) 694-2121. www.woodbrothersracing.com. Hours: Museum: Weekdays 9:00am-Noon & 1:00-5:00pm. Also open Saturdays of Winston Cup Martinsville races. Admission: FREE. Note: Racing gift shop.

One of the most successful racing teams in NASCAR history, Stuart's Wood Brothers have won races on every major track in the country. Their Race Shop and Museum contains memorabilia spanning 50 years of racing. They have a variety of trophies, helmets, uniforms, etc. from drivers like Pearson, AJ Foyt and Dale Jarrett. Also several classic race cars are displayed.

VIRGINIA PEACH FESTIVAL

Stuart - Rotary Field. (276) 694-6012. www.patrickchamber.com. The festival celebrates Patrick county agriculture and especially, peaches. Local farmers conduct orchard tours and have peaches and produce for sale. There are games and pony rides for the children. (August, first full long weekend)

BLUE RIDGE PARKWAY

Vinton - 2551 Mountain View Road (Vinton Ranger Station 24179. Phone: (540) 857-2458. www.BlueRidgeParkway.org. Hours: Activities run from (mid-June to October). Campgrounds, concessions & lodges open (May-October). The parkway closes by section during severe conditions. Admission: FREE to drive parkway. Some sites have minimal fee. Note: Camping, hiking, fishing, bicycling, picnicking. Detailed camping & hiking sites found online. Many longer trails are moderate to strenuous -too much for a young family hike. Easy to moderate "leg stretching" loops can be found all along the Parkway, esp to points of interest.

The Parkway runs parallel to I-81 and begins in Waynesboro at Milepost 0, and ends in Cherokee, NC. It connects the Shenandoah National Park (Skyline Drive) to the Great Smoky Mountains National Park. The parkway follows the Appalachian Mountain chain and provides some of the most spectacular scenery in the world, ranging from 650 to 6,000 feet in elevation. A hundred species of trees, a variety of flowering shrubs and wildflowers as well as 54 different mammals and 59 species of birds live along the parkway, more than the entire European continent! The speed limit is 45 MPH and the drive warrants "taking your time" to see the seasonal foliage. Even better, pull off the road and spread out a blanket and have a picnic.

Look especially for these mile marker sites:
- Hogback Overlook (milepost 21)
- Logging RR exhibit (milepost 34.4)
- Humpback Rocks (milepost 8.4) has Visitors Center, pioneer mountain farm.

South Central Area

- Fallingwater Cascades National Scenic Trail (milepost 83.1) is a 1.5-2.5 mile hiking loop. Moderate.
- Cave Mountain Lake Recreation Area (Natural Bridge area) has lake swimming, beach, hiking, picnicking and camping. Small vehicle admission. (540) 291-2188.
- James River Restored Canal Lock (milepost 63.6)at US 501, James River Visitors Center in Big Island (586-4357). Battery Creek Lock #7 was part of the James River and Kanawha Canal System. May-October.
- Peaks of Otter Area (milepost 84) has a Visitors Center, historical farm, trails, picnicking and camping. Mile 86 in Bedford is where the Johnson Farm is demonstrating southern mountain interpretive farming demos. Accessible from Peaks of Otter by trail. (August-November, 540-586-3707).
- Rocky Knob (milepost 169) has picnicking, camping, Visitor Center, trails&cabins.
- Meadows of Dan town has an old general store, Mabry Mill (mp 176.1) and Nancy's Candy Company (see separate listing).
- Groundhog Mountain Overlook (milepost 188.8) is a high point with 360 degree view and observation tower.
- Puckett Cabin (milepost 189.9) the home of Grandma Puckett, the storied local midwife who helped birth 1000 babies.

Chapter 5
South East

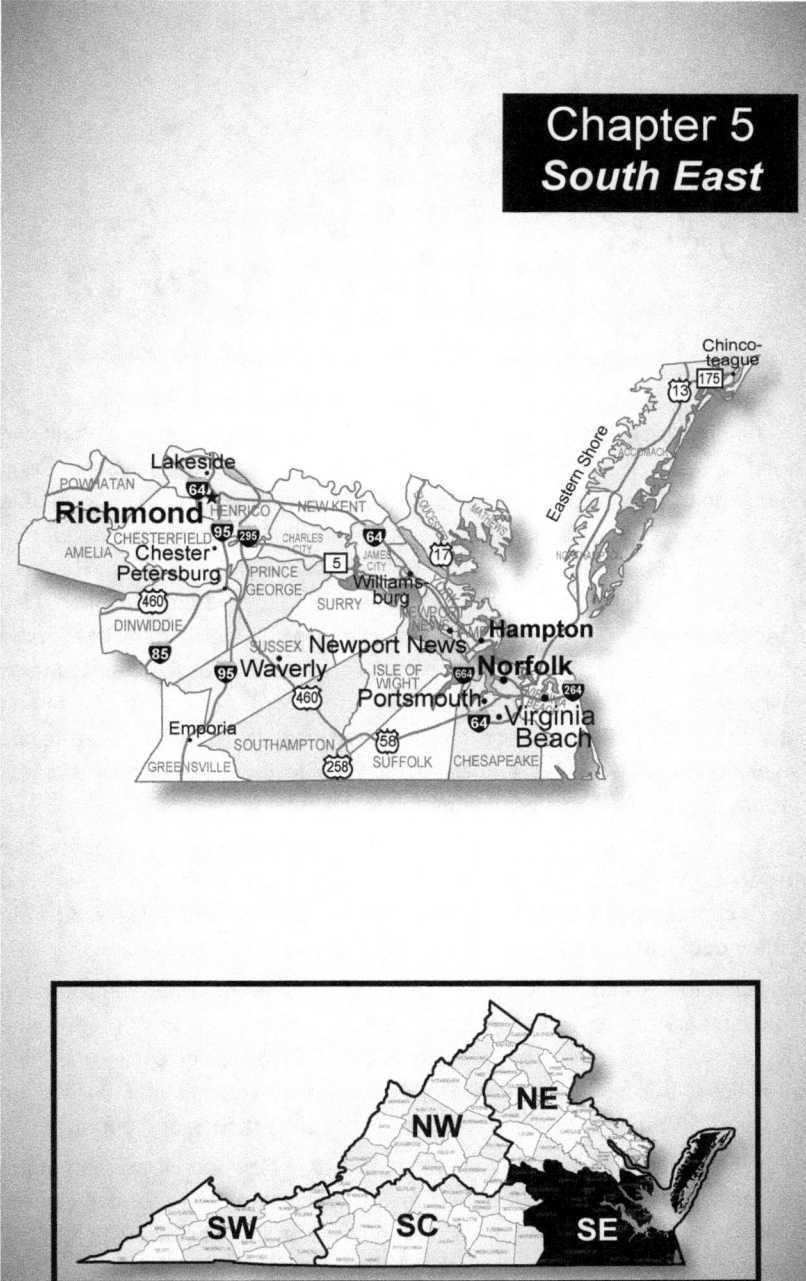

A Quick Tour of our Hand-Picked Favorites Around...

South East Virginia

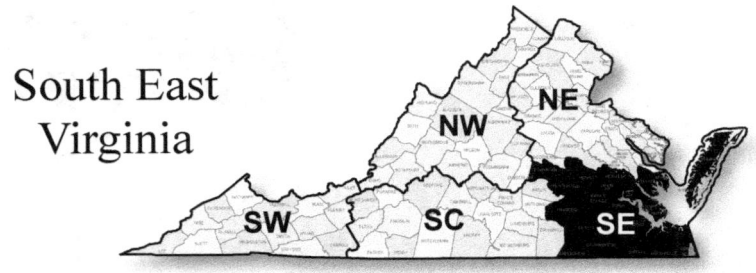

America's Historic Triangle of Williamsburg, Jamestown and Yorktown offers adventure at every turn in the place where America began and independence was won. Visit **Colonial Williamsburg** when your favorite "characters" are in residence. Don a tri-corner hat or bonnet and grab an old-fashioned root beer and pretzel roll (to feel Colonial, my child). At **Historic Jamestowne**, the new Archaearium is the place where kids can play detective while "walking" over real excavations. Maybe do a cartwheel in the fort yard, just like Pocahontas used to do. Nearby **Jamestown Settlement** is where the colorful re-created action is. Grind corn, put on armor, or hang out with the Sailors on life-size ships. **Yorktown** takes you forward to the Revolutionary War battles and even right inside camp as military soldiers prepare for the battle that would end the war.

Too much history in one day? Try Williamsburg's amusements like **Busch Gardens** Europe and **Water Country USA**. Forecast predicting rain or cool temps? Go inside at **Great Wolf Lodge** and splash and slide at the indoor waterpark.

Hampton Roads area has a world-class museum celebrating soaring achievements in air and space, maritime leadership, and the marine environment. Hampton's **Virginia Air & Space Center** gives new meaning to an out-of-this-world vacation! Here you can try your piloting skills in an official NASA Shuttle Landing Simulator or see a Mars rock or moon rock.

What better way to start your vacation day in Newport News than at the **Virginia Living Museum**. Stop at the touch tank and feel the wonder of the underwater world or take a walk outside on the boardwalk to see red wolves, river otters, birds and more, all in a natural wooded setting. Watch a pelican feeding, or explore the spooky world of an underground cave. The nearby **Mariners' Museum** offers visitors a look into the world of seafaring adventure. Go to see the turret of the Civil War ironclad USS Monitor, which is currently being displayed and restored at the museum in a new "walk-on" ship.

Most people know Norfolk as one theme: naval boatyards and **Nauticus**. The maritime-themed science center features hands-on exhibits, theaters with live actors, touch tanks, digital hi-definition films, and actually boarding a real battleship – the USS Wisconsin. Feel the unique texture of a nurse shark's skin, touch a tornado, design a battleship, or participate in a simulated naval battle aboard an Aegis-class destroyer. It's like being in a giant Navy ship experiment!

Home to the world's largest naval installation, visitors can enjoy a fascinating and entertaining commentary aboard several **Navy-themed Tour Boats**. Two-hour cruises depart daily from the Nauticus docks. Venture into the smooth waters of Hampton Road's historical harbor or board a bus tour narrated by naval personnel. Did you know supply ships glide up next to a battleship and send supplies secretly, underwater? Thrill to the sights of aircraft carriers, nuclear submarines, guided missile cruisers and all of the other ships that form the world's most powerful armada as you pass by them – up close!

Want to still be by the water but in a more natural setting? Cross the **Chesapeake Bay Bridge Tunnel** that actually takes you underwater to get to the other side! Escape to the quiet, laid-back land by the Bay with outdoor activities, day cruises, crabbing from the pier, nature walks, biking and delicious seafood. Travel along Rte. 13 to the tip – Chincoteague. You'll soon know why you felt called to come here – and the other tens of thousands others who are led each year – the **Chincoteague Ponies**! Reading stories about Misty or the romance of wild ponies from far-away lands will only enhance the journey. Across the inlet bridge on **Assateague Island**, go in search of the famous ponies either on foot, by bike or on a guided tour. Kids might want to try crabbing in the inlet, too. If you plan in advance, the Pony Swim, Parade and Auction is definitely one of those must-do festivals to attend.

What do a horseshoe crab's mouth and a toothbrush have in common? Where do playful bottlenose dolphins go for summer vacation? Where do juvenile humpback whales winter? Virginia Beach is a regular visitation spot for these, and other marine animals...in the ocean or at the **Virginia Aquarium**. You'll find "touch points" around seemingly every turn in this museum.

Ever wonder what it was like to be a Civil War soldier? **Pamplin Historical Park** lets you travel back 140 years and become a buck private. And, the kids get to use their personal MP3 players (or on site borrowed) to participate in drills, experience being fired upon (with air bursts), and play period games. Sleep in a platform tent, eat the Civil War era meals (hardtack, yuk!), or learn military codes and communications. Think you can cut it as a soldier in the 1860s?

Finally, wrap up all of this history at the **Virginia Historical Society** in Richmond. Any Virginian or anyone who wants an overview of the state's historical highlights needs to visit here. Discover the entire "Story of Virginia" through videos, storyphones, computer games and other interactive devices that make learning fun for the whole family. To finish you Natural History lesson of Richmond, take a canal boat trip along right through downtown Richmond! Or find a calmer section for fishing or swimming in the magnificent James River.

Sites and attractions are listed in order by City, Zip Code, and Name. Symbols indicated represent: 🍴 Restaurants   🛏 Lodging

Cape Charles

CHESAPEAKE BAY BRIDGE TUNNEL

Cape Charles - PO Box 111 (Rte. 13 between Hampton Roads and Eastern shore) 23310. Phone: (757) 624-3511 or (757) 331-2960. www.cbbt.com. Hours: The bridge is always open (except for poor weather or accidents). Seagull Restaurant and Gift Shop hours are 7:00am to 6:00pm, mid-September through mid-May; and 6:00am to 10:00pm, mid-May through mid-September. Admission: Toll for cars is $14-$18.00, one way. Small fee for return trip.

> This bridge/tunnel must be completely inspected for safety every 5 years. Well, it takes about 5 years to complete an inspection... so it's **a never ending job**!

For updates visit: www.KidsLoveTravel.com

Both a tourist attraction and a travel convenience, the Chesapeake Bay Bridge-Tunnel connects the Virginia mainland at Virginia Beach near Norfolk with Virginia's Eastern Shore. At 17.6 miles long, it carries US 13 across the mouth of the Chesapeake Bay using bridges, tunnels (underwater!) and 4 man-made islands. Direct crossing time is approximately 25 minutes. Sea Gull Island is located on the southernmost of the Bridge - 3-1/2 miles from Virginia Beach. This island provides the traveling public an opportunity to stop and stretch their legs. Birdwatch, or just take in the natural beauty and sounds of the Chesapeake Bay. Observe Navy and commercial ocean-going ships gliding gracefully through one of the world's busiest shipping channels. An interpretive display of the construction of the Bridge-Tunnel is located just outside the Gift Shop. This is quite a unique experience!

View from the stopover pier, looking out at the water we're about to go under...

EASTERN SHORE OF VIRGINIA NATIONAL WILDLIFE REFUGE VISITORS CENTER

Cape Charles - 5003 Hallett Circle 23310. www.fws.gov/refuge/eastern_shore_of_virginia/. Phone: (757) 331-2760. **Visitor Center Hours: Daily 9:00am-4:00pm (April-November). Daily 10:00am-2:00pm (December and March). Saturday-Sunday only (January and February).**

Located at the tip of the Delmarva Peninsula, this area is one of the most important avian migration funnels in North America. Each fall the refuge is the scene of a spectacular drama as millions of songbirds and monarch butterflies and thousands of raptors converge on their voyage south. The birds wait here until favorable winds assist them in crossing the Chesapeake Bay. This "funneling effect" provides excellent viewing opportunities for visitors between late August and early November. The refuge has a state of the art visitor center with interactive exhibits and foot trails, wildlife observation platforms and a photography blind. Three-dimensional displays depict the four critical habitats the refuge was established to protect - Chesapeake Bay, Barrier Islands, Salt Marshes, and Upland Forests. Get a close-up look and feel of the skulls, bones, feathers and other amazing natural discoveries at the Please Touch table. The Wise Point boat ramp is open to the public.

KIPTOPEKE STATE PARK

Cape Charles - 3540 Kiptopeke Drive (Eastern Shore, 3 miles north of Chesapeake Bay Bridge Tunnel on US 13, then west on SR 704) 23310. Phone: (757) 331-2267. www.dcr.virginia.gov/state_parks/kip.shtml. Admission: $7.00 per car. No parking fee for camping and cabin guests, up to two vehicles.

On Virginia's beautiful Eastern Shore, originally first explored by Capt. John Smith in 1608, Kiptopeke offers recreational access to the Chesapeake Bay along with an opportunity to explore a unique habitat featuring a flyway for migratory birds, rarely seen animals & a coastal dune environment. The park offers five new sun-filled cabins that sleep 16, RV and tent camping, a group camping lodge, a yurt (part cabin, part tent) and camping trailers. There's also a boat ramp, a lighted fishing pier, picnic areas, 4.2 miles of hiking and biking trails, a playground, a beach bathhouse and a swimming beach. Seasonal interpretive and educational programs focus on natural history, birding and bay ecology.

BIRDING & WILDLIFE FESTIVAL

Cape Charles - Best Western & Sunset Beach. www.esvafestivals.com. This festival takes place during the Fall migration of neo-tropical songbirds and raptors. It provides an opportunity for birdwatchers to witness incredible numbers of birds congregated in preparation for their flight to the tropics. (October, mid-month long weekend)

JAMES RIVER PARADE OF LIGHTS

Chester - (804) 706-1340. Celebrate Christmas traditions at the festive 1611 Citie of Henricus. Enjoy the annual James River Parade of Lights as boats compete for the holiday light decorations. (December, second Saturday evening)

Chincoteague

ASSATEAGUE EXPLORER

Chincoteague - (Departs daily from the dock at East Side Marina, on Chincoteague, just northeast of the Pony Swim area) 23336. Phone: (757) 990-1795 or (866) PONY SWIM. www.assateagueisland.com/explorer.htm. Admission: Rates: Pony Express or Birdwatching Nature Tours - $59.00, child (3-11) receive a $10.00 discount. Schedule: Pony Express Nature Tours: several times daily. Circle (Chincoteague) Island Nature Tour: 2-3 times daily. Check out the area map of expeditions online. Reservations recommended. (mid-May thru mid-October).

Assateague visitors often drive to the island and say, "Where are the wild ponies?" The National Park Service has placed miles of fence along the roadways to keep the wild horses away from roads and back in their natural habitat. About 95% of the wild ponies are found far away from the roads and these pony sighting trips take you to these productive areas. Your boat captain and guide is a commercial fisherman and native of Chincoteague Island. You will voyage into secluded wildlife refuge areas and learn about wild ponies and their behavior as you cruise up close. Get your best view of Assateague's lighthouse and have a great chance of seeing bald eagles, dolphin & other wildlife along miles of the refuge. This is an action-packed adventure and recommended for families who want to experience tons of wild ponies. The boat is large and stable with a quick and shallow water running capability.

ASSATEAGUE ISLAND NATIONAL SEASHORE/ CHINCOTEAGUE WILDLIFE REFUGE

Chincoteague - 8586 Beach Road (Toms Cove Visitor Center) 23336. Phone: (757) 336-6122. www.nps.gov/asis/index.htm Hours: Daily 6:00am-6:00pm (open til dark April-October). Visitors Ctr open 9am-4pm. Admission: $10.00 per vehicle for one day. $25.00 per vehicle for one week. Note: Pets are prohibited in the entire Virginia portion of Assateague Island, even in your car. Educators: The mystique of wild ponies: https://www.nps.gov/asis/learn/kidsyouth/online-activities-for-kids.htm for activities and https://www.nps.gov/asis/learn/education/lesson-plans.htm for lesson plans.

Which theory about how the ponies got on the island do you believe? A Sunken Spanish Galleon or a Colonial Natural Corral?

One in a chain of barrier islands along the Atlantic coast with many species of migratory birds like snow geese, great blue herons, balk eagles and osprey. The Refuge is famous for birdwatching due in part to its prime location along the Atlantic Flyway which makes it a vital resting and feeding area for hundreds of different kinds of migratory birds. Many visitors choose to bike along the bike paths while others enjoy the miles of Assateague and Chincoteague coastline by taking wildlife voyages by boat.

Wild Ponies (approximately 150 on the Virginia end of the island), horseshoe crabs, shellfish, waterfowl and a great variety of birds can be found while you explore the natural features of this unique ecosystem. Several paved trails of wildlife viewing are open to walkers and bikers during the day and automobiles after 3:00pm to dusk. The Lighthouse Trail is a 1/4 mile foot path through the woods to the historic Assateague Lighthouse. It is for walking only. The 1 1/2 mile Woodland Trail takes hikers and bikers through a beautiful pine forest and leads to an overlook where you can sometimes see wild ponies.

Camping at Assateague Island National Seashore is permitted only on the Maryland side of Assateague. Assateague State Park is also located on the Maryland side of Assateague and provides over 300 campsites.

INTERNATIONAL MIGRATORY BIRD CELEBRATION

Chincoteague - Chincoteague National Wildlife Refuge. Eastern Shore National Wildlife Refuge. Attention is focused on bird migration during the spring when migrants may be seen throughout North America. Thousands of shore birds, numbering more than 20 different species, use Chincoteague National Wildlife Refuge and Fisherman Island to feed and rest during the spring migration before moving on to their final destination. Lighthouse and canoe trips are featured. (May, second weekend)

CAPTAIN BARRY'S BACK BAY CRUISES

Chincoteague - Capt. Barry's boat is docked off Main Street in the Landmark Plaza) 23336. Phone: (757) 336-6508. www.chincoteague.com/captainb/ Admission: $35.00-$40 for Sea Life Cruise Tours: Expedition leaves 4x/day. Reservations necessary. Note: No prior experience on the water is necessary.

Choose your tour based on age of kids and interest in nature. Participants can get their hands dirty and their feet wet as they identify aquatic animals and plants. Catch Crabs by pulling pots, looking for jelly fish, learning about clams and oysters, how they are caught and grown, learning inter-tidal biology, navigation, weather forecasting, bird identification, netting, beach combing for shells, hearing about the history (hear tales about pirates, smugglers and movie stars), swimming, sunbathing, photography, or just hanging out.

MUSEUM OF CHINCOTEAGUE ISLAND

Chincoteague - 7125 Maddox Blvd. (north on Main, then east on Maddox to right before the bridge to Assateague) 23336. Phone: (757) 336-6117. www.chincoteaguemuseum.com. Hours: Daily 11:00am-5:00pm (Memorial-Labor Day). Friday-Sunday only (March-May, September-November) Admission: $5.00 per person (age 13+).

The only one of its kind in the US, they feature live marine exhibits (fresh live oysters, clams, and fish from the nearby waters), shell specimens (touchables), historical maritime artifacts and most uniquely, tools from the seafood industry. Did you know that Native Americans were the first oysterman? Young kids will have their eyes wide open looking at the giant clam or the huge first-order Fresnel lens from the Assateague lighthouse. Oyster memorabilia here and there and everywhere in this area. Watch a 4-minute oyster processing video - amazing that this is still a manual process.

South East Area

CHINCOTEAGUE PONIES / PONY SWIM & AUCTION

Chincoteague - Memorial Park Fireman's Carnival Grounds (tip of Chincoteague Island where it looks onto Assateague Island. www.chincoteague.com/pony_swim_guide.html (Visit this website on swim day for almost live pictures!). FREE. Tens of thousands of people from around the world line the banks of Assateague Channel to watch approximately 125 Chincoteague ponies make the swim from Assateague Island to Chincoteague. Part of the immense attraction are the romantic stories of where the wild ponies first came from: Some believe the colonists hid the livestock on the island to avoid taxes. Another theory holds that pirates used the island to hide. And, another (even more) romantic, story tells of them swimming ashore from a Spanish galleon that wrecked nearby.

The ponies are auctioned to keep the herd to a workable size so the island ecology system is balanced. The ponies travel in bands, freely, each with a stallion leading the herd. During the month before the swim day, the local fire department holds a carnival with entertainment, rides and food (even clam & oyster sandwiches). Between 7:00am-11:00pm on Wednesday morning, local Saltwater Cowboys round up the ponies, a veterinarian inspects their health, then the cowboys drive the ponies into the water where they take a brief swim to Chincoteague. They reach land, rest a little, and are then driven through the streets to the carnival grounds to be penned and auctioned the next day. By the way, the first foal to reach land is crowned King or Queen Neptune and auctioned for a special charitable cause.

HERE'S THE INSIDE SCOOP FOR THE BEST DAY - If you want to see the ponies

Huge crowds gather early to watch...

up close, arriving by 6:00am is a must. Otherwise, you can be a cheerleader from afar (bring some binoculars and arrive by 7:30am, or you'll miss it!) as you watch the 5 minute swim. You do get your chance later to see the ponies up close as they are paraded through Main Street and then penned up at the carnival. The carnival is wonderfully organized and very family friendly. By noon, you may be ready to wander around the islands. Don't forget sunscreen, bug repellent, snacks, rain gear if it's damp, and some games or activities to keep the kids occupied while waiting. The free shuttle service is wonderful and highly recommended - although it stops running early afternoon...and it's about a 5 mile walk if you miss it! (last Wednesday and Thursday of July).

CHRISTMAS PARADE

Chincoteague - (757) 336-6161. www.chincoteaguechamber.com. Enjoy a Christmas parade featuring floats, marching bands, color guards, saltwater cowboys, fire companies from around the Eastern Shore and Santa. (December, first Saturday)

IRON PONY ADVENTURE PARK

Chincoteague - 4368 Pension Street (US 13 to SR 175 on the island) 23336. https://www.ironponyci.com/. Phone: 757-336-7118 Hours: Tuesday-Saturday (seasonally) Admission: $35.00-$45.00.

Iron Pony Adventure Park is an aerial adventure course with over 30+ obstacles on 2 full levels. Visitors maneuver from platform to platform by traversing obstacles like ladders, tight ropes, balance beams, wobbly bridges, cargo nets, and, finally, try the pony plunge, a 26-foot-high leap of faith.

NASA VISITOR CENTER

Chincoteague (Wallops Island) - Wallops Flight Facility (US 13 to SR 175 west next to the Main Base of NASA) 23337. http://sites.wff.nasa.gov/wvc/. Phone: (757) 824-2298. Hours: Tuesday-Saturday 10:00am-4:00pm. Admission: FREE.

Wallops Flight Facility, located on Virginia's Eastern Shore, is NASA's premier site for suborbital and small orbital flight projects, Earth Science research, technology development, and home to NASA's only owned and operated launch range. They showcase the world of the past and carry you to the present where you will learn about Sounding Rockets Program, Scientific Balloon Projects, Orbital Tracking Station and much more. Attend one of their fun children's programs, participate in an exciting model rocket launch or even view an actual rocket launch from the observation deck. Best to visit during a special program like Model Rocket Launch (first Sat of each month at 1:00pm), Puppet Shows (weekends at 11:00am), or daily "Space Ace" Activities.

The Virginia Space Flight Adventure Camp (weeklong all summer for a program fee) - Wallops Island is the place for students, 11-15, to enjoy model rocketry, robotics and flight simulation. The students can see plenty of F-18s, C-130s, P-3s, research aircraft as well as Coast Guard and Navy aircraft taking off and landing every day!

Eastern Shore

HOPKINS & BROTHERS STORE & MALLARDS RESTAURANT

Eastern Shore (Onancock) - 2 Market Street, waterfront. (757) 787-3100 https://eatatmallards.com/restaurant/. Historic Onancock is 40 miles north of the Chesapeake Bay Bridge Tunnel, and four miles off the Chesapeake Bay up Onancock Creek.

For updates visit: www.KidsLoveTravel.com

Boaters who tie up just for the day or a weekend can walk to 11 restaurants, a dozen shops and galleries, several B&Bs and a historic hotel. The adjacent Mallard's on the Wharf restaurant inside the historic Hopkins and Bros. store has dockside dining. One of the oldest general stores on the east coast, they still sell merchandise ranging from groceries and dry goods to locally made arts and crafts. Waterfront restaurant serves mostly seafood (locally caught) with a kids' menu.

TURNER SCULPTURE

Eastern Shore (Onley) - US 13, PO Box 128 23418. Phone: (757) 787-2818. www.turnersculpture.com. Hours: Call ahead for best viewing hours as they change monthly. Admission: FREE. Note: Gift gallery with items for sale. (Although the least expensive fine art sculptures are around $50.00)

You've probably seen a lot of Turner sculptures in your travels to the White House, Chicago's Botanical Garden, Philadelphia (and Chicago, Salisbury, New York, North Carolina) Zoo, and the Virginia Marine Science Museum. Most admirers of the art appreciate nature's creatures because the Turners (father & son) capture snapshots of it (especially waterfowl). The process of making these works is fascinating for children. First, the mold is fabricated around the original clay model. Step two is the wax casting followed by dipping a ceramic mold around the wax cast. Next, the wax is removed and 2000 degree molten bronze is poured into the hollow mold. The ceramic mold is then removed, the bronze is cooled and the pieces are welded together. Finally, artists apply patina for detail and color. Hopefully, you'll get to meet the artists or maybe be fortunate enough to see the pouring stage where the men wear "spacesuits" that are heat and fire retardant.

VIRGINIA PEANUT FESTIVAL

Emporia - (434) 348-4219. One of the regions top crops gets its due with a colossal peanut-themed parade, a fireworks show, fun for little ones and a free tour of a local peanut farm. FREE. (3rd or 4th weekend in September)

CAPE HENRY LIGHTHOUSES

Fort Story - 583 Atlantic Avenue (east of US 13 via US 60, then northeast on SR 305) 23459. Phone: (757) 422-9421. www.nps.gov/came/cape-henry-lighthouses.htm. Hours: Daily 10:00am-4:00pm. Closed most winter holidays. Admission: FREE by visitor pass issued by military personnel.

Cape Henry Lighthouse is the first lighthouse structure authorized, fully completed, and lighted by the newly organized Federal Government. It is an octagonal stone structure, faced with hewn or hammer-dressed stone. The oil-burning lamps of the Cape Henry Lighthouse were first lighted late in October, 1792. Climb the many stairs, once you reach the summit, enjoy a panoramic view of the Atlantic Ocean and the Chesapeake Bay. Across the dune line, you'll find the new Cape Henry Lighthouse, built in 1881. It's the tallest iron-encased lighthouse in the country. Adjacent to the lighthouses is a replica of the First Landing Cross, planted by the first settlers to give thanks for a safe voyage after arriving here in 1607.

GLOUCESTER POINT BEACH PARK AND VIMS WETLANDS

Gloucester Point - 1208-1255 Greate Road (East of Coleman Bridge on the York River) 23062. https://www.gloucesterva.info/1295/Gloucester-Point-Beach-Park. Phone: (804) 642-9474 or (804) 684-7000 (aquarium). Hours: Beach: Seasonally, dawn to dusk. Aquarium: open seasonally for marsh walk tours and events. Admission: FREE. Note: Boat Ramps, Fishing Pier, Charcoal Grills, horseshoes, Playground, and Volleyball.

Gloucester Point Beach Park is located on the bank of the York River. This park offers a large, shady, and grassy Park area with picnic areas and a shelter. The swimming area and sandy beach are perfect for sunbathing, wading, and beach fun! The Beach House has a concession stand, restrooms, and outdoor shower. The Aquarium and Visitor Center offers visitors opportunities to observe marine life and learn about VIMS scientists' current research. Self guided exhibits include current issues in marine research, eight aquaria ranging in size from 50 to 3,000 gallons, and life-sized models of marine mammals and fishes (Discovery Labs - www.vims.edu/cbnerr/education/)

Hampton

BUCKROE BEACH

Hampton - North First St (I-64 exit 268, Mallory Street to Pembroke Ave., turn right) 23664. Phone: (757) 850-5134. www.facebook.com/buckroe Hours: Open year-round: Daily. Summer season runs Memorial Day through Labor Day, daylight hours. Admission: FREE. Small parking fee.

Bordering the Chesapeake Bay, Buckroe Beach offers eight acres of family-friendly sandy beach, a playground for children, picnic shelters with tables and grills by reservation, a great walking and bike path, a Bark Park, and spacious car park area. Enjoy the wide, clean beach and gentle surf of this Chesapeake Bay beach. Lifeguards on duty during the summer season. The park pavilion is the site of big band concerts and an outdoor movie series during the summer. Beach chair, umbrella, kayak and paddlecraft rentals are available.

BLUEBIRD GAP FARM

Hampton - 60 Pine Chapel Road 23666. www.hampton.va.us/bbgf/. Phone: (757) 727-6739. Hours: Open year-round: Wednesday-Monday, 9:00am-5:00pm. Closed Thanksgiving, Christmas Day and New Year's Day. Admission: FREE. Note: Picnic facilities, playground. Please do not feed the wildlife as they should remain wild.

Bluebird Gap Farm offers an exciting adventure and educational experience in an urban environment. Designed to resemble a working farm, this 60-acre site is home to bobcats, cows, horses, sheep, goats, mountain lions and other domesticated and wild animals familiar to traditional Virginia farmers. Look for Saturday special activities like hayrides. Late winter and early spring, the babies are born - check out the website to see what the newest babies are.

HAMPTON HISTORY MUSEUM

Hampton - 120 Old Hampton Lane (downtown) 23666. Phone: (757) 727-1610 or (800) 800-2202. www.hampton.gov/history_museum/. Hours: Monday-Saturday 10:00am-5:00pm. Sunday 1:00-5:00pm. Closed Thanksgiving, Christmas and New Year's Day. Admission: $4.00-$5.00.

The museum interprets Hampton's past spanning from its inhabitance by the Kecoughtan Indians through the 20th century. Learn about folks like Captain John Smith, Blackbeard the pirate, Booker T. Washington and astronauts. Part of an old tavern and a replica of a pirate's skeleton that was unearthed during Hampton's waterfront renovation are highlights. 400 years of Hampton history including inventive galleries on the Antebellum, Civil War and Reconstruction periods. Topics in the Civil War gallery include the Battle of Big Bethel, the Burning of Hampton and the effort of Union Gen. Ben Butler to declare escaped slaves. See the full-scale reproductions of the USS Monitor's gun turret and a portion of the CSS Virginia's (Merrimack) casemate.

LANGLEY SPEEDWAY

Hampton - 11 Dale Lemonds Drive (I-64 exit 262) 23666. Phone: (757) 865-RACE. www.langley-speedway.com. Hours: Each Saturday gates open at 4:00pm and races begin at 7:00pm. Admission: $12.00 adult, $5.00 child (6-12). Family Night - 2 adult/2 Kids get in for $30.00.

April through October, Langley Speedway offers thrilling NASCAR Dodge Weekly Racing action. Experience the excitement of high-speed racing on a 4/10-mile track. Eight divisions race at Langley: Late Models, Grand Stocks, Super Streets, Super Trucks, Legends, Ucars, Modifieds and Wolf Trucks.

SANDY BOTTOM NATURE PARK

Hampton - 1255 Big Bethel Road (I-64 to Hampton Roads Center Pkwy exit 26A) 23666. Phone: (757) 825-4657. www.hampton.gov/sandybottom. Hours: Open year-round: Daily sunrise to sunset. The nature center is open from 9:00am-6:00pm (May-September) and 9:00am-4:30pm (October-April). Admission: FREE, fees for rentals.

This 456-acre recreational facility features two lakes, wetlands areas, trails for hiking and biking, fishing, non-motorized boating, picnic areas, children's playground, a campground, tent cabins for rent and a beautiful nature center with creature displays. Call about special nature programs.

VIRGINIA AIR & SPACE CENTER

Hampton - 600 Settlers Landing Road (I-64 exit 267) 23669. Phone: (757) 727-0900 or (800) 296-0800. www.vasc.org. Hours: Monday-Wednesday 10:00am-5:00pm, Thursday-Sunday 10:00am-7:00pm (Memorial Day to Labor Day). 10:00-5:00pm daily rest of year (except Sunday opens at Noon). IMAX daytime and evening shows. Closed only Thanksgiving and Christmas. Admission: $22.50 adult, $20.50 senior (65+), $19.00 child/student (3-18). IMAX shows extra $8.00-$10.00. Note: IMAX presentations are often related to space travel or science fiction. The famous 1920 restored Hampton Carousel is next door and gives old-fashioned rides (seasonally).

The official visitor center for NASA Langley Research facilities, this place houses flight and space artifacts, hands-on exhibits (like a Crater Maker or Rover Races) and historical displays. See a real moon rock or a Mars rock!

See the Apollo 12 Command Module that journeyed to the moon and back; and a replica of the Lunar Orbiter, which mapped the moon's surface for future landings. Travel high-tech at the Inter-planetary Travel Agency.  The kids can actually Launch-a-Rocket where they learn about the stages of preparation for a launch and then, send a model rocket shooting up into the clouds. The 94 foot high ceiling is full of hanging military aircraft and NASA spacecraft (one aircraft was actually struck by lightning 700 times in research!) Feeling adventuresome? The Adventures in Flight gallery takes visitors on an aviation adventure when they "wing walk" on a bi-plane, see a replica 1903 Wright Flyer, explore a DC-9 passenger jet, ride in a WWII bomber, become an air traffic controller, sit in the cockpit of a fighter jet, or pilot an airplane. Also, try your piloting skills on the Shuttle Landing Simulator, or Lunar Landing and Module Simulators. Lots of "wows" from the kids here!

INTERNATIONAL CHILDREN'S FESTIVAL

Hampton - Mill Point Park. Prepare for sensory overload as you experience the sights, sounds and tastes of different cultures from more than 25 countries. This unique festival provides an opportunity to experience diversity as participating countries showcase their heritage through educational exhibits, entertainment, food and fun. www.hampton.gov/parks/icf/ (Saturday mid-April)

VIRGINIA ARTS FESTIVAL

Hampton - Hampton Roads. www.virginiaartsfest.com. This 25-day festival showcases a diverse array of artists renowned in the fields of classical music, chamber music, dance, world music, opera, gospel music, international acts & family entertainment. Admission. (mid-April to mid-May)

AFRIKAN AMERICAN FESTIVAL

Hampton - Mill Point Park. www.hamptoncvb.com. This alcohol-free, family-oriented event is held in conjunction with the Hampton Jazz Festival and celebrates America's diverse African-American heritage. Enjoy ethnic foods, arts and crafts, kids activities and live music. Admission fee. (June, fourth weekend)

AIR POWER OVER HAMPTON

Hampton - Langley Air Force Base. (757) 764-2018 or www.airpoweroverhamptonroads.com. Air show of Hampton Roads. Dozens of military and civilian aerial demonstrations, displays, vendors. Admission: Free. (June, third weekend)

BLACKBEARD PIRATE FESTIVAL

Hampton - Downtown. www.facebook.com/blackbeardfestival. Set sail for Hampton's Blackbeard Festival where living history and family go hand-in-hand. Immerse yourself in 1780's Hampton with live entertainment, pirate camp, children's activities, sea battles, fireworks and more, as Hampton reenacts and celebrates the demise of Blackbeard, one of the fiercest pirates ever known. Pirate-themed artists, water-based activities with live actors acting out pirate battles, food and vendors. Arrrr..gg..hh, mateys! (June, first weekend)

HAMPTON CUP REGATTA

Hampton - Mercury Boulevard bridge between Phoebus and Fort Monroe. The Hampton cup is the oldest, continuously run powerboat race in the country and the largest inboard hydroplane race in the U.S. The National Championships, sanctioned by the American Powerboat Association, feature 10 classes of hydroplanes and competition in excess of 140 mph. Live entertainment, concessions and kids' activities are included. FREE. www.hamptoncupregatta.com. (August, second long weekend)

HAMPTON BAY DAYS

Hampton - Downtown. (800) 800-2202. www.baydaysevents.com. Festivities highlighting the Chesapeake Bay include educational exhibits, a carnival, children's FUNtastic Junction, an Extreme Arena, fireworks and four stages of musical entertainment, including national acts. Also featured are antique cars, the military area and sports events. (September, first full weekend)

CASEMATE MUSEUM AT FORT MONROE

Hampton (Fort Monroe) - PO Box 51341 (off I-64 to Bernard Road) 23651. Phone: (757) 788-3391. www.nps.gov/fomr/index.htm Hours: Daily, 10:30am-4:30pm, except MOndays. Closed Thanksgiving, Christmas Day and New Year's Day. Admission: FREE.

The largest stone fort ever built in the U.S., Fort Monroe is headquarters for the U.S. Army Training and Doctrine Command. Within the historic fort's stone walls is the Museum, which chronicles the history of the fort and the Coast Artillery Corps. During the Civil War, Fort Monroe was a Union-held bastion in the center of a Confederate state. In the museum's Civil War area, learn how Freedom's Fortress helped shelter thousands of slave refugees and see the cell where Confederate President Jefferson Davis was imprisoned.

Hopewell

CITY POINT OPEN AIR MUSEUM WALKING TOUR

Hopewell - City Point (Hopewell) Historic District (begins on Cedar Lane at St. John's Church, exit 9 or 15, follow signs) 23860. Phone: (800) 541-2461 or (800) 863-8687. https://historichopewell.org/city-point-museum/ Guided tours of the house and grounds are available year round, Monday – Saturday from 10AM to 4:30PM and Sunday from 1PM to 4:30PM. Group tours are available by appointment. The grounds are open to the public free of charge and the pier provides access to the Appomattox River. Small admission for inside tours of some buildings, if desired. Note: Union fort breastworks and Weston Manor are nearby, as are Sears Mail-Order Houses. Hopewell offers a selection of Sears, Roebuck & Company Mail-Order homes in its Crescent Hills neighborhood. Visitors can drive through this area and view homes built from 1926-1937.

This self-guided tour (brochures available at the Visitors Info Center, exit 9 off I-295) captures the people and events of City Point during the Civil War. Walk down the same streets that Union Generals Grant, Sheridan, and Sherman or President Lincoln did and stop to read insights at 25 wayside exhibits. Of interest to kids along the tour are the St. John's Episcopal Church (505 Cedar Lane), where black and whites were baptized prior to the Civil War and the Union army used the church temporarily as a signal station, a Union stockade, and a place of worship - open to view most weekday mornings; Appomattox Manor (currently being renovated by NPS); City Point Early History Museum at St. Dennis Chapel (exhibits show visitors the 10,000 plus year history of old City Point). At certain sites, children can explore the interior of a Civil War hospital tent, or have photos taken with life size figures of a wounded soldier, President Lincoln, or an Appomattox Indian. Products as diverse as the first automatic dishwasher, the first Kraft paper and cardboard boxes, china and artificial silk have been manufactured in Hopewell. Without a visit to some buildings, the kids might find the tour a little boring.

WESTON MANOR

Hopewell - (Weston Lane & 21st Avenue, Exit 15A of I-295 off Rt. 10 East) 23860. Phone: (804) 458-4682. https://historichopewell.org/weston-manor/. Guided tours of the house and grounds are available year round, Monday – Saturday from 10AM to 4:30PM and Sunday from 1PM to 4:30PM. Group tours are available by appointment. The grounds are open to the public free of charge and the pier provides access to the Appomattox River.

Weston was owned by the Eppes family of City Point, originally presented as a wedding gift. Heirs linage includes ties to the Appomattox Plantation and Pocahontas. During the Civil War, Weston was the residence of 12 year old Emma Wood and her family. Later, she wrote a journal of her wartime experiences. Be sure to listen for stories about little Emma's adventures, occupation by Union Troops, and post-war tall tales.

Newport News

PENINSULA SPCA PETTING ZOO

Newport News - 523 J. Clyde Morris Blvd. (I-64 exit 258A) 23601. Phone: (757) 595-1399. www.facebook.com/pg/PSPCAPettingZoo. Hours: Monday-Friday 10:00am-5:00pm, Saturday 10:00am-4:30pm. (Weather Permitting) Admission: $2.00 adult, $1.00 child (3-12).

The Peninsula SPCA's Petting Zoo has a variety of exotic animals including a black panther, mountain lion and a charming family of lemurs. Meet "Tiger Lily" a Siberian tiger and "Pascanelli," an African mandrill. The petting zoo has an exotic area with a lion, jaguar, otters, kangaroo, badgers, crocodiles, alligators, etc. The kids will love the opportunity to pet the deer and goats and to meet a peacock and even a leopard.

VIRGINIA LIVING MUSEUM

Newport News - 524 J. Clyde Morris Blvd. (I-64 exit 258A) 23601. Phone: (757) 595-1900. www.thevlm.org. Hours: Daily 9:00am-5:00pm. Closed all major winter holidays. Admission: $19.95-$23.95 adult, $16.95 child (3-12). Planetarium or laser shows are $6.00 extra. Note: Summertime weekend safaris and Adventure Clubs. Wild Side Café & picnic areas.

The museum building's living exhibits showcase Virginia's natural history from the mountains to the sea. Explore the underwater realm of the Chesapeake Bay and the underground world of a limestone cave. Follow the trail along a wooded lakeside boardwalk where you visit raccoons, bobcats, foxes (specifically Virginia's red fox), otters, butterflies, and beavers in their natural habitats. You'll find a meadow, bald eagles, endangered red fox, beautiful blue heron (searching for food in the wetlands/swamp aviary) and native wildflower gardens. Indoors at the Touch Tank, meet sea stars, horseshoe crabs, a fossilized dinosaur track and other marine life common to the Chesapeake Bay. Visitors can open the jaw of a pit viper model, watch a frog jump, create a chorus of nighttime

A GIANT turtle friend... it was amazing to be this close....

sounds and do a virtual dissection of a frog. Walk through the James River, a giant ocean aquarium full of fishes and loggerhead turtles, an indoor songbird aviary, and a nocturnal animal exhibit featuring bats, flying squirrels, screech owls (surreal!) tree frogs and other creatures of the night. In the springtime thru early summer, you can see many bugs and butterflies all native to the Eastern Coast Plains. When you arrive, check the listings for live animal & sky shows. Step up to the observatory and view the sky through a 14-inch telescope. Study spectacular views of the sun from the observatory and travel the universe in a planetarium show. We heard lots and lots of "Look...look..., mom and dad!"- here.

NEWPORT NEWS PARK

Newport News - 13564 Jefferson Avenue (I-64 exit 250B) 23602. Phone: (757) 888-3333 or (800) 203-8322. https://www.newport-news.org/visitors/things-to-do/outdoors-and-recreation/6/newport-news-park/. Hours: Daily, year-round. Park open dawn-dusk. Admission: FREE, fees for campsites.

This 8,000 acre park with two fresh water reservoirs is one of the largest municipal parks east of the Mississippi. Rent a paddleboat, try your hand at some freshwater fishing, take a pleasant bike ride through beautiful woodlands, play a round or two of disc golf and hike one of the nature trails. Other Features: aeromodel flying field, 5-star archery range, bicycle rental, boat ramp, boat rental, 180-site campground, Civil War battle site, golf course, horse show arena, interpretive programs, wildlife rehabilitation center, picnic shelters, playground, ropes and initiatives course, Tourist Information Center. Picnic shelters are available. Discovery Center with Civil War and wildlife exhibits. Campground is a 180-site full-service campground located in a natural wooded setting adjacent to the Lee Hall Reservoir.

CHILDREN'S FESTIVAL OF FRIENDS

Newport News - Newport News Regional Park. Children of all ages are the focus of this festival filled with hands-on activities, rides, food, exhibits, and entertainment. Admission fee. (May, first Saturday)

FALL FESTIVAL OF FOLKLIFE

Newport News - Newport News Regional Park. Southeast Virginia's biggest celebration of traditional crafts, trades and entertainment features 200 crafts people, craft demonstrations, free children's activities, food vendors and continuous entertainment. Parking fee. (October, first weekend)

ENDVIEW PLANTATION

Newport News - 362 Yorktown Road (I-64 exit 247) 23603. Phone: (757) 887-1862. www.endview.org. Hours: Thursday-Saturday 10:00am-4:00pm. Admission: $8.00 adult, $7.00 senior (62+), $6.00 child (7-18) Note: Visit nearby Lee Hall Mansion for additional glimpse at plantation life. 163 Yorktown Road. (757) 888-3371. Especially good for re-enactments and seasonal open houses. Civil War Children's Camps and Miss Sallie's Academy in summer.

Built in 1769 by Colonel William Harwood, the house has witnessed the Revolutionary War, the War of 1812, and the Civil War. It was used as a field hospital by Confederate and Union troops and as the headquarters for Union General McClellan during the 1862 Peninsula Campaign. Endview was used as a resting place or campground in September 1781 by 3000 Virginia militia en route to Yorktown and the climatic revolutionary War battle. During the War of 1812, it was a campground for members of the Virginia Militia. By the outbreak of the Civil War, Endview had passed to the Curtis family and was the home of confederate Captain Humphrey Harwood Curtis. First Confederate, and then Union forces used the home and its grounds as a hospital during the 1862 campaign.

CIVIL WAR RE-ENACTMENT

Newport News - Endview Plantation. (757) 887-1862. www.endview.org. Visitors can experience living history programs, battles each day, sutlers, ladies' activities & house tours. Admission fee. (March or April weekend)

MARINERS' MUSEUM

Newport News - 100 Museum Drive (I-64 exit 258A) 23606. Phone: (757) 596-2222 or (800) 581-SAIL. www.mariner.org. Hours: Daily 9:00am-5:00pm, Sunday 11am-5:00pm except Thanksgiving and Christmas. Admission: $1.00 general admission. Note: 550 acre park with picnicking and a walking trail with fishing. Museum Café. The Mariners' Museum Backpack Program contains all you need for a self-guided walk of the Noland Trail, from information on the history of the park, plants and animals, and environmental concerns. Gallery Hunts too.

Capture the spirit of seafaring adventures by following Captain Cook and Captain John Smith's maps of the Age of Exploration. Take a journey in an African canoe or a Jazz Age runabout in the International Small Craft Center; or examine the small details of the miniature ships display. Catch a wink from the colorful figureheads (mermaids to polar bears) from the great Age of Sail. Study the US Navy and examine life on the water in the Chesapeake Bay gallery. Meet historical interpreters portraying a female pirate, an 18th century sea captain, and a crewman from the Civil War ironclad Monitor. Learn boat-building techniques from the master craftsmen of the Wooden boat School. The giant Cape Charles lighthouse lamp greets you and many audio stations allow you to visit with some of the watermen. Kids will also be attracted to many of the miniature dioramas and the giant buoy.

> **Seabag Tour** is a hands-on scavenger hunt through the USS Monitor Center. Using objects, visitors will be able to explore the story of the creation, battle, life aboard, sinking, rediscovery, and conservation of the USS Monitor.

USS MONITOR CENTER: Visitors to this $30 million center will be able to literally step back in time and walk the deck of the legendary Civil War ironclad. Start with the action up close in the high-definition battle theater. Visitors can then walk along a recreated gun deck of a classic wooden warship where they learn about technological advances in naval warfare and design that led them to the creation of the first true ironclad warships. Discover artifacts from the wreck of the USS Monitor (anchor, signal light, propeller, and engine - seen in restoring tanks or special cases). Come aboard the Monitor... Smell the gunpowder. Feel the excitement of being responsible for the most revolutionary piece of military weaponry of the day. Experience what it was like to do something no one had ever done before: guide tons of metal through an armada of wooden ships that cannot hope to compete with your might!

PENINSULA FINE ARTS CENTER

Newport News - 101 Museum Drive (I-64 exit 258A, across from Mariner's Museum) 23606. Phone: (757) 596-8175. https://www.virginia.org/listing/peninsula-fine-arts-center/14732/ Hours: Tuesday-Saturday 10:00am-5:00pm, Sunday 1:00-5:00pm. Admission: $7.50 adult, $6.00 senior, student, military $4.00 child (6-12).

See some of the best in contemporary and fine art with exhibits changing every two months - some local or historical in nature. Do you like sculpture, paintings and photography? How about creating art on your own? The Hands On For Kids area is where kids put on a smock and paint, draw, color or make sculpture at Rocky's Diner, play games in the attic or paint in the studio. They can also put on a puppet show or fingerpaint with sound (something really different).

HUNTINGTON PARK / VIRGINIA WAR MUSEUM

Newport News - 9285 Warwick Blvd. (I-64 exit 263A or 258A) 23607. Phone: (757) 247-8523 war museum or (757) 886-7912 park. www.warmuseum.org or www.nngov.com/parks-and-recreation. Hours: Thursday-Saturday 9:00am-4:30pm. Admission: $2.00 adult, $1.00 senior (65+), military, child (6-15). Museum: $8.00 adult, $7.00 senior (62+) and military, $6.00 child (7-18).

HUNTINGTON PARK - Features: Ballfields, basketball, Tennis Center, public beach with swimming (attendants Memorial Day - Labor Day), picnic shelters, large playground area "Fort Fun" (a 13,000 sq. foot climbing hide-and-seek area), public boat ramp and children's fishing pier.

WAR MUSEUM - The museum interprets American military history from 1775 to the present. Its collection of over 60,000 artifacts includes uniforms, insignias, vehicles, weapons and one of the nation's greatest collections of propaganda posters. See a 10x10 foot section of the Berlin Wall, one of General Colin Powell's Desert Storm uniforms, an 1883 brass Gatling Gun and a portion of the outer wall from Dachau Concentration Camp. The newest exhibit, Marches Towards Freedom, traces the role of African-Americans in the United States military, beginning with the Revolutionary War.

STARS IN THE SKY

Newport News - Victory Landing Park. Stars in the Sky. 25,000+ attendance for children's rides, national entertainment and fireworks. FREE. (4th of July)

U.S. ARMY TRANSPORTATION MUSEUM

Newport News (Fort Eustis) - Bldg. 300, Besson Hall, Washington Blvd. (I-64 exit 250A to Rte. 105) 23604. Phone: (757) 878-1115. www.transportation.army.mil/museum/ Hours: Monday-Saturday 9:00am-4:30pm. Closed Federal holidays. Admission: FREE.

Most kids probably don't think of Army transportation as being the key to victory. Inside, the exhibits lead you from early mule-drawn wagons to modern HUMMVEEs. Models, dioramas of typical war scenes and films explain

South East Area 153

transportation technology and its contributions to the growth of our nation. Look for the "jeep that flies" or the "truck that walks" or the "flying saucer". Outside, the Marine Park displays DUKWs and a tugboat; the Cargo Yard has many trucks including the newest Tactical Vehicles; the Aviation Pavilion exhibits aircraft from the Korean War to present including parachute and vertical take off/landing airplanes; and the Rail Yard includes many locomotives, box cars and cabooses used in several wars. Hovercraft, Skycraft, "Destruction", and the Cybernetic Walking Machine are some of the most popular vehicles.

Norfolk

NORFOLK SPORTS

NORFOLK TIDES BASEBALL - www.norfolktides.com. (757) 622-2222. (follow I-264 west, exit 11A-Brambleton Ave-left at Park Ave.) Take yourself out to the ball game at beautiful Harbor Park, the 12,000 - seat home of the AAA Norfolk Tides, the Baltimore Orioles' top minor league team. Harbor Park is perched on the banks of the Elizabeth River along Norfolk's downtown waterfront. "Rip Tide," the large and fuzzy blue mascot roams the stands to entertain visitors. Major League style stadium with full service restaurant. Season: (April thru Labor Day weekend).

NORFOLK ADMIRALS HOCKEY - www.norfolkadmirals.com or (757) 640-1212.

ELIZABETH RIVER FERRY

Norfolk - HRT, PO Box 2096 (departs from the Waterside Marketplace) 23501. Phone: (757) 222-6100. www.goHRT.com. Tours: The ferry departs every 30 minutes with 15 minute service at peak times on weekends. Fare: $1.50, Seniors and $0.75 for Persons with Disabilities.

Enjoy the panoramic harbor view from the Elizabeth River Ferry while traveling between downtown Norfolk and Portsmouth by paddlewheel boat. This charming pedestrian ferry operates between The Waterside Festival Marketplace in Norfolk and High Street Landing and North Landing Ferry Docks in Portsmouth. If you've ever been caught in congested traffic between these two cities, you know this mode is a welcome alternative during peak rush hours or as a leisurely way to park and enjoy both city's attractions.

VIRGINIA SYMPHONY / VIRGINIA YOUTH SYMPHONY ORCHESTRA

Norfolk - 861 Glenrock Road, Suite 200 (Norfolk's Chrysler Hall-performances) 23502. Phone: (757) 466-3060, (757) 892-6366 box office or (757) 640-7541 (youth symphony). www.virginiasymphony.org. Concerts: (Fall to mid-Summer) Note: The Virginia Symphony encourages parents to bring their children to the Peanut Butter & Jam Family Concert Series, which is open to children of all ages; but all other concerts are restricted to children age 6+.

Founded in 1920, the Virginia Symphony Orchestra serves the communities of Hampton Roads, and has grown to become one of the nation's leading regional symphony orchestras. The symphony performs over 140 concerts annually including Classical Masterworks, Pops, Mozart & More. They offer Young People's Concerts in conjunction with area schools and a popular Peanut Butter & Jam Series for families. Youth Symphony performs occasionally throughout the city and at special events.

VIRGINIA ZOO

Norfolk - 3500 Granby Street (I-264 west to downtown Waterside exit to St. Pauls Blvd to Monticello Ave) 23504. Phone: (757) 441-5227. www.virginiazoo.org. Hours: Daily 9:30am-4:00pm. Closed New Year's Day, Thanksgiving, Christmas Eve & Christmas Day. Seasonal hours may apply. Admission: $17.95 adult, $15.95 senior (62+), $14.95 child (2-11). Note: Café, Safari shop, concessions. Norfolk Southern Express - train feature that gives visitors a narrated tour of the Zoo.

Come stroll along the towering boardwalk on a walking safari through Africa, while you'll see animals big and small living in their naturalistic habitat. See the majestic giraffes, magnificent elephants and kingly lions. Keep a look out for the frog lab and reptile nursery. One direction leads you to the Waterfowl Pond and the Botanical Gardens. Another direction wanders past the Large Animals Exhibit and the Tiger Exhibit where the popular Siberian Tigers are (born from cubs at the zoo). Farthest back from the entrance are the Okavango Delta exhibits of African animals set in unobstructed naturalistic settings similar to the largest inland delta in the world. They have monkeys to delight you, mandrills to amaze you and more than 30 other incredible creatures from snakes and sloths to a 7-pound lizard named Bobby. Children love the Prairie Dogs - the interactive habitat has underground tunnels and viewing bubbles allowing kids to safely come nose-to-nose with playful prairie dogs.

NAVAL STATION NORFOLK

Norfolk - 9079 Hampton Blvd. (all tours depart from the Naval Tour and Information Center) 23505. Phone: (757) 444-7955. www.norfolkvisitor.com/norfolknavy/. Hours: Call for tour times. During heightened national security or US battle times, no tours are offered. Admission: $10.00 adult, $5.00 senior(60+) & child (3-11).

Home port to more than 75 ships and 100 aircraft of the Atlantic Fleet - this is the world's largest naval installation. The bus tour is 45 minutes long and narrated by naval personnel. It passes by submarines, destroyers, cruisers, amphibious assault ships, aircraft carriers and an airfield. Along the way, you'll also pass by historic homes from the 1907 Jamestown Exposition.

AMERICAN ROVER TALL SHIP CRUISES

Norfolk - (departs at the Marina at the Waterside) 23510. Phone: (757) 627-7245. www.americanrover.com. Admission: Tickets may be purchased at the blue gazebo on the dock. $22-$28 adult, $12-$18 child-under 12. Tours: Daily 1:30pm, 7:00pm sunset Wednesday-Sunday (spring and fall). 6:30pm sunset (daily, summer).

Sail across the sparkling Elizabeth River and Hampton Roads harbor on the American Rover. This majestic 19th-century cargo schooner sports modern amenities important to passengers of the 21st century. Venture into the smooth waters of Hampton Roads' historical harbor and rich maritime heritage. Sail by giant merchant and navy ships, tugs, fishermen, yachts, or, lend a hand at the sails, take a try at the helm, roam the decks, or relax, as the Captain points out the highlights around you. Live Entertainment available during certain cruises (try for the folk singers - sailing tunes).

CHRYSLER MUSEUM OF ART

> Mermaids on Parade is a display of more than a hundred 10-foot sculptures created by local artists. The mermaids are proudly displayed throughout the streets of downtown Norfolk and surrounding areas. Map available on www.norfolk.gov/index.aspx?NID=1962

Norfolk - 245 West Olney Road (at Mowbray Arch) 23510. Phone: (757) 664-6200. www.chrysler.org. Hours: Tuesday-Saturday, 10:00am-5:00pm. Sunday Noon-5:00pm. All facilities closed Mondays and major holidays. Admission: FREE Educators: Complete historical unit studies related to museum art online under Learning pages. Note: Restaurant. Museum Shop.

Maybe pretend your family is on safari to explore the artistic interpretation of animals in the Chrysler Museum of Art's collections. Then, follow a theme such as Costumes (Explore the ways that people expressed their wealth, social status, individuality, and practical needs throughout the ages by the clothes they wore); Glass Art; Ancient Worlds: Egyptian mummies and art stations. They are taught the "recipe" that the Chinese discovered for making porcelain and some of the techniques involved in applying the colors and designs; or Sculpture: including a Glass studio with free daily demos at noon.

MACARTHUR MEMORIAL

Norfolk - City Hall Avenue, MacArthur Square (I-264, exit 10, head west) 23510. Phone: (757) 441-2965. www.macarthurmemorial.org. Hours: Tuesday-Saturday 10:00am-5:00pm. Closed New Years, Thanksgiving, and Christmas. Admission: FREE. Educators: A History Scavenger Hunt is a wonderful way to engage the kids and teach them mapping and observation skills. Note: A 24 minute film on MacArthur's life is shown in the theatre. Gift shop displays 1950 Chrysler Imperial limousine which he used from 1950 to end of his life.

General Douglas MacArthur was one of the most colorful and controversial men in American history. The General's final resting place is where he lies surrounded by nine separate galleries arranged in two levels, each portraying the principal periods of the General's life. The MacArthur Memorial's extensive collection of military and personal artifacts allows visitors to discover the compelling story of General of the Army Douglas MacArthur and the millions of American men and women who served our nation during the Spanish American War, World Wars I, World War II, the Occupation of Japan, and the Korean War. The memorial's goal is to renew your faith in those American values of Duty, Honor, Country.

NAUTICUS

Norfolk - One Waterside Drive (I-264 west, Waterside Drive exit) 23510. Phone: (757) 664-1000. www.nauticus.org. Hours: Daily 10:00am-5:00pm (Memorial Day-Labor Day). Tuesday-Saturday 10:00am-5:00pm, Sunday Noon-5:00pm (Rest of Year). Closed winter holidays. Admission: $15.95 adult, $14.95 senior and military, $11.50 student (4-12). Educators: Education/Online Curricula. Kids Games & Puzzles (Education/For Kids icon). Note: Iron Whale Café and Banana Pier Gift Shop.

Journey through the world's oceans at the large maritime science and technology center that explores the power of the sea. Stand on the actual bridge of the USS Preble and scan the Elizabeth River through a real periscope. Kids can do lots of hands-on like chart and steer across treacherous waters, drill an oil well, or design a ship (can take the plans home to build in the backyard!). At the

South East Area

AEGIS Battle Simulated Theatre, you can sit in a command control room and help make decisions in battle - try not to mess it up or your ship will blow up! Watch "The Living Sea" in the giant screen theatre and then (since you're in the mood), touch live sharks (small ones!) and horseshoe crabs in the touch tanks. Now, forecast the weather, predict hurricanes and warn ships of potential dangers via The Weather Channel. You and your family can control an actual 9-foot long robotic arm to collect samples and artifacts from the seabed, or operate a remote-controlled camera to explore the wreck site at Secrets of the Deep. Be sure to try your hand at a game "Design Chamber: Battleship X", see the lifestyle exhibit "City at Sea", or enjoy a virtual tour of the battleship with very high techBattleScopes. The theatre presents: "The Last Battleship".

On the same premises are several other related museums: Hampton Roads Naval Museum (naval history and why Hampton Roads became the largest naval base). 1907: The Jamestown Exposition and the Launching of the Steel Navy is the newest permanent exhibit. It examines the period from 1880, when the Navy began to recover from a post-civil war decline, to 1907, when President Theodore Roosevelt sent the Great White Fleet around the world as an affirmation of American naval strength.

Or, experience the pride of exploring the USS WISCONSIN mighty military vessel that earned five battle stars during WWII and more recently Desert Storm. Berthed at Nauticus, the Battleship Wisconsin is one of the largest and last battleships ever built by the U.S. Navy. Explore its deck through a self-guided or audio tour that will take you back in time to experience this majestic ship. Once aboard, docents and exhibits, and a video on board, invite you in. See giant chains (for the anchors) and guns (large enough to propel a shell the weight of a Volkswagen over 26 miles!).

VICTORY ROVER

Norfolk - One Waterside Drive (depart from Nauticus Docks) 23510. Phone: (757) 627-7406. www.navalbasecruises.com. Admission: $19.00-$29.00 per person. Tours: 2 Hour Narrated Naval Base Cruises Depart Daily. 11:00am & 2:00pm, (Early April - Memorial Day Weekend). 11:00am, 2:00pm and 5:30pm (Memorial Day Weekend - Labor Day). 11:00am & 2:00pm. (Labor Day - Late October). 2:00pm Cruise, Tuesday-Sunday (November & December).

A big ship in "drydock" where it is raised out of the water for repairs...

Your Front Row Seat to the Naval Fleet. Enjoy an entertaining commentary along the way aboard this Navy-themed vessel. See the sight of Aircraft Carriers, Nuclear Submarines, Guided Missile Cruisers, and all of the other ships that form the World's most powerful Armada. Most fascinating: Supply Ships - They glide up next to a battleship and send supplies underwater! Drydocks - To see a boat nearly 1000' longraised (there is a secret) from the water is amazing! "Cranky" cranes - are always loading and unloading containers somewhere, Aircraft Carriers - The one we saw was nearly 1000' feet long, had 4 ½ acres of deck space, a barber shop…and was the home to 6000 crew! Pseudo Submarine Decoys - sonar boats that pickup war missiles, Nauticus & USS Wisconsin. Excellent narration. Great way for youth to get the feel of the naval shipyard without being overwhelmed.

VIRGINIA STAGE COMPANY

Norfolk - 110 E Tazewell St (Housed in the Wells Theatre) 23514. Phone: (757) 627-1234. www.vastage.com. Admission: $25.00+ Note: At 1919 Monticello Ave, nearby is the home of the world's original ice cream cone making machine - Doumar's (757) 627-4163.

Virginia Stage Company at the Wells Theatre is nationally recognized for fine productions of contemporary and classic drama, comedies and Broadway bound premiers. Virginia Stage Company resides in the beautifully restored Wells Theatre, a National Historic Landmark in the heart of Downtown Norfolk. Six major productions each season as well as children's educational theater programs with productions like Romeo & Juliet or Jungle Book. Best for a holiday treat of the annual "A Christmas Carol".

For updates visit: www.KidsLoveTravel.com

South East Area 159

NORFOLK BOTANICAL GARDEN

Norfolk - 6700 Azalea Garden Road (I-64 exit 279B-Norfolk Airport) 23518. Phone: (757) 441-5830. www.norfolkbotanicalgarden.org. Hours: Daily 9:00am-9:00pm. Guided train and boat tours 10:00am-4:00pm daily, weather permitting. Admission: $16.00 adult, $14.00 youth (3-17). Admission includes a complimentary tram tour (April-mid-October). Note: Visitor Center with maps, interpretive exhibit, orientation video and gift shop. Garden House Café. Educators: http://norfolkbotanicalgarden.org/education/teacher-resources/

Discover one of the largest collections of azaleas, camellias, roses and rhododendrons on the East Coast. This is the only botanical garden in the country offering tours by boat or trackless train. Kids will probably like the Butterfly Garden, Japanese Garden, Colonial Herb Garden and the lakes and Friendship Pond. Parents like the 12 miles of pedestrian pathways to walk, skip and stroller on. They even have designated Bike Nites where biking the trail is encouraged.

World of Wonders Children's Garden is a three-acre garden dedicated to families and children. After spilling out of an underground tunnel, kids can splash their way around the world! Through fountains, bubblers, foggers and jet sprays, they will explore the oceans and other major waterways on Earth. Don't forget the water spray fountain and a dirt factory!

NORFOLK HARBORFEST

Norfolk - Town Point Park. www.festeventsva.org. (757) 441-2345. This festival celebrates the region's rich maritime heritage in grand style. This three-day family event begins with a parade of sail into Norfolk's harbor and continues all weekend with live national entertainment, spectacular fireworks, on-the-water action and an entire area just for children. Free. (June, first or second weekend)

SPIRIT OF NORFOLK FIREWORKS DINNER CRUISE

Norfolk - Fireworks Dinner Cruise. www.spiritofnorfolk.com. Enjoy a cruise along the Elizabeth River while enjoying great food, and entertainment. Watch the spectacular fireworks up close and personal from the observation deck. Admission. (July 4th)

VIRGINIA CHILDREN'S FESTIVAL

Norfolk - Town Point Park. (757) 441-2345. Children's events all day. (October Saturday)

GREAT AMERICAN INDEPENDENCE DAY CELEBRATION

Norfolk. Town Point Park & Oceanview Beach Park. Great American Independence Day Celebration.

Portsmouth. North Landing / Crawford Pkwy. Fireworks between downtown Portsmouth and Norfolk waterfronts over the Elizabeth River. FREE.(July 4th)

Petersburg

PAMPLIN HISTORICAL PARK & THE NATIONAL MUSEUM OF THE CIVIL WAR SOLDIER

Petersburg - 6125 Boydton Plank Road (I-85 exit 63A) 23803. www.pamplinpark.org. Phone: (804) 861-2408 or (877) PAMPLIN. Hours: Tuesday-Sunday 9:00am-5:00pm (March - November) except Thanksgiving, Christmas, and New Years Day. Admission: $15.00 adult, $12.00 senior, $8.00 child (6-12). Educators: www.pamplinpark.org/schoolprograms.html#resources. History & Civil War Day Camps. Tours: Self-guided tours presented on MP3 technology tell the stories of Tudor Hall Plantation, the Military Fortifications Exhibit and the Breakthrough Battlefield. Note: Gift shop.

Pamplin Historical Park delivers a fresh approach to historical museums by combining a blend of new technology and old-fashioned storytelling that immerses visitors in the war and the day-to-day lives of very common soldiers. THE NATIONAL MUSEUM OF THE CIVIL WAR SOLDIER is where visitors can wear a personal audio device and become intimately acquainted with their own comrade, such as Delevan Miller, a 13-year-old drummer boy, throughout the tour. Your soldier/guide (by MP3) takes you to "A soldier's Life" which is the room packed full of artifacts and models and soldiers in army regimen. "Pack Your Knapsack" is where a sergeant tells you how to pick items essential to carry but not weighing more than 16 pounds - it's hard to discard a pot and pan and just bring "light-weight" tin cups, blankets, etc. The "Trial by Fire" display reveals sounds of the war: martial music, marching feet tramping, cannon fire, ground trembling, and PRAY that you don't get shot - Mommy did with a powerful puff of air to the chest! Ending at "A test Of Faith", where names of those who survived or were discharged or POW's is revealed - what was the fate of your chosen "soldier comrade"?

Help pack your soldier's knapsack...
© Photo courtesy of Pamplin Historical Park

South East Area 161

Now, venture outdoors for some more "life-like" experiences.

TUDOR HALL PLANTATION - take a short path to the 1812 house that reflects both civilian and military history. One side of the house is furnished as a family would have known it. The other side is outfitted to suit the needs of a Confederate general and his staff.

MILITARY ENCAMPMENT AND FORTIFICATIONS EXHIBIT is a scale, authentic-looking scene of daily costumed programs where visitors mingle with soldiers as they spend a typical day in camp, cooking, cleaning equipment or mending clothes and playing games. Listen for the cannon blast every now and then...or learn soldier lingo. What artillery do you use as the enemy gets closer?

At The BATTLEFIELD CENTER, kids can enter "The Discovery Tent" and sample Civil War uniforms and period clothing that is just their size. They can also try their hand at interactive computer kiosks that feature fun learning games and quizzes based on what they have seen at the Park.

The BREAKTHROUGH THEATER is a multi-media show on the breakthrough battle presented in surround sound with bullets whizzing past and the ground shaking from artillery fire.

© Photo courtesy of Pamplin Historical Park

BREAKTHROUGH TRAIL winds through the battlefield of April 2nd, 1865 where General Grant's Union army broke thru the Confederate lines, ending the 10 month Petersburg Campaign and setting in motion the events leading to Lee's surrender at Appomattox one week later. Plan on a 3-4 hour minimum stay. Our family's favorite Civil War museum, by far!

ANNIVERSARY OF THE BREAKTHROUGH BATTLE

Petersburg - Commemorate the anniversary of the April 2, 1865 Petersburg Breakthrough by participating in a pre-dawn tour of the Breakthrough Battlefield followed by a hot breakfast at the Hardtack & Coffee Cafe. Reservations and fee required. (last Saturday in March)

CIVIL WAR WEEKEND

Petersburg - The rattle of musketry and the roar of cannon rally visitors to this educational and entertaining commemoration of the Civil War era. Living history demonstrations, lectures and book signings, storytelling, and musical performances engage all your senses and help the Civil War era come to life. Free with Park admission. (third weekend in June)

PETERSBURG NATIONAL BATTLEFIELD

Petersburg - 1539 Hickory Hill Road (I-295 south to Rte. 36/Fort Lee exit) 23803. Phone: (804) 732-3531 & (804) 458-9504 & (804) 265-8244. www.nps.gov/pete/. Hours: Grounds open from 8:00am-dusk. Grant's Hdqts. (City Point) / Eastern Front/ Five Forks Battlefield open 9:00am - 5:00pm. Petersburg National Battlefield is closed on Thanksgiving Day, Christmas Day and New Year's Day. Admission: FREE. Educators: Petersburg National Battlefield lessons to explore the state of the country prior to the Civil War: www.nps.gov/pete/forteachers/upload/2013-2014-Educator-Guide-Final-2.pdf. Note: Biking, hiking, auto tour and horseback riding.

Can you imagine spending almost ten months of the Civil War fighting in one area? Why were the soldiers here for so long? How did they pass their days? What was it like living in the trenches around Petersburg? Learn why Petersburg, Virginia, became the setting for the longest siege in American history when General Ulysses S. Grant failed to capture Richmond in the spring of 1864. Grant settled in to subdue the Confederacy by surrounding Petersburg and cutting off General Robert E. Lee's supply lines into Petersburg and Richmond. On April 2, 1865, nine-and-one-half months after the siege began, Lee evacuated Petersburg. Begin your tour at the park entrance Visitor Center viewing exhibits about the Petersburg campaign, an audiovisual map presentation, battlefield relics, maps, etc. The 4-mile self-guided Tour begins at this point, with some areas reserved for "walk-on" sites only. The Siege Line Tour picks up where the initial tour ends and leads to park areas south and west of Petersburg. An audiotape of the 35+ mile driving tour is available. Summertime is especially fun because costumed interpreters depict army life during the siege.

VIRGINIA MOTORSPORTS PARK

Petersburg (Dinwiddie) - 8018 Boydton Plank Road 23803. Phone: (804) 862-3174. www.virginiamotorsports.com. Hours: Weekly Drag Racing Program: March to November with local promotional activities. Admission: $11.00-$40.00 Specialty Events: NHRA Virginia Nationals, Mopar Madness, Pontiacs in the Park, AMA Prostar Spring Nationals, Super Chevy Show, Fun Ford Weekend, Virginia Bike Fest, Street Outlaw Series, Nite of Fire, Truckin Nationals, NHRA Xplod Sport Compact, and more.

The Park has become known as one of the top drag race strips in the nation. Built For Speed, Virginia Motorsports Park was built in 1994 to showcase the most exciting Motorsports events with the fastest racecars in the world. Drag Racing, Truck & Tractor Pull and Motocross events - you choose your racing style. Ever hear of Mud Bog Racing? Well, if you haven't, get on out and watch the trucks sloshing around in the mud pit! If you have a 4x4 with big tires, you, too, can be a Mud Bogger! Or you can enter the race on your ATV.

QUARTERMASTER MUSEUM

Petersburg (Fort Lee) - (just inside main gate of Fort Lee) 23801. Phone: (804) 734-4203.   www.qmmuseum.lee.army.mil.   Hours: Monday-Friday 10:00am-5:00pm, Saturday 11:00am-5:00pm. Closed Thanksgiving, Christmas and New Years Day. Admission: FREE.

This supply center was founded only two days after the Army itself in 1775. The Quartermaster is responsible for almost every service function in the Army: food, clothing, transportation, aerial supply, petroleum supply and mortuary services. See the wagon supply vehicle used from the 1890s to WWII. When autos replaced horse-drawn vehicles, the Quartermaster Corps developed the jeep, which became one of the most famous of all military vehicles. They have a jeep used by General George S. Patton, Jr. in WWII. You'll also see a kitchen which could be pulled directly onto the battlefield providing hot meals to soldiers in WWI.

Portsmouth

CHILDREN'S MUSEUM OF VIRGINIA

Portsmouth - 221 High Street (I-264 exit 7 or I-664 south exit 9 - downtown, Olde Towne) 23704. Phone: (757) 393-8393. www.childrensmuseumva.com. Hours: Tuesday-Saturday 9:00am-5:00pm, Sunday 11:00am-5:00pm. Closed winter holidays. Open summer Mondays. Admission: $11.00 adult, $10.00 military, seniors, child (2-17). Note: Planetarium. Strollers are welcomed. Family Fun Saturdays.

Up close with a model train

The Children's Museum of Virginia in Portsmouth is the largest children's museum in the commonwealth. The most popular exhibit here is the antique toy and model train collection, one of the largest on the East Coast.

Two floors packed with over 90 hands-on displays to stimulate imagination through science (physics of Bubbles - you can even be "inside" a giant one), art (check out the Harmonograph), and music (giant musical instruments like drums and guitars). See a pretend grocery store, ride a "waterbed raft", climb into the cab of a fire engine or bus (with dress up clothes), hard hat stack up area, electrifying weird, and funny science in motion.

LIGHTSHIP PORTSMOUTH MUSEUM

Portsmouth - 420 High Street (I-264 exit 9 to downtown/old towne at the foot of London St on the waterfront) 23704. Phone: (757) 393-8741. www.portsmouthnavalshipyardmuseum.com/lightship/index.html. Hours: Monday-Saturday 10:00am-5:00pm, Sunday 1:00-5:00pm (summers). Reduced hours off season. Admission: $4.00 general (includes both Naval & Lightship admission).

Lightships were built to help mariners avoid dangerous shoals and enter the harbor safely. Sometimes, a land lighthouse wasn't visible, so, lights were  instead fixed to masts of ships that anchored for months in strategic locations off the coastline. Typically, the ship would anchor at a strategic location at sea and remain there for months at a time. The maximum crew for the Lightship Portsmouth during her half-century in service was 15 men. Your family can actually board the vessel and see the most important object aboard - the lantern. The Fresnel lens had to be strong enough to be seen for 12 miles or more. You'll also see the galley/dining hall, the efficiently designed captain's quarters and crew's bunks.

NAVAL SHIPYARD MUSEUM

Portsmouth - 2 High Street Landing in Olde Towne (I-264 exit 7) 23704. Phone: (757) 393-8591. https://portsmouthnavalshipyardmuseum.com/. Hours: Wednesday-Saturday 10:00am-4:00pm, Sunday Noon-4:00pm. Open on Mondays during the summer and occasional observed Monday holidays. Admission: $4.00 for both museums (Naval & Lightship included in one fee). Discounted rates off season.

Established in 1949 within the nation's oldest shipyard, on the Elizabeth River. Visitors will experience a steady stream of vessels from pleasure craft to carriers, and a collection of antique cannons.

For updates visit: www.KidsLoveTravel.com

During the Revolutionary War, the shipyard was described by the British as "the most considerable one in America."

It's been burned three times by retreating armies because of its strategic importance. Many historic ships have been built here, including the CSS VIRGINIA, the first ironclad to engage in battle; the nation's first battleship, the TEXAS; and the world's first aircraft carrier, the LANGLEY. The shipyard is also home to the country's first drydock, still in use.

SEAWALL FESTIVAL

Portsmouth - Portsmouth Waterfront. www.portsvaevents.com This family festival features a children's park, craft show, regional cuisine, golden oldies and beach music. A recreational vehicle park is available for motorcoaches. (June, first weekend)

UMOJA FESTIVAL

Portsmouth - Old Towne Portsmouth waterfront. (757) 393-8481, (800) POR-TSVA or www.umojafestportsmouth.com. This event is an African-American cultural celebration, featuring national musical entertainment, an African marketplace, children's activities a community forum, heritage trolley tours, Afrocentric foods, and exhibits. FREE (Memorial Day weekend)

Richmond

CANAL WALK, RICHMOND

Richmond - Visitor Center at Hillcrest & Riverside Drive (Tredegar Iron Works to 12th St. and James River and Kanawha from 12th to Triple Crossing) 23219. Phone: (804) 648-6549. https://venturerichmond.com/explore-downtown/riverfront-canal-walk/. Hours: Daily sunrise to sunset. Admission: FREE. Charge for boat rentals or guided boat tours. (804) 788-6466.

Enjoy a leisurely walk along the restored Kanawha and Haxall canals, with History Medallions pointing out the rich history of Richmond's waterfront. Or take a guided bateau boat tour (April-October) on the restored Kanawha Canal, originally designed by George Washington. By linking the James River with the Kanawha River in western Virginia, which in turn flowed into Ohio, he hoped to improve transportation and trade with the west. The first section of the canal system circumvented the seven-mile falls near Richmond. First envisioned in 1774, these canals were to be part of a continuous transportation route from the Atlantic Ocean to the Mississippi River. Did you know that in 1888 Richmond built the first commercially successful electric streetcar system.

FEDERAL RESERVE MONEY MUSEUM

Richmond - 701 East Byrd Street (Federal Reserve Bank) 23219. Phone: (804) 697-8110. www.thefedexperience.org. Hours: Tuesday-Friday 9am-4pm. Admission: FREE. Educators: Online lesson plans under "For Teachers" icon.

A self-guided tour exhibits forms of currency, rare bills (even $100,000 bills!) and gold and silver bars (a favorite of the kids). A great virtual tour of the museum with a view of the gold bar is available on the website. 500 items depict the history of currency including such items as compressed tea bricks which could be spent or brewed or an actual coin of the Kingdom of Lydia, the birthplace of coinage.

MAGGIE L. WALKER NATIONAL HISTORIC SITE

Richmond - 600 North 2nd Street 23219. www.nps.gov/malw. Phone: (804) 771-2017. Hours: Tuesday-Saturday 9:00am-4:30pm. Closed major winter holidays. Admission: FREE. Tours: offered every hour. Educators: Curriculum guides online "For Teachers". Note: The visitor's center has a short film presentation to begin your tour. The film talks from Maggie's point of view talking to children.

The site honors Maggie Walker, a prominent businesswoman, who overcame social obstacles of her time - being physically impaired, black and a woman. She founded the St. Luke Penny Savings Bank, the first chartered bank in the country started by a woman, and became a success in the world of business and finance. Her home, next to the visitor center, has been completely restored to the 1930's appearance with many Walker family furnishings to view. The house has 28 rooms - rather large and ornate. She showed her wealth with a chauffeured limousine, diamond rings and many gold-leafed furnishings. She also was very generous and gave most extra money away. Learn how she helped fellow African-Americans "turn nickels into dollars". The main interpretive exhibits feature the story of her life. The exhibits include many historical photographs, a recreation of the St. Luke Penny Savings Bank teller window, displays of museum artifacts such as Mrs. Walker's dress and St. Luke regalia, and a child's personal St. Luke savings bank (like the ones she gave children in the area). The opening of the new exhibits changes the way visitors view Mrs. Walker's home. Previously, tours left the visitor center and angled across the courtyard entering the home from the rear porch. Now visitors will view the exhibits, then exit onto Leigh Street and enter Mrs. Walker's home from the front door just as invited guests would have arrived during her lifetime.

South East Area   167

THE WHITE HOUSE OF THE CONFEDERACY

Richmond - 1201 East Clay Street (downtown, 2 blocks north of Broad Street) 23219. Phone: (804) 649-1861. https://acwm.org. Hours: Daily 10:00am-5:00pm. Closed Major winter holidays. Admission (separate for each museum) $15.00 adult, $13.00 (62+ and military ID), $8.00 child (6-17). Combo tickets help you save $2-5.00 on admission to both museums. Tours: Guided of the White House start in the basement and cover the first and second floors are daily and last about 40 minutes.

Take a guided tour of the White House, the Civil War residence of Confederate President Jefferson Davis. The home has been restored to its wartime elegance. Museum: 500 wartime flags, 250 uniform pieces and the personal belongings of many Confederate generals like Jefferson Davis, Robert E. Lee, J.E.B. Stuart and Stonewall Jackson. Displays on the lives of free and enslaved African Americans and the giant, 15 foot painting of "The Last Meeting of Lee and Jackson" are here also. White House: The executive mansion of President Jefferson Davis and his family during the Civil War. Children's Activities Days (hands-on activities, games with guide), Civil War encounters (costumed living historian will portray an "eyewitness" to various events), and day camps for kids, too.

RICHMOND SYMPHONY

Richmond - 300 W. Franklin Street (venue varies by production) 23219. Phone: (804) 788-1212 Ticket office. www.richmondsymphony.com. Admission: **$15.00 for family style pops concerts. Special events tickets start at $20.00.**

Founded in 1957, the Richmond Symphony offers a variety of performances ranging from classical to pop. Kid Classics (like Bugs Bunny on Broadway), Family Concerts and Handel's Messiah each year.

ST. JOHN'S CHURCH

Richmond - 2401 East Broad Street   23219. www.historicstjohnschurch.org. Phone: (804) 648-5015. Admission: $12.00 adult, $10.00 child (7-18). Tours are conducted Monday through Saturday from 9:30am-4:00pm. Sunday hours are 12:30pm-4:00pm. Weekends only each winter. Tours are on the hour and half-hour and last approximately 20 minutes. Last tour leaves one half hour before closing. Closed New Years, Easter, Thanksgiving and Christmastime.

> Built in 1741 (the first church and largest building built in town), Patrick Henry delivered his famous "Liberty or Death" speech in favor of independence at this site.

Tours are also subject to close for weddings, funerals, or other church functions. Educators: Wonderful and easy PDF downloadable Activities on their online Education pages. It is best to visit here after the children have studied the Revolutionary War. Then, they are very impressed.

You can experience the historic significance of St. John's Church by taking a tour led by one of their expert guides. The tour includes a history of the buildings on the grounds of St. John's, highlights of the graveyard, where numerous individuals prominent in Richmond and Virginia history are buried, a tour of the inside of the Church, and a description of the vigorous debate of the Second Virginia Convention, during which Mr. Patrick Henry delivered his famous speech, which has lived on as the most famous cry for freedom in the world - "Give me liberty or give me death." Reenactments of the Second Virginia Convention of 1775 are held Sundays at 2:00pm during the summer. The costumed guide gives excerpts of the speech as it applies to the times.

ANNIVERSARY RE-ENACTMENT OF PATRICK HENRY'S FAMOUS "LIBERTY OR DEATH" SPEECH

Richmond - St. John's Church. Eleven actors recreate the 1775 Second Virginia Convention. Free, donations accepted. (Sunday closest to March 23rd, the actual date of Henry's speech)

VALENTINE MUSEUM - RICHMOND HISTORY CENTER

Richmond - 1015 East Clay Street 23219. https://thevalentine.org/ Phone: (804) 649-0711. Hours: Tuesday-Sunday 10:00am-5:00pm. Closed all winter holidays. Admission: $10.00 adult, $8.00 senior/student (7-18).

"The Museum of the Life and History of Richmond" focuses on urban and social history, decorative arts, costumes and architecture. The 1812 Wickham house is refurnished and offers mostly architectural history. What types of tools might a 19th century artist use? Who was Valentine? How did an elegant Richmond home handle the heat before air conditioning? The self-guided Wickham House basement examines the slaves' private spheres. A timeline in the shape of a river highlights important events as it winds across the gallery floor.

VIRGINIA STATE CAPITOL

Richmond - Capitol Square (9th & Grace Streets) 23219. Phone: (804) 698-1788. www.virginiacapitol.gov. Hours: Monday-Saturday 9:00am-5:00pm, Sunday 1:00-5:00pm. Admission: FREE. Tours: One hour long. Last tour leaves at 4:00pm. Gallery seating is also available on a first come, first serve basis. Note: Capitol Café & Gift Shop.

The Capitol was designed by Thomas Jefferson and houses the second oldest legislative body in the western hemisphere. Highlights are: the Houdin statue of George Washington, the hidden interior dome, seen only from inside the building, and busts of the eight Virginia born presidents; the Old Senate Hall and the Old Hall of the House of Delegates, where Aaron Burr was tried for treason in 1807, Robert E. Lee received his commission as commander of the VA troops and the Confederate Congress met during the Civil War. If you have time, guided tours offer more insight into the state's governmental historical figures and stories. Look for the doorknobs throughout the building with the State Seal on them - how many can you count? The Governor's Mansion is the oldest continuously occupied governor's home (1814) in the country. These tours are probably a little long for the young ones.

CHILDREN'S MUSEUM OF RICHMOND

Richmond - 2626 West Broad Street (I-95/I-64 exit #78 south, adjacent to the Science Museum) 23220. (at website you can go to other two satellite locations) www.c-mor.org. Phone: (804) 474-CMOR or (877) 295-CMOR. Hours: Daily 9:30am-5:00pm. Admission: $9.00 general (age 1+). Seniors pay $1.00 less. Admission is the same at Chesterfield & Short Pump locations. Daily science and crafts.

It's a museum where you can touch everything! Kids learn through interactive play - they can chase butterflies with Shadow Play, tinker in an inventor's lab, be a star at the CMOR Playhouse, or build sand castles in the Backyard exhibit. Here's the highlights: Treehouse - climb to treetops to look in an eagle's nest, explore a limestone cave, or float on the James River. Town Square - become a paramedic or shop at the market. Little Farm - a special area dedicated for creeping, crawling, tumbling - preschoolers only. See the waterplay area, too where young engineers can jump waterfalls and hop into water jets. The noticeable focus here is the crawling and climbing aspects - an educational playplace!

NEW YEARS EVE BASH

Richmond - Richmond Children's Museum. Song and dance, make a hat and fun noise makers and join the CMOR parade. Admission. (early New Years Eve afternoon)

MAYMONT

Richmond - 2201 Shields Lake Drive (I-195 Maplewood exit, follow signs) 23220. Phone: (804) 358-7166. https://maymont.org. Hours: Exhibits: (Maymont House, Nature Center, Children's Farm Barn & Maymont Shop): Tuesday-Sunday, 12:00-5:00pm. Grounds, Gardens & Visitor Center: Daily, 10:00am - 5:00pm Admission: $6.00-$8.00 suggested donation at Nature Center, Children's Farm & Maymont House Note: Café. Tram, Carriage Rides (Sundays, Noon-5:00pm) and Hayrides (weekends in summer, 1:00--4:00pm) are $5.00 fee per person per ride.

A visit to Maymont is best started at the Robins Nature & Visitor Center - Maymont's front door. A history lover will soon find a path to the 1893 Maymont House Museum. A plant lover will find the elaborate Japanese and Italian gardens. For animal lovers there are the Nature Center, Wildlife Exhibits and the Children's Farm. In the Nature Center, many linked aquariums are home to playful river otters, many species of fish, turtles and other creatures. Interactive galleries include a replica of Richmond's flood wall, a weather station and a fish ladder. The Children's Farm introduces little ones to all sorts of barnyard animals. Children are welcome to feed and pet many animals on display. Be sure to bring quarters for the feed dispensers. The Farm is home to a variety of goats, sheep, pigs, chickens, donkeys, rabbits, peafowl (peacocks and peahens), turkeys, cattle, horses, geese and ducks. Rare breeds include Scotch Highland and Dutch Belted cows, the Barbados Blackbelly sheep and others. The envy of zoologists across the nation, Maymont's bear habitat alone is worth a visit. The large terrain includes a rock scramble, a pond, and multiple areas for climbing, sleeping, hiding and eating. There are also exhibit areas to view bison, red fox, and hundreds of other animals. Also, explore the opulent Victorian mansion, gardens, and other wildlife exhibits.

The otters are always so much fun to watch...

VICTORIAN HOLIDAYS AT MAYMONT

Richmond - Maymont. It's Christmas Day in 1893 with tours of the lavishly decorated House, carriage rides, carolers, bell ringers, Father Christmas, Yule logs, wassail and more. Candlelighting Ceremony & Community Sing. www.maymont.org/events/annual.asp. Admission. (December, second week)

RICHMOND INTERNATIONAL RACEWAY

Richmond - 602 E. Laburnum Avenue 23220. Phone: (804) 345-7223 (RACE). https://www.richmondraceway.com/

A ¾ mile "D" shaped asphalt oval surrounded by the greatest number of seats of any VA sport complex. Twice annual admissions exceed 170,000 to NASCAR Nationwide Series and Sprint Cup series race weekends. Admission varies with event.

RICHMOND KICKERS SOCCER

Richmond - City Stadium 3201 Maplewood Avenue 23221. Phone: (804) 644-5425. www.richmondkickers.com. Season: (mid-April to mid-August) Admission: $8.00-$15.00

The Richmond Kickers are a professional USL-Division 2 team. Kids nights feature Kids Kicks and Kicker for a Day.

SCIENCE MUSEUM OF VIRGINIA

Richmond - 2500 West Broad Street (off I-95 and I-64, exit #78 south towards Broad Street) 23220. Phone: (804) 367-6552. www.smv.org. Hours: Tuesday-Sunday 9:30am-5:00pm. Closed Thanksgiving and Christmas. Admission: $16.00 adult, $13.50 senior (60+) and child (6-12), $10.00 preschool (3-5). Military FREE. Dome: $4.00 extra. Note: Café. Shop4Science gift shop. Educators: Teachers Guides- www.smv.org/teachers/teachers-guides.

In a former 1919 train station, the museum offers 250 + hands-on exhibits and demonstrations. Subjects covered include aerospace, speed, electricity, physical sciences, biology, telecommunications, and an IMAX Dome. See rats play basketball. Play laser pool. Watch a giant-screen film in the museum's IMAX® DOME & Planetarium. In BodyHuman, start at the "Very Small Gallery" (microscopic cells and DNA) to "my size" systems of the human body. Look at dozens of cells, then start "Seeing Things". At Question Power, jump on a stationary bike to see if you can generate as much electricity as the wind does turning a windmill. Check out a small house that's different from yours. Explore Newton's laws, gravity, momentum, potential and kinetic energy in whole-body experiences! The Speed and Going Places exhibits examine movement and travel technology. Float on air. Find the perfect chemistry as you mix science and technology with art! Look for the Tabletop Science Sites and Demonstration Stations (different each day). Note: to take advantage of the many demonstrations and theatre science presentations, check the announcement board as you enter.

VIRGINIA REP'S CHILDREN'S THEATRE

Richmond - 114 West Broad Street (Empire Theatre - the oldest theater in Virginia & venues around town) 23220. Phone: (804) 344-8040. www.theatreiv.com. Admission: Regularly priced tickets are around $20.00-30.00.

Theatre IV presents two performance series: The Family Playhouse Series of plays, musicals and puppet shows for the entire family and the Broadway series with more mature themes. The Family Series includes favorites like: Charlie Brown, A Christmas Carol, The Secret Garden, and Beauty and the Beast.

VIRGINIA HISTORICAL SOCIETY

Richmond - 428 North Arthur Ashe Boulevard (I-95/ I/64 East to Exit 78 (Boulevard). Turn right onto Boulevard (heading south) to the corner of Kensington) 23220. Phone: (804) 358-4901. www.vahistory.org. Hours: Monday-Saturday 10:00am-5:00pm, Sunday 10:00-5:00pm. Closed major holidays. Admission: $10.00 adult, $8.00 senior (65+) or military, $5.00 child & student (6-17). Tours: Gallery Walks take place in the galleries of the Virginia Historical Society. All walks begin at noon unless otherwise indicated. Walks are free with admission and free to members. Reservations are not required. Educators: The Story of Virginia themes are separated online, each with a teachers guide accompaniment. Note: Museum Shop full of Virginia history items and crafts.

Any Virginian or anyone who wants an overview of the state's historical highlights needs to visit here (and more than once to get it all). Discover the entire "Story of Virginia" at the Virginia Historical Society through videos, storyphones, computer games and other interactive devises that make learning fun for the whole family. You'll start at the orientation theatre. The film shown is an "easy to follow" path of state history. Now, move on to the first inhabitants (Powatan Indians) including a dugout canoe, a wooden musket, and Pocahontas portraits (even a piece of her hat). Move on from the settlers to the Conestoga Wagon display and the move out west (most Virginians who left went towards Ohio). As you progress past the early 1800's (see Revolutionary War stuff along the way), move to the Civil War gallery, and then it's on to the 1900's. Here you'll see an actual streetcar theatre and famous native Virginians (especially sports figures).

VIRGINIA MUSEUM OF FINE ARTS

Richmond - 2800 Grove Avenue @ Blvd (I-195 Boulevard exit) 23221. Phone: (804) 340-1400. www.vmfa.museum. Hours: Daily 10:00am-5:00pm plus some evenings. Admission: Donations. Educators: Teacher packets and inspiring materials will help bring art into any classroom. See Educational Resource Room online for details. Note: Cafeteria and gift shop.

You'll find the largest art collection in the Southeast as well as the largest public display of Faberge Russian Imperial eggs outside of Russia. This art museum focuses on collections of art nouveau, art deco, Himalayan, contemporary, impressionist and British sporting art. Kids Studios are designed to follow what your child is learning in school. The hands-on process makes new links between art and other experiences, and makes them all more meaningful to children. Family Studio and Studio Sundays bring the art in the galleries to life with related performances, storytelling, art activities, and more. They're free and open to all; no registration needed.

RICHMOND NATIONAL BATTLEFIELD PARK

Richmond - 3215 E. Broad Street (I-95: take exit 74C west then follow signs to Civil War Visitor Center located at 470 Tredegar Street) 23223. Phone: (804) 771-2145. www.nps.gov/rich. Hours: Park battlefields are open sunrise-sunset. Visitor centers at Tredegar Iron Works, Chimborazo and Cold Harbor are open Wednesday through Sunday, 9am to 4:30pm. Cold Harbor is closed December-Feb. Admission: FREE for most sites. Civil War Center has parking fees. Educators: Followup activities available when you book a themed tour.

Richmond's story is not just the tale of one large Civil War battle, nor even one important campaign. Instead, the park's resources include a naval battle, a key industrial complex, the Confederacy's largest hospital, and dozens of miles of elaborate original fortifications.

CHIMBORAZO MEDICAL MUSEUM: The museum stands on the eastern end of downtown Richmond, at the site of the Civil War's famous Chimborazo Hospital. Between 1861 and 1865 more than 75,000 Confederate soldiers received treatment at this spacious facility. The medical museum tells the story of those patients and the hospital and physicians that cared for them. Using artifacts, uniforms, and documents, the exhibits describe the state of medicine in 1860 and the care of wounded and sick soldiers on the battlefields and in the many large centralized Richmond hospitals like Chimborazo. A short film supplements the exhibits.

AMERICAN CIVIL WAR VISITOR CENTER AT TREDEGAR IRON WORKS: serves as the gift shop and information center for the War aspects of the James River. The Center's mission is to tell the whole story of the conflict that still shapes our nation. The main exhibit space titled: In the Cause of Liberty, explores the war's causes, course, and legacies through artifacts, media, and programs looking at three essential perspectives—Union, Confederate, and African American. Three floors of exhibits and artifacts are on display. Orientation film is shown every half hour. In 2019 the Civil War Museum opens: www.tredegar.org. $18.00 adult, $16.00 military and senior, $9.00 child (6-17). (next to the NPS Tredegar site)

ANNIVERSARY OF THE SEVEN DAYS BATTLES

Richmond (Mechanicsville) - Gaines' Mill Battlefield. www.nps.gov/rich/. (804) 226-1981. The Richmond National Battlefield Park commemorates the Seven Days Battles with living history programs and ranger-led tours. Encampment, rifle firing demonstrations and walking tours throughout the weekend. (long Weekend before July 4th)

THREE LAKES NATURE CENTER

Richmond - 400 Sausiluta Drive (off Wilkerson Road, east of Chamberlayne Avenue) 23227. https://henrico.us/rec/places/three-lakes. Phone: (804) 501-1470. Hours vary by season but Visitors Center always open Tuesday-Sunday Noon-4:30pm. Admission: FREE.

Three Lake Nature Center and Aquarium brings together three worlds - air, land and water. A 50,000-gallon freshwater aquarium, wetland exhibits, aquatic animal/plant life, forest animals, etc. give you "Nature's" view of the world. Features also include a variety of exhibits designed to give the visitor hands-on knowledge of local plant and animal life.

LEWIS GINTER BOTANICAL GARDEN

Richmond - 1800 Lakeside Avenue (I-95 North take Exit 80, the Lakeside Avenue exit) 23228. Phone: (804) 262-9887. www.lewisginter.org. Hours: Daily 9:00am-5:00pm. Closed Thanksgiving, Christmas, and New Years. Admission: $13.00 adult, $11.00 senior (55+), $8.00 child (3-12) Note: Gift shop and café (lunch). Children's Discovery Programs and Family Fun Calendar with seasonal events.

Lewis Ginter Botanical Garden brings you new horticultural displays each season. The more than 25 acres of gardens includes the Conservatory glass-domed showcase with exotic and tropical displays; an elegant Victorian-style garden; Asian Valley; the Island Garden, a wetland environment with a stunning display of pitcher plants, water irises and lotuses; a Children's Garden with colorful and interesting plants to attract butterflies and birds, a TreeHouse, international village, Farm and Sand & Waterplay areas. Good to take a stroller along the winding paved paths.

For updates visit: www.KidsLoveTravel.com

South East Area

CAPITAL CITY KWANZAA FESTIVAL

Richmond - Richmond Convention Center. (804) 644-3900. www.efsinc.org. This year end celebration features performances, special children's activities, discussion groups and The African Market of eclectic merchandise and African-inspired cuisine. Admission. (December, close to the 30th)

EMBASSY SUITES

Richmond - 2925 Emerywood Pkwy., I-64 exit 183. www.embassy-suites.com. (804) 672-8585. Each suite lets the family spread out with a separate living room with sofa bed, galley kitchen with wet bar, microwave, refrigerator and coffee maker, two phones and two TVs. Your stay includes a complimentary full breakfast (cold and hot, made-to-order foods) plus an evening snack/beverage reception. The hotel also has a tropical atrium indoor pool and whirlpool. Rates start around $175.00

HENRICUS HISTORICAL PARK

Richmond (Chester) - 251 Henricus Park Road, 601 Coxendale Road 23836. Phone: (804) 706-1340. www.henricus.org. Hours: Wednesday-Sunday 10:00am-5:00pm (Feb-December) Admission: $12.00 adult, $8.00 child (age 3-12). Note: **Visitors Center and Museum Store.**

Henricus was home to Pocahontas, the beginnings of the early plantations and the first English hospital in America. It was built along the James River on land inhabited by the Appomattocks tribe, where Pocahontas grew up. Harsh battles were fought when the English first arrived in America. Henricus Historical Park is where Pocahontas lived and was courted by John Rolfe! It was the marriage between Pocahontas and John Rolfe that helped bring a peaceful coexistence between the two warring factions. Children learn history as costumed interpreters work in the 1611 Citie of Henricus, Virginia's second successful English settlement after Jamestown. Every month carries out a different theme, for example: Harvest, Holidays, Native Americans, Government, Environment, Militia, Archaeology and Colonial. Enjoy nature hikes, birding and fishing at the Dutch Gap Conservation Area.

METRO RICHMOND ZOO

Richmond (Chesterfield) - 8300 Beaver Bridge Road 23219. Phone: (804) 739-5666. www.metrorichmondzoo.com. Hours: Monday-Saturday 9:30am-5:00pm. **Closed winter holidays and icing condition days. Admission: $23.95 adult, $22.95 senior (60+), $17.95 child (2-11). Skyride, train and carousel $2.00-$3.00 extra. Educators: live Cheetah Cam.**

This privately owned zoo features exotic animals such as endangered lemur, ostriches, giraffes, penguins, lions, tigers, chimpanzees and a nocturnal exhibit featuring bats, a sloth, and more than 200 monkeys. Visit their herd of giraffe up close, and let these gentle giants eat right out of your hand! Feed and pet many barnyard animals. Various hand-raised antelope reside in the petting area. Learn about their African penguins at the daily feedings. Take the Treetop Zoofari Zipline (extra fee) high above the zoo to see the animals from this scenic viewpoint! Carousel and other rides are also fun for the kids.

POCAHONTAS STATE PARK

Richmond (Chesterfield) - 10301 State Park Road (I-95 to SR 288 north, then SR 10 east to Rte. 655 west) 23832. Phone: (804) 796-4255. www.dcr.virginia.gov/parks/pocahont.htm. Admission: $7.00 per vehicle.

Located 20 miles from downtown Richmond, this park has pool swimming, boating, bicycling, camping and group cabins. The Civilian Conservation Corps Museum is dedicated to the Depression-era volunteers who helped to build the state's park system. Algonquin Ecology Camp is available for overnight group camps as is the Heritage Center and the new amphitheater on a sloping hillside. There's also hiking and bridle trails.

KINGS DOMINION

Richmond (Doswell) - 1600 Theme Park Way (I-95 EXIT 98) 23047. Phone: (804) 876-5000. www.kingsdominion.com. Hours: Weekends (April-Memorial Day), Daily (Memorial Day-Labor Day), and Weekends (Labor Day - first few weekends in October). Generally opens at 10:00 or 10:30am and closes around 8:00-10:00pm. Admission: One-Day General Admission: $46.00-$56.00. Discounts online. Tips: The Eiffel Tower makes a great meeting place and is easy to find from anywhere in the park. Additionally, they provide strollers and wheelchairs for a small rental fee.

During the spring and summer months, you won't want to miss Kings Dominion in nearby Doswell north of Richmond, a 400-acre theme and water park and world-class roller coasters. Dominator. The innovative 4,210-foot steel coaster is the longest floorless coaster in the world and has the largest roller coaster loop. Kings Dominion brings the best of amusements to the Mid-Atlantic with one of the largest coaster collections on the East Coast; two children's areas; and Soak City, a 19-acre water park included with admission. Try the new Stunt Coaster. Soak City features 4-8 awesome slides, Tidal Wave Bay wave pool, Tornado, Zoom Flume raft adventure, Surf City Splash Playhouse, Kiddie Kove, Lil' Barefoot Beach and Lazy Rider. Adults may be supervising, but, kids are in charge at: PLANET SNOOPY: fun theme rides like Boulder Bumpers, Raceway, Scrambler, Boo Blasters, Cars, Planes, Trains, an old-fashioned carousel and Backyard Circus!

Many shows throughout the day vary from Country, to Today's Hits, to Yesterday's Favorites, to hot Latin Beats, or maybe Summer Jam songs.

MEADOW FARM MUSEUM

Richmond (Glen Allen) - 3400 Mountain Road (I-95 exit 84 to I-295 west to Woodman Road South exit to Mountain Road) 23060. Phone: (804) 501-5520. https://henrico.us/rec/places/meadow-farm. Hours: Wednesday-Sunday Noon-4:00pm (early March-early December). Weekends only (December, mid-January to early March). Closed many holidays. Admission: FREE. Small fee for some events. If you want to "visit" with living history farm hands, come on theme weekends.

Step back in time at Meadow Farm Museum with its 19th-century farmhouse, gardens and more than 150 acres of woodlands. Costumed interpreters perform domestic and agricultural tasks throughout the year. Start your visit at the orientation center with everything from old wooden farm tools to hand-made paper dolls. Many of the displays are at a child's eye-level and short storyboards help to explain customs and traditions of the time. The story of the Sheppard family through the seasons is a great video to watch at least once. Walk around the farm and see the cows, horses, sheep, pigs and fowl that are typical of the nineteenth century. Watch farmhands planting the crops every spring and many other chores including pickling, harvesting, or Dr. Sheppard preparing homemade medicine for his patients. Also, outside on the farm, you'll find a barn, smokehouse, doctor's office and blacksmith. You might see the women churning butter and learn how you can make your own at home using one cup of heavy whipping cream-along with a marble-in a jar with tight fitting lid. Shake it hard for a while, pour off liquid and the solid part is sweet, creamy butter. Spread it on fresh bread for an authentic 19th century lunch!

HARVEST FESTIVAL

Richmond - Meadow Farm. Celebrate fall with the whole family at Meadow Farm and Crump Park. Enjoy music, dancing, living history exhibits, a petting zoo, scarecrow making and more.

OLD-FASHIONED CHRISTMAS AND LAMP LIGHT TOURS

Richmond - Meadow Farm. (804) 501-5520. The cooks prepare dinner as the Sheppard family greets their guests. Visit with an 1840's style St. Nick along with music, period games and hot cider. Cooking demonstrations, lantern tours of the farm. Free. (December, first Sunday)

Smithfield

FORT HUGER

Smithfield - 15080 Talcott Terrace 23430. Phone: (757) 357-2291. www.historicisleofwight.com/fort-huger.html Hours: Friday-Sunday 10:00am-4:00pm. Admission: FREE. Guided tours monthly. Grounds open dawn to dusk.

Fort Huger, the gateway to the Confederate Capital, is located in the northern reaches of Isle of Wight county off route 10. View the ghost fleet on the James River, take the self-guided walking tour through the new trails and see the cannon mounted along the edges of the fort.

ISLE OF WIGHT COUNTY MUSEUM

Smithfield - 103 Main St. 23430. Phone: (757) 357-7459. www.historicisleofwight.com Hours: Monday-Saturday 10:00am-4:00pm. Sunday Noon-4pm. Closed New Years, Thanksgiving and Christmas. Admission: $2.00 adult (age 18+). Note: In the same small town of Smithfield, there is the Old Brick Church (St. Luke's Church) said to be the oldest Gothic Church in America, and Boykin's Tavern Museum on Monument Circle or the Old Schoolhouse (part of walking tours).

In a circa 1900 country store, see prehistoric fossils, Native American and colonial artifacts, Civil War history thru the area, a miniature plantation house and the famous Smithfield Ham galleries. See the "World's Oldest Smithfield Ham" and the world's oldest peanut among this exhibit of historical ham memorabilia. The city walking tour, approximately one mile in length, begins at the museum and will whisk you back to the days of dusty roads, plank sidewalks and a bustling riverfront.

OLDEN DAYS FESTIVAL

Smithfield - Downtown. (757) 357-5182. www.smithfield-virginia.com. Visitors can see blacksmiths, colonial herbalists, kettle corn poppers and quilters perform their heritage craft. On Friday and Saturday night, visitors are introduced to Smithfield's more famous, and often infamous forefathers, as well as their eccentricities, during the lantern-lit guided Ghost Walks. Entertainment. (June, last weekend)

GREAT DISMAL SWAMP NATIONAL WILDLIFE REFUGE

Suffolk - 3100 Desert Road (I-664 to Rte. 58 west to Rte. 337 to Rte. 642, White Marsh Rd., follow signs) 23434. . Phone: (757) 986-3705. www.fws.gov/refuge/great_dismal_swamp Hours: The Washington Ditch and Jericho Lane entrances are open Daily 6:30am- 8:00pm (April 1-September 30) and 6:30am-5:00pm (October 1-March 31). Note: Hiking, biking, photography, wildlife observation, fishing and boating. A variety of unpaved roads provide opportunities for hiking

South East Area

and biking, with Washington Ditch Road the best suited for bicycle traffic. An interpretive boardwalk trail meanders almost a mile through a portion of the Swamp. All vehicles must pay a $5.00 daily fee for entry to the Wildlife Drive for touring or for boating.

Many weird and wild tales have been told about the Great Dismal Swamp and its mysterious circular lake, a biological wonder. The Refuge consists of Lake Drummond, a 3,100 acre natural lake in the center of the Swamp. The Swamp supports a variety of mammals, including otter, bats, raccoon, mink, gray and red foxes, and gray squirrel. White-tailed deer are common, and black bear and bobcat also inhabit the area. Yellow-bellied and spotted turtles are commonly seen, and an additional 56 species of turtles, lizards, salamanders, frogs, and toads. About 100 bird species have been reported as nesting on or near the Refuge. Birding is best during spring migration from April to June. Other birds of interest are the wood duck, barred owl, pleated woodpecker, and prothonotary warbler.

SUFFOLK PEANUT FEST

Suffolk - (757) 539-6751. www.suffolkfest.org. Fireworks, commercial, military and county exhibits, arts and crafts, amusement rides and the Nationwide Demolition Derby are featured at this event to celebrate the peanut. Other events include tractor pulls, yo-yo contest and favorite festival foods. "Gooberland" provides an area for family activities. (October, second long weekend)

Surry

CHIPPOKES PLANTATION STATE PARK

Surry - 695 Chippokes Park Road (access via SR 10 to Rte. 634) 23883. Phone: (757) 294-3625. www.dcr.virginia.gov/state_parks/chi.shtml. Hours: Mansion guided tours: Saturday 10:00am-4:00pm, Sunday 1:00-4:00pm (April-October). Grounds open daily (seasonally) along with Farm Museum self-guided tours. Admission: $7.00 per vehicle. Note: Playground, swimming and picnicking.

Chippokes Plantation State Park borders the creek named for an Indian Chief who befriended early English settlers. This park offers a working farm for more than 370 years. Visitors may tour an antebellum mansion, stroll the gardens, or view a collection of antique farm and forestry equipment in the Farm and Forestry Museum. The park has 3.5 miles of hiking and bicycling trails, (a half-mile of which is accessible), through the historic area, as well as an auto farm tour road. The park also has an equestrian area with 10 miles of riding fun around farm fields and two multiple-use trails. The park has a visitor center with a gift store, interpretive programs. A new campground and three overnight cottages allow visitors to spend the night on the historic grounds.

CHIPPOKES STEAM AND GAS SHOW

Surry - Chippokes Plantation State Park. (804) 786-7950. Come celebrate the early days of the modern farm with an exciting and educational weekend. The event includes tractor pulls, vintage trucks, steam engines, kids' activities, demonstrations, farm animals, arts and crafts, a flea market, entertainment, peanut-picking, blacksmithing, food and more. Fee. (mid-June weekend)

JAMESTOWN-SCOTLAND FERRY

Surry - 16289 Rolfe Highway (Rte. 31 between James City and Surry counties) 23883. Phone: (800) VA FERRY. www.virginiadot.org/travel/ferry-jamestown.asp. Hours: Daily Every 20 minutes in the summer. Less often the rest of the year. Schedule online. Admission: FREE.

Passenger vehicle ferry service, Surry County to Jamestown. Fun way to first look onto Jamestown with similar angle as the explorers.

SMITH'S FORT PLANTATION

Surry - 217 Smith's Fort Lane (SR 31/641 across the river from Jamestown, 2 miles from the ferry dock) 23883. Phone: (757) 294-3872. http://preservationvirginia.org/visit/historic-properties/smiths-fort-plantation. Hours: Friday-Saturday 10:00am-5:00pm, Sunday Noon-5pm (March-December). Admission: $15.00 adult, $12.00 senior (65+), $10.00 student (ages 6-17).

In 1609, Captain John Smith built a fort on land directly across from Jamestown as a refuge in event of a Indian attack. When John Rolfe married Pocahontas in 1614, the Indian chief Powhatan presented this land as part of her dowry. The house is furnished with early English and American furniture. A footpath leads to the original fort site. Neither Pocahontas, John Smith, nor John Rolfe ever permanently lived here, but they do weave much history of all three throughout the tour.

Virginia Beach

FIRST LANDING STATE PARK

Virginia Beach - 2500 Shore Drive (US 60 at Cape Henry) 23451. Phone: (757) 412-2316. www.dcr.virginia.gov/state_parks/fir.shtml. Hours: Dawn-Dusk Admission: $9.00 per vehicle. No parking fee for camping and cabin guests, up to two vehicles.

In April of 1607, some 100 English settlers landed here and established the first government in English America before heading up the James River to establish Jamestown. Along with its historical significance, the park offers recreational activities to explore lagoons, large cypress trees and rare plants and critters. 19 plus miles of hiking trails wind through the natural area. The most popular, the first section of the Bald Cypress Trail, is one-mile, crosses dunes and ponds, and is handicapped accessible. Trail walks are conducted by interpreters throughout the year, and trail guidebooks are available in the Trail Center. Bicycles allowed on Cape Henry trail only. The park's Bay Store rents bikes. Climate controlled cabins, campsites, picnic areas, a swimming beach, boat ramps and a bicycle trail are offered too. The Chesapeake Bay Center showcases a historical exhibition of the first landing of settlers in 1607, plus aquariums, environmental exhibits, a wet lab and touch tank. It also has supplies and equipment rentals so visitors can participate in programs such as sea kayaking in the Chesapeake Bay. This is one of the most popular state parks in Virginia because of its significance and tourism location.

HUNT CLUB FARM - PETTING FARM

Virginia Beach - 2388 London Bridge Road 23451. (757) 427-9520. Hours: Daily 9:00am-5:00pm (Feb-November). Admission: $15.00 per person, children under 2 are free. Pony rides $10.00 per ride.

Hunt Club Farm's Petting Farm gives visitors an opportunity to visit a wide variety of farm animals. You can chase a chicken, feed a goat, or moo with the cows! Come out and meet llamas, donkeys, cows, sheep, goats, baby goats, chickens, turkeys, guinea hens, roosters, peacocks, swans, ducks, geese, miniature horses, donkeys, rabbits, pot belly pig, cats, dogs and more. They also have a play area, Treewalk Adventure and BirdWalk. Easter Egg Hunt and Fall Pumpkins.

OCEAN BREEZE WATERPARK

Virginia Beach - 849 General Booth Blvd. (1.5 miles south of the resort area, just past the Virginia Marine Science Museum) 23451. Phone: (757) 422-4444 or (800) 678-WILD. www.oceanbreezewaterpark.com. Hours: Park generally opens around 10:00am and closes between 5:00-8:00pm (longer hours when school's out) (Memorial Day-Labor Day) Admission: Online $39-$49 general (ages 10+). Twilight and senior, child and military discounts. Free parking, sunscreen and tubes. Note: Arcade, food court, locker rentals and a Caribbean grill restaurant.

Ocean Breeze Waterpark is Virginia Beach's only water park. Enjoy 19 acres of fun. Choose from winding waterslides, relaxing waves or experience over-the-edge intensity with the new thrill ride THE HURRICANE. Fly from Bamboo Shoots, let the current drift you along the Jungle Falls or explore the pirate ship in the Buccaneer Bay Children's Section. Slither down your choice of 16 water slides, shoot the rapids on an inner tube, or sprawl on the spacious sundeck. Enjoy the waves in a million-gallon Runaway Bay Wave Pool, or enjoy the Paradise Pipeline water slide. For the more adventurous, try the Bahama Mamma speed slide. Or, for leisurely fun, Dive In Movies.

VA BEACH SURF & RESCUE MUSEUM

Virginia Beach - 24th Street & 2401 Atlantic Avenue (just off the boardwalk) 23451. Phone: (757) 422-1587. https://vbsurfrescuemuseum.org/ Hours: Monday-Saturday 10am-5pm, Sunday Noon-5:00pm (spring & summer). Closed Mondays rest of year. Closed major winter holidays. Admission: $5.00-$8.00 (ages 6+).

The restored 1903 Lifesaving/Coast Guard station traces life-saving and Guard services in history. The quaint museum is probably most noted for artifacts and displays about shipwrecks that have occurred off the coast. Don't leave without taking a peek through TOWERCAM, a roof-mounted video camera that zooms in on passing ships dotting the horizon (can also be viewed from home at: www.vabeach.com). The camera transmits its pictures to a television monitor, affording museum visitors the same view crewmen had from the tower nearly 100 years ago.

VIRGINIA AQUARIUM

Virginia Beach - 717 General Booth Blvd. (I-64 exit Rte. 44 east, get off on the Birdneck Road exit and head south) 23451. www.VirginiaAquarium.com. Phone: (757) 425-FISH. Hours: Daily 9:00am-5:00pm. Closed Thanksgiving and Christmas. Admission: $29.95 adult, $24.95 senior (65+) and child (5-17), $22.95 military. IMAX films are $7.95 each or discounted if combo tickets purchased. Note: IMAX films are show several times daily with subjects of whales, dolphins, dinosaurs and nature. Adventure Park Zip/Climb (3 hr $31-$56). The Osprey Café offers breakfast, lunch and snack items. There are two museum stores. Getting Here: VB Wave Trolleys regularly make stops at the Bay & Ocean Pavilion and Marsh Pavilion. Educators: Try one of several On Your Own Worksheets online on the Teachers Page. Discovery Days and Camps year-round.

The marine museum takes visitors on a journey of water through different habitats. Aquarium visitors are taken on two journeys: a journey across water that focuses on the diverse natural habitats across Virginia today and a journey through the habitats of Virginia's past. You'll find "touch tanks" around seemingly every turn in this museum. Does a stingray really feel like wet bologna? What do a horseshoe crab's mouth and a toothbrush have in common?

RESTLESS PLANET: - Immersive habitats look, feel, sound and smell like a

South East Area

Malaysian peat swamp, a coastal desert, the Red Sea and an active volcano.

CHESAPEAKE BAY AQUARIUM - houses the largest collection of Chesapeake bay fish in the world, 30 species in all, so you're bound to see something new or different. Look for the fish with the human-like bucked teeth!

ATLANTIC OCEAN PAVILION - explore the depths of the open ocean with sharks, sea turtles, jellies, lobster and stingrays. Here is where you'll find the 300,000 gallon aquarium which re-creates the Norfolk Canyon. Look for the funny "follow the leader" schools of fish, watch sea turtle hatchlings, or interact at oceanographic exhibits. Understand simple exhibits like sand scapes and waves & water. Build-your-own hurricane and tong for oysters.

MARSH PAVILION - focuses on plants and animals in a salt marsh that is the last undeveloped salt marsh in Virginia with direct access to the ocean. Get there by walking the one-third mile long nature trail. In the pavilion, you'll love to watch the antics of a live river otter habitat with over and underwater viewing; an aviary and insect micro marsh; and live jellyfish from around the world, a giant Pacific octopus and a touch pool with Indo-Pacific invertebrates. Don't miss the Secret Life of Owls Creek 9-minute film that introduces you to what appears to be a muddy, murky environment.

RUDEE BOAT TRIPS

200 Winston Salem Ave 23451. (757) 425-3400 Adm: $28.95 per person with reservations. Tours: several tours daily, by reservations. Highly recommended! Where do playful bottlenose dolphins go for summer vacation? Where do juvenile humpback whales winter? Virginia Beach is a regular visitation spot for these, and other marine animals. Seasonal boat trips lasting 30 minutes (Pontoon Cruises along Creek) to 2 hours are educational and eventful. Trips leave from Rudee Inlet Fishing Center (one mile down the road from the AQUARIUM) mornings and afternoons, and, while dolphin or whale sightings aren't guaranteed, you'll for sure see some historic landmarks and take samplings of ocean marine life collected, displayed in temporary tanks and then released back. All that watery excitement and you don't have to get wet. We saw over 60 dolphins on our early morning trip (July & August are the best months for dolphin). Even babies (that little fin is so-o-o cute!) and pods (groups) fishing. When in the area, please fit a boat trip into your plans. You'll find screams of excitement and education about "dolphin family groups" at the same time. It's also a great, relaxing way for parents to recover before beginning the next adventure.

VIRGINIA BEACH BOARDWALK

Virginia Beach - 1st thru 40th Streets, along Atlantic Avenue 23451. Phone: (800) 822-3224. www.vabeach.com/virginia-beach-boardwalk

This resort city features family attractions, outdoor recreation, year-round events, 28 miles of beaches, a boardwalk/resort area and a diverse selection of restaurants and shopping. Stretching from Rudee Inlet on the south end of the resort area up to 40th Street. Lifeguards are on duty from mid-May to mid-September, 9:30am-6:00pm. Permanent restrooms are adjacent to the boardwalk at 17th, 24th, and 30th Streets and open all year. They do not contain changing facilities. Foot showers are available along the oceanfront. Parasailing, bicycle and surfing providers ticket booths line the boardwalk shops. Oceanfront pilots free summer shuttle service. Riders hail the compact Freebee vehicles via a mobile app and can enjoy courtesy transportation throughout the oceanfront district for twelve hours daily.

Beachstreet USA is comprised of a diverse array of street performers along the sidewalks of Atlantic Avenue from 17th to 25th Streets from 8:00pm-11:30pm nightly (midnight on summer weekends!). Puppets, bands, jugglers, magicians, and others entertain on the sidewalks of Atlantic Avenue! Live concerts & theatrical productions take place seven nights a week from 6:00-11:00pm on stages at 7th, 13th, 17th, 24th, and 25th Streets along the oceanfront.

<u>Virginia Beach Amusement Park</u> is on the Boardwalk at 15th Street. Full-scale rides include roller coasters, ferris wheels, games of chance and picnic tables. Arcades, go carts and mini-golf complexes are on or just off Atlantic Ave.

ATLANTIC COAST KITE FESTIVAL

Virginia Beach - Oceanfront, 17th Street Park. (800) 822-3224. April is National Kite Month. Appropriate for all ages, the Atlantic Coast Kite Festival combines several unique activities into a day-long festival held right on the beach. Featured activities include kite demonstrations and ballets, kite building, and lessons on flying all sorts of kites. Prizes will be awarded for kite building and kite flying skills! (last weekend of April)

STARS & STRIPES EXPLOSION

Virginia Beach - Beachside. Inspiring concerts, rock performances, tribute bands, fireworks, and more featured at this annual Hampton Roads held on Independence Day! A rousing concert by Virginia Beach Symphony Orchestra - Almost 80 musicians, all volunteers, play combined with the Virginia Beach Chorale. free event. (July 4th)

FALSE CAPE STATE PARK & BACK BAY NATIONAL WILDLIFE REFUGE

Virginia Beach - 4001 Sandpiper Road (5 miles south of Sandbridge, no vehicular access) 23456. www.dcr.virginia.gov/state_parks/fal.shtml. Phone: (757) 426-7128 or (757) 721-2412. Hours: Trials & Refuge: Daily, Dawn-Dusk. Visitor Stations: Monday-Friday 8:00am-4:00pm and Weekends 9:00am-4:00pm (April-September). Open again after the 1st week of October through the end of October. Admission: $5.00 per vehicle entrance fee. Tram fees: $8.00 adult, $6.00 child (under 18) and senior. FREE for child able to sit in parent's lap. Tours: Tram service is a 4 hour tour departing Tuesday, Thursday - Sunday from Little Island Park at 9:00am. (April-October). Reservations needed (757) 498-BIRD. Winter Terra Gator tours are $8.00 per person.

This 4,321-acre area is a mile-wide barrier split between Back Bay and the Atlantic Ocean, in the extreme southeast corner of Virginia Beach. It has 6 miles of unspoiled beaches, 12 primitive campsites, and 7.5 miles of hiking / biking trails. The park also features Wash Woods Center - an extensive environmental educational program and group overnight facility in one of the last undisturbed coastal environments on the East Coast. To get a taste of the park, the Back Bay operates a tram that leaves from Little Island City Park, drives through the wildlife refuge and lets visitors explore the park for two hours in the Barbour Hill area. Summers are full of birds, Fall lures concentrations of waterfowl, shorebirds and raptors. Approximately 10,000 snow geese and a large variety of ducks visit Back Bay Refuge during the peak of fall migration, usually in December. A stopover at False Cape allows you to climb one of two observation towers located in the park entrance for bird watching.

MILITARY AVIATION MUSEUM

Virginia Beach - 1341 Princess Anne Road, Virginia Beach, VA 23457. www.militaryaviationmuseum.org. Hours: Daily 9am-5pm. Admission: $7.50-$15.00.

The Military Aviation Museum, located at the Virginia Beach Airport is home to one of the largest private collections of World War 2 and Korean War era fighters, bombers, trainers and seaplanes. Many aircraft have been restored to their World War II condition and are available for flight demonstration*, static display or movie production or commercials. The Fighter Factory is the aircraft recovery and restoration component of the museum dedicated to the preservation of historical aircraft before they are lost forever. To view the current fleet of aircraft online, you can visit the Fighter Factory website. Guided tours occur four times daily. *Aircraft are not always available for flight demonstrations. For inquiries, please call 757-721-PROP.

NAVAL AIR STATION OCEANA

Virginia Beach - Oceana Blvd. (only open to employees and tour vehicles) 23460. Phone: (757) 433-3131. www.cnic.navy.mil/Oceana.

One of the Navy's four master jet bases, it is home to 19 aviation squadrons, including the F-14 Tomcat fighter planes and the A-6 Intruder medium attack bombers. The Aviation Historical Park located just inside the Main Gate on Tomcat Blvd is open daily to military and DOD employees and people on the base tour. Park includes 13 aircraft on display. Watch training sequences, too. There are two observation parks located near the runways to watch aircraft take-off and land. One is located on Oceana Boulevard at the POW/MIA memorial, and the other is off London Bridge road on the opposite side of the air station (blue circles).

NEPTUNE FESTIVAL / OCEANA AIR SHOW

Virginia Beach - Oceana Naval Station. www.oceanaairshow.com. (757) 427-8000. Visitors thrill to the sight of aerobic stunts, vintage warbirds and modern military aircraft. Internationally known flying teams. Admission. (September weekend)

MOUNT TRASHMORE PARK

Virginia Beach - 310 Edwin Drive (off I-264 west) 23462. www.vbgov.com/parks. Phone: (757) 473-5237.

World-renowned Mount Trashmore Park is 165 acres, 60 feet high, over 800 feet long, and was created by compacting layers of solid waste and clean soil. Recognized for its environmental feat, the park features the Water Wise demonstration garden that boasts xeriscaping where you can learn how to create a beautiful garden with minimal water requirements. Park is open from 7:30am until sunset. Facilities include picnic shelters, playground areas, basketball court, volleyball areas, parking, vending machines and restrooms, plus an extensive street course Skate Park which includes a seven-foot deep bowl and a massive 13.5 ft tall vert ramp. The park also has a walking trail that measures approximately 1.45 miles. Trail maps are available at Park Office. No private boats are allowed on this lake, but fishing is allowed.

AIRFIELD 4-H CENTER

Wakefield - 15189 Airfield Road (I-95 to Rte. 460) 23888. Phone: (757) 899-4901. www.airfieldconference.com. Admission: Lodging ranges $15.00-$40.00 per person each night. Wildlife tours and Challenge Course are additional small fee. Most recreational facilities are included in lodging or group fees. Note: Food catering available.

For updates visit: www.KidsLoveTravel.com

The Airfield Center is located on 113 scenic and wooded acres, surrounded by a 105 acre lake. Recreation facilities include: Olympic size outdoor swimming pool, Fishing on the lake (state license required), outdoor tennis courts, Campfire circle, Softball, Canoes, Nature trail, Paddle boats, Horseshoes, Basketball, and 100 stalls for horse show functions plus two rings with outdoor lighting. You can also sign up for Wildlife Tours: includes a unique variety of animals and the Challenge Course: a combination of obstacle course activities, coupled with individual and group initiatives.

MILES B. CARPENTER MUSEUM COMPLEX

Waverly - 201 Hunter Street (Rte. 460 west near Rte. 40) 23890. Phone: (804) 834-3327. http://milesbcarpentermuseum.com/ Hours: Open Daily except Tuesday and Wednesday 2:00-5:00pm. Admission: FREE. Note: Herb Garden, Art Studio (sign up for programs with folk artists) and nature trail. See local folk art and visiting artists and exhibits at the annual Folk Art Festival on Mothers Day weekend.

> Located in a Victorian house, you'll see that Mr. Carpenter's whittled work is folksy and is best known for "the watermelon with a bite".

This cute, small town museum complex is run by retired townsfolk who personally knew Mr. Carpenter (or worked in the peanut or woodworking industry). Begin in the Miles B. Carpenter Home and Museum. As you walk from room to room, you'll see many of Mr. Carpenter's whimsical wooden carvings. We found his animal and people figurines were the best. By taking a branch or limb from a tree, he formed snakes, birds, and funny looking people - just from some rough carving and paint. (The kids will certainly get some new ideas about crafting here!) Next, visit the first peanut museum in America. Here, you'll actually see how peanuts grow (really...did you know that they grew underground?) and are harvested (then & now). The original seeds came from Peru in 1830, but a hearty seed (the heart of the peanut) was grown until 1842 in Waverly? Finally, walk inside the Wood Products Museum and see different species of wood. What started as a sawmill eventually became Mr. Carpenter's famous workshop.

Williamsburg

WATERCOUNTRY USA

Williamsburg - 176 Water Country Pkwy (off Rte. 50, follow signs) 23147. Phone: (757) 253-3350 or (800) 4ADVENTURE. www.watercountryusa.com. Hours: Weekends (May, September). Daily (Memorial Weekend to Labor Day). Park opens at 10:00am (May to mid-September). Admission: $65.99 per person. Save w/ advance flex tickets. Note: Gift shops, food service, picnic pavilion, locker rental, bathhouse and free use of life vests and inner tubes.

Water Country USA is the largest outdoor waterpark in the mid-Atlantic and features state-of-the-art water rides and attractions, entertainment, shopping and restaurants - all set in a colorful 1950s and '60s surf theme. More than 1,000 lounge chairs are available throughout for parents to rest. Several pools are climate-controlled for comfort. They start with a classic Wave Pool but add an Aquatic Dive Show. There's the easy-goin' Hubba Hubba Highway and wild Big Daddy Falls with plenty of flumes and tunnels in between. Other popular activities include the obstacle course, Adventure Isle. Also, slide over to the Tots area, superspeed Beach Blanket Slide, 4 person high speed toboggan, dark tunnel tube rides, sci-fi kids interactive area, whitewater rafting, 2 person flume ride, surf boggans, lazy river floating or the other classics - waterslides and twisty tubes. Our favorites: the Wave Pool and Lazy River encourage life jackets vs. traditional tubes for floating. The water and grounds are super clean and the staff very friendly, too.

KINGSMILL RESORT

Williamsburg - 1010 Kingsmill Road 23185. Phone: (757) 253-1703 or (800) 832-5665. www.kingsmill.com.

Upon checking into one of their villa room (s), the kids can pick up a "kid's fun map" to all the activities they offer (especially in the summer). Kingsmill Kampers is for kids ages 5-12 (all day or half day) and Junior Kampers for preschoolers ages 3-4. Different sports are played, also crafts, cooking, reading, and meals provided for a fee. Some nights (especially weekends) they have "Kids Night Out" where parents can enjoy an evening out while the kids have supervised play like the Game Room, Beach Party, Pool Party, or Nite Golf (with glow in the dark balls). We also loved the Treasure Hunt around the property, pool games, poolside bingo on Sundays and they even offer complimentary golf, tennis and fishing clinics for the young-uns. Great "family-friendly" eats at Elements and deli market. This great location is just a shuttle drive away from Busch Gardens, Water County, and Williamsburg. Many family packages include admission (unlimited) and meal to Busch Gardens/ Water Country and greens/court fees (around $300.00 per night for family stay). A great place also to settle in and enjoy top-notch sports facilities.

BUSCH GARDENS WILLIAMSBURG

Williamsburg - US 60 (I-64 exit 242A) 23187. Phone: (757) 253-3350 or (800) 832-5665. www.buschgardens.com. Hours: Park Opens at 10:00am, closing times vary seasonally between 6:00pm-11:00pm (peak season June-August with latest closing times daily). Open weekends only in late March, early April, September and October. See website for exact times. Admission: ~$100 for general all inclusive admission. Good online discount tickets. Flex Combos with Water Country USA. Parking fee. Note: Picnic areas are located in each parking lot. Picnics and coolers may not be taken in the park.

The European-themed adventure park is an action-packed park with 17th century charm and the technology and conveniences of the modern age. All the 50+ thrill or kiddie rides are based on the theme of the area you are journeying through. By the way, parents, you'll love the well-maintained landscapes and clean facilities, not to mention, the yummy European-themed food concessions and restaurant food! Here's the six European areas you'll visit:

IRELAND, KILLARNEY - Virtual Reality Ride (a white-knuckle, 4-D adventure ride through mythical Celtic lore of a land of giants where you become one of the main characters!); or powerful dance production celebrating Irish heritage; or resident leprechaun roaming act; Irish fare of corned beef, smashed potatoes, soda bread and Irish stew.

SCOTLAND, HEATHERDOWNS - Loch Ness Monster steel roller coaster with interlocking loops; Highland Stables, home to the famous Clydesdales horses; Li'l Clydes kiddie ride.

ENGLAND, BANBURY CROSS - Aeronaut Skyride is a scenic aerial tour of the park; Royal Preserve and Menagerie Petting Zoo offers guests viewing and contact with miniature breeds; the Globe Theatre has a changingadventure film that puts guests in the middle of the action. SESAME STREET FOREST OF FUN is nearby and a great play park designed for youngins. Animals: Greystone Tower viewing of gray wolves' unique habits; Lorikeet Glen where guests become perches as the brilliant birds land on arms, shoulders and heads; and Eagle Ridge sanctuary for American balk eagles presentations.

KIDS LOVE VIRGINIA

FRANCE - test drive classic European race cars through tunnels and across bridges at Le Mans Raceway; The Royal Palace Theatre showcases entertainment on selected summer evenings. The floorless coaster, Griffon, is here for the brave. Shows combine favorite Canadian dances and music from the 50's to today.

GERMANY, OKTOBERFEST - Bavarian hamlet has the Big Bad Wolf, a suspended roller coaster and many cute, creative kiddie rides dot; "Oktoberfest" has a cast of musicians and dancers celebrating. Guests may dance and sing along.

GERMANY, RHINEFELD - cruise down the Rhine to rides including Alpengeist inverted steel roller coaster, Land of Dragons magical play area designed for kiddies, Kinder Karussel antique merry-go-round, march along with "the Boogie Band"; many sweet treats are available here too. This will probably be the younger kids favorite play, climb, and crawl place.

ITALY, FESTA ITALIA - home to the high-speed hypercoaster, Apollo's Chariot and several festive themed rides and games including Roman Rapids white-water raft journey through choppy waters, raging water falls and geysers.

ITALY, SAN MARCO - tour the ruins of Mt. Vesuvius on Escape from Pompeii thrilling water ride with special effects; Da Vinci's Garden of Inventions features rides for children like the Flying Machine and the Battering Ram.

COLONIAL WILLIAMSBURG

Williamsburg - 101 Visitor Center Drive 23185. Phone: (800) HISTORY or (757) 220-7645 or (757) 229-7193 for theme tours. www.colonialwilliamsburg.org. Hours: Daily 9:00am-5:00pm but may vary by season and special evening events. Admission: Average $35.99 adult, $19.99 child (6-12) Day Pass;  Discounts online and during Winter season. Without admission, you may only enter the shops and taverns selling wares. Note: Start at the Visitors Center to get oriented, otherwise it will be a chaotic day. Make reservations for tavern

South East Area

meals and evening programs upon arrival. Evening programs, children's tours, and special events are particularly fun for repeat guests. We know one family that regularly visit and promise the best way to do it is to stay overnight in one of the historic homes on site. They like the ease of parking and discount access to evening programs and meals. School-aged kids and parents will like the 35 minute film "Williamsburg-The Story of a Patriot" to get "in the mood". Strollers welcome or can be rented on first come, first serve basis. Be sure to pick up the guide for families (a simple brochure to steer you in the right direction). With the help of the Colonial Williamsburg Explorer app, creating an adventure has never been easier. Educators: Excellent "Learn" pages with online games and Lesson Plans & Research Materials for teachers.

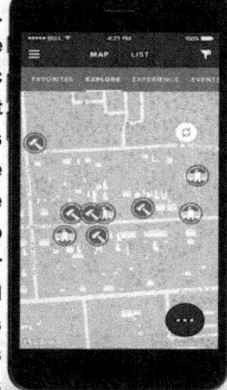

Explore a typical day in the life of an 18th century child blending English and Colonial cultures and, Revolution. Costumed characters ply their trades and re-enact and interpret aspects of colonial life. Tour the Costume Design Center and Millinery to see the effort they put into authenticity (you can even rent costumes for the day!). Discuss the day's chores, independence and freedom with "People of the Past" at the Capitol or get the highlights of the final days of the last royal governor at the Palace. Lots of leisurely games - like lawn bowling and tops - can be played on the side lawn. Be sure to try the Garden Maze while in this area as well. At the Wythe House, go around back to visit with the slave cook or visit the stable and laundry.

Many buildings house trades that kids can help with like: the Geddy Site (craft brass, bronze, silver and pewter), the Carpenter's Brickyard (help knead clay that is molded into bricks), and the Fire Engine bucket brigade. Grab your tricorn hat and head to the Peyton Randolph Yard for Patriots at Play! This interactive program offers fun, hands-on activities that immerse children in 18th-century life (including chores!).

Song and Dance are heard and seen throughout the day with special storytelling, dance and music of African-Americans; 18th century dance by youth where, once demonstrated, kids can participate; Palace Green musicians; and the Fife & Drum Corps perform in parades.

Four taverns explore the connection between 18th century foodways and operation of eating establishments. Each tavern offers 18th century lunch and dinner menus served in authentic colonial surroundings (George Washington's favorite spot was the Campbell's Tavern). Check out an 18th century "time out" spot at the stockade (good photo ops) or step inside the courthouse for a mock trial.

Words of advice: First, be sure to plan on a full (9:00am-5:00pm) day. This is the only way to visit with the characters of the day and tour all the buildings that interest you. Second, as soon as the children are "involved", purchase or rent them hats (and maybe clothes) - you'll be amazed at how much more they learn "in character". Third, characters like "Martha Washington" help (she invited us to "sit for a spell" and taught the children morals and manners plus gave us the "skinny" on Thomas Jefferson!). The house cooks also really give you the best interpretations on a kid's level and teach about the tasks of the day. We learned all about the meals of the day - midday being the largest, followed by leftovers at supper and breakfast the next day. Fourth, if you want to snack, purchase some tavern rolls and apple cider and eat like fellow colonists.

JULY 4TH CELEBRATION

A salute to the 13 colonies, a reading of the Declaration of Independence, a garden party at the governor's Palace and a fireworks display as a finale. Admission.

100 MILES OF LIGHTS

In colonial Williamsburg, celebrate with holiday programs, tours, concerts, feasts, illuminations and incredible decorations along with the annual holiday exhibit of antique toys. The magic of the season comes to life with enchanting holiday décor and an extraordinary cast of musicians, singers and dancers. Special Kids Only activities planned. Admission fee. (Thanksgiving weekend thru January 1)

GREAT WOLF LODGE INDOOR WATERPARK RESORT

Williamsburg - 549 East Rochambeau Drive (I64, take the Lightfoot/Route 199 exit, 234 or 234(A). On Rte. 199, take the second Mooretown Road exit. At first light, turn left) 23188. Phone: (800) 905-WOLF. www.greatwolflodge.com. Note: MagiQuest interactive Treasure Hunt game. Wipeout- Preteens and up may want to try this - you'll be surprised how well they do. The new activities are geared towards the kids that are getting too big to just splash.

Forecast predicting rain or cool temps? Who cares - the 301-suite destination, Great Wolf Lodge has an array of amenities including: a huge indoor Waterpark, an Arcade, Cub Club activity/crafts room, Spa (with teen ice cream

spa treatments), Ropes Course, Mini-golf, 4D movies, Fitness Room, Pizza & snack concessions, The Loose Moose Bar & Grille gourmet buffet and food court, Claw Café confectionery and an animated Great Clock Tower to greet you. The full-service resort is designed to capture the atmosphere and adventure of the northwoods. What you'll notice as parents is the casual resort layout that is clean, cozy and all family. Although they do have a hot tub area for adults only, everything else is about the kids (or the kid in you!). Attractions at the 84-degree indoor waterpark include eight waterslides, six pools, a tipping bucket, a giant indoor wave pool and a new four-person raft ride. Our kids especially loved the Gigantic indoor wave pool and water toy areas. Both had comfortable water temps. We liked the family tube slide but it was scary being in total darkness the whole time - best for the adventuresome craving an edge to normal water rides. The Cub Club activity sheet is given to each patron upon check-in. Many of the all day activities are really fun for the young ones and the evening storytime by the giant fireplace is something to look forward to. Want a real treat and lots of space? Try the Loft Fireplace Suite. It sleeps 6-8 and the loft offers parents some privacy. Seasonal Specials. Rates (include admission to waterpark) for lodging run $199-$300 per night depending on package.

SNOWLAND

Williamsburg - Great Wolf Lodge. The lodge is decorated in a winter scene. It snows 3x daily, hot cocoa and live music, clock tower sing along, Rowdy the Reindeer Storytime. Attend the North Pole University for Elves. Admission (includes lodging and indoor waterpark passes). (month-long in December)

YORK RIVER STATE PARK

Williamsburg - 5526 Riverview Road (I-64 to Croaker exit, north on SR 607 to SR 606) 23188. Phone: (757) 566-3036. www.dcr.state.va.us/parks/yorkrive.htm. Admission: $5.00 per vehicle. Note: Visitors Center plus more than 20 miles of hiking, biking and equestrian trails to explore a marsh up close. Boat ramp, fishing (fresh & saltwater), picnicking, and seasonal bike and boat rentals.

This park is known for its rare and delicate environment where freshwater and saltwater meet to create a habitat rich in marine and plant life. Taskinas Creek and the surrounding marsh are designated as a Chesapeake Bay National Estuarine Research Reserve. Activities here focus on the history and preservation of the York River and its marshes.

BERKELEY PLANTATION

Williamsburg (Charles City) - 12602 Harrison Landing Road (off SR 5 west) 23030. Phone: (804) 829-6018. www.berkeleyplantation.com. Hours: Daily 9:30am-4:30pm (mid-March thru Jan 1). Shorter winter hours. Closed Thanksgiving and Christmas Day. Admission: $16 adult, $14.50 senior (60+), $7.50 student (6-12).

This is the site of the first official Thanksgiving in 1619 (two years before the Pilgrims in Massachusetts.). It is also the ancestral home of two U.S. Presidents: Benjamin Harrison V, a signer of the Declaration of Independence and William Henry Harrison, ninth President. "Taps" was composed here in 1862 during the Civil War. The original Georgian mansion, built in 1726 of brick fired on the plantation, occupies a beautifully landscaped hilltop site overlooking the historic James River. Knowledgeable and enthusiastic guides in period costumes conduct tours of the original 1726 mansion, furnished with a grand collection of 18th century antiques. The tour includes an audio-visual program and museum.

FIRST THANKSGIVING FESTIVAL

Williamsburg (Charles City) - Celebrate the 1619 landing of the original colonists at Berkeley Plantation. Join them at the site of the First Official Thanksgiving in America, for a day dedicated to history, food and fun with tours of the 1726 manor house, walks in the colorful autumn gardens and a formal living history program. Admission. (first weekend in November)

South East Area 195

CENTURIES OF CHRISTMAS AT BERKELEY PLANTATION
Williamsburg (Charles City) - The elegant 1726 mansion will be beautifully decorated with fresh greenery from Berkeley's gardens for special tours. Costumed guides will add a special touch to your holiday season with stories of Christmas at Berkeley through four centuries of history. (first Saturday in December thru January 1)

SHERWOOD FOREST PLANTATION
Williamsburg (Charles City) - 14501 John Tyler Hwy. (I-295 south to exit #22A heading east on SR 5 for 10 miles) 23030. www.sherwoodforest.org. Phone: (804) 829-5377. Hours: Open daily 9:00am-5:00pm, except Thanksgiving and Christmas. Admission: $10.00 adult (age 16+) for self guided grounds tour. Tours: Guided tours of the president's big house by registration and payment ($25.00-$35.00).

This house was the home of the 10th President, John Tyler (1841-1845) and the Tyler family since 1842. It is known to be the longest frame house in America and the tour features mid-19th century plantation life. Ten points of interest are included in the self-guided tour of the grounds and original out-buildings. Look for the ancient tree plantings (1850 ginkgo), the ballroom, the milk house and the restored slave house on tour.

SHIRLEY PLANTATION
Williamsburg (Charles City) - 501 Shirley Plantation Road (I-295 south to exit #22A heading east on SR 5 for 10 miles) 23030. Phone: (804) 829-5121. www.shirleyplantation.com. Hours: Daily 9:30am-4:00pm. Closed Thanksgiving, Easter, and Christmas Days and winter months. Tours: Grounds and outbuildings $11 adult, $9.50 senior (60+) and military, $7.50 student (7-16). Guided tour of Home: $25 adult, $22.50 senior (60+), $17.50 youth (7-16), $20 military.

Shirley was founded six years after the settlers arrived at Jamestown in 1607 to establish the first permanent English Colony in the New World. It was granted to Edward Hill I in 1660. The famous square-rigged, flying staircase rises three stories with no visible means of support and is the only one of its kind in America. During the Revolution, this plantation served as a supply center for the Continental Army. During the Civil War, Shirley survived two Campaigns.

Ann Hill Carter, mother of Robert E. Lee, was born and raised at Shirley (she married Henry "Light-Horse Harry" Lee in the parlor). Outbuildings include a large two-story kitchen house, laundry house, and two L-shaped barns, one with the ice cellar beneath it, stable, smokehouse and root cellar. The original early 18th century kitchen has new interpretation that sheds light on the lives of slaves and house servants. An archaeology room showcases 40 years of excavations. Archeological excavations are ongoing seasonally.

CHICKAHOMINY POW-WOW/FALL FESTIVAL

Williamsburg (Charles City) - Native Americans from all over will join the Chickahominy Tribe for their annual pow-wow on the Tribal Grounds in Charles City featuring Native American dancers, drummers, traditional crafters, historical and cultural demonstrations, food and more. This is the longest running traditional pow-wow in Virginia, dating back to 1951. This is a family-friendly educational and cultural event. Free. Web site: www.chickahominytribe.org. (September, third weekend)

HISTORIC JAMESTOWNE

Williamsburg (Jamestown) - 1368 Colonial Parkway (I-64 exit 242A, Rte. 199 west to Colonial Pkwy or Rte. 31 via the Jamestown Ferry) 23185. www.nps.gov/colo/. Phone: (757) 229-1733. Hours: 9:00am-5:00pm daily except Thanksgiving, Christmas and New Years. Admission: $15.00 adult (16+). Weeklong pass to the site and Yorktown Battlefield. Note: Nearby, the ruins of the original glass furnace of 1608 may be seen and glassblowing demos are given regularly by costumed craftsmen in a re-created period type glasshouse. Educators: The most popular programs for kids are their Colonial Junior Ranger or Pinch Pot Programs. Kids can make their own clay pinch pot (takes 20 minutes) daily in the summer. Use the same techniques as Pocahontas did as written by Captain John Smith in his journal (this is a wonderful, hand-made souvenir). Educators: www.wjcc.k12.va.us/tahg/sites/jamestowne.html.

This is the actual ORIGINAL site of the first permanent English settlement in the New World. You can explore Jamestowne in many ways. If you are the athletic type you can walk, run or bike the three/five mile loop drive of the island. The five mile Island Loop road winds through 1500 acres of woodland and marsh, looking much as it would have in the 1600s. Interactive museum exhibits tell the story of Jamestown's 92 years as the early capital of Virginia, including the arrival and melting of three cultures – the Virginia Indians, English and Africans. An audio-visual "immersion" experience provides a multi-media overview of Jamestown's rich history and personalities in a 180-degree theater setting. Another museum on the property, The Archaearium (literally, "a place for archaeology"), showcases artifacts and findings of the Jamestown Rediscovery archaeological excavation that has uncovered the site of the original 1607 James Fort. Under unique glass structures, visitors are able to see excavated areas of Jamestown's last Statehouse underneath their feet, and view re-created 17th century landscapes through virtual viewers overlooking the site. The skeleton room is really interesting. See what detective work goes into new "finds." Try to figure out clues to determine JR's death (a skeleton named the Jamestown Recovery dude). Any time you visit, we highly recommend the Park Ranger or Living History tours. It's a quick study of the fascinating and true stories about John Smith and Pocahontas. Afterwards, observe the excavations going on and maybe do a cartwheel in the fort yard, just like Pocahontas used to do. All the ground you walk on is historic dirt formed from the earth and artifacts left behind. Use your imagination here... Pocahontas and the Colonial settlers will probably appear in your dreams that night!

JAMESTOWN SETTLEMENT

Williamsburg (Jamestown) - PO Box 1607 (I-64 exit 242A, between SR 31 and Colonial Pkwy) 23185. www.historyisfun.org. Phone: (757) 253-4838. Hours: 9:00am-5:00pm daily, until 6:00pm (mid-June to mid-August). Closed on New Years and Christmas. Admission: $18.00 adult, $9.00 child (6-12). Combo ticket with Yorktown Center add only $6.00-$12.00.

Jamestown Settlement tells the story of Jamestown, America's first permanent English Colony, from its beginnings in Europe through the first century of its existence. The museum has two elements: American Evolution: an indoor theater and exhibits (they are very engaging and present wonderful historical facts and artifacts) which orient guests to the time and place recreated outside the center. Now that you're oriented, board the Discovery, Godspeed and Susan Constant, re-creations of the three ships that colonists navigated across the Atlantic during their four-month winter voyage to the New World. It's fun watching the kids try to imagine a journey (yet alone across the ocean) in these wonderful reproductions. Explore a re-created Powhatan Indian village and a re-created fort built by the Jamestown colonists. A 4D experiential theater and a new interactive exhibit allows visitors to delve into Pocahontas's life and legend. Costumed interpreters invite kids to climb into a sailor's bunk (or steer the rudder and help set sail); grind corn (then make cornbread pancakes or grind shells to make beads); make cordage (from hemp) in an Indian village; try on armor and play a game of Quoits in a colonial fort. Kids can also try their hand at 17th century map-making, navigation and ship design in the gallery hall.

JAMESTOWN LANDING DAY

Jamestown Landing or the Original Site. Sailing demonstrations and interpretive activities explore contact between English colonists and American Indian cultures on this anniversary of the founding of America's first permanent English colony. Special tickets. (May, second Saturday)

COLONIAL CHRISTMAS

Jamestown Settlement & Yorktown. Holiday traditions of 17th and 18th-century Virginia are recalled through special interpretive programs. At Jamestown Settlement, a film and guided tours compare and contrast English Christmas customs of the period with how the season may have been observed in the difficult early years of the Jamestown colony. (Thanksgiving week thru early January)

AMERICAN REVOLUTION MUSEUM AT YORKTOWN

Williamsburg (Yorktown) - PO Box 1607 (I-64 to Exit 247. Turn left onto Route 143. Turn left at the first traffic light, onto Route 238) 23187. Phone: (757) 253-4838 or (888) 593-4682. www.historyisfun.org. Hours: Daily 9:00am-5:00pm, until 6:00pm in the summer. Admission: $18.00 adult, $9.00 child (6-12). Combo pricing with Jamestown Settlement available. Educators: Teacher Packets and Lesson Plans online under Learn (cover the period well with a variety of different approaches).

The Yorktown Victory Center has transformed into the AMERICAN REVOLUTION MUSEUM at YORKTOWN. The museum presents a renewed national perspective on the meaning and impact of the Revolution through an introductory film, timeline, expansive gallery exhibits, interactive displays and an experiential theater, and new settings for hands-on interpretive experiences in expanded re-creations of a Continental Army encampment and Revolution-era farm.

They use Witness Gallery - wonderful short stories - as seen through the eyes of ordinary men and women of the time. Characterized by life-size cast figures, graphics and artifacts representative of their lives, the witnesses include two African-American slaves who supported opposite sides, a Mohawk chief who struggled to remain neutral, and a Virginia plantation owner loyal to Britain. "Yorktown's Sunken Fleet" area has a re-creation of the bow portion of the excavation site of the British supply ship Betsy. Kids can try on 18th century clothing in "A Children's Kaleidoscope" discovery room (games and schooling...the young ones will want to spend at least a half hour here!).

Outdoors, visitors can join a cannon crew, see the crews "kitchen in the dirt", and learn about 18th century medical care (ex. blood letting) in a Continental Army encampment. Visitors can explore the soldiers' tents and try on a military coat, and are sometimes recruited to participate in drills with wooden muskets or serve on an artillery crew. The re-created 1780s farm completes a museum visit. Kids can water and weed the garden at a 1780s farm (and smell the cooking over the open-hearth), or view an archeological excavation site. You'll fully understand this point of history by attending the orientation film. Set in an encampment at night during the Siege of Yorktown, the film dramatizes the musings and recollections of an array of individuals.

LIBERTY CELEBRATION

Yorktown Center. Tactical drills, military exercises and role-playing demonstrations salute America during the Fourth of July holiday. Visitors can learn about the sacrifices of our nation's founders, including those who signed the Declaration of Independence. (July 4th weekend)

YORKTOWN VICTORY

Yorktown Center. (888) 593-4682. Anniversary of Washington's victory over the British at Yorktown. Parade, tactical demos, encampment, hands-on activities, walking tours. Some free, some admission. (October, third weekend)

A COLONIAL CHRISTMAS

Yorktown Center. Holiday traditions of 17th and 18th-century Virginia. At Jamestown Settlement, a film and guided tours compare and contrast English Christmas customs of the period with how the season may have been observed in the difficult early years of the Jamestown colony. At the Yorktown Victory Center, hear accounts of Christmas and winter in military encampments during the American Revolution and glimpse holiday preparations on a 1780s Virginia farm. (Thanksgiving thru early Jan)

ALLIANCE TALL SHIP DAY SAILS

Williamsburg (Yorktown) - 425 Water Street (Riverwalk Landing Pier) 23690. Phone: (757) 639-1233. www.sailyorktown.com. Tours: 3 times daily morning, afternoon and evening (April - October). $41.00 adult, $31.00 child (12 and under). Evening sunset cruises may be extra with no child discount in June and July.

The Tall Ship ALLIANCE is a 105' gaff topsail schooner that takes daily sailing cruises from Riverwalk Landing Pier in historic Yorktown. This is your opportunity to explore the Chesapeake Bay tidewaters for a few hours. Join the tallship and step back into history aboard this three masted schooner as she sails down the York River under a cloud of canvas. Or, try a family Pirate Cruise aboard the SERENITY and get to dress up, raise sails, steer the ship or fire a cannon.

WATERMEN'S MUSEUM

Williamsburg (Yorktown) - 309 Water Street (off SR 238 east) 23690. Phone: (757) 887-2641. www.watermens.org. Hours: Tuesday-Saturday 10:00am-5:00pm, Sunday 1:00-5:00pm (April-late December). Admission: $5.00 adult, $4.00 senior (62+) and student (grades K-12).

The museum tells the story of Virginia's working Watermen and their families who, for generations, have harvested the rivers and tributaries of the Chesapeake Bay for its abundant seafood year round. Indoor exhibits include models of workboats, tools of the trade, nautical artifacts, and paintings and photographs of life on the bay. Outdoor exhibits feature a 100-year-old Poquoson 5-log canoe as well as other boats. Visitors can also tog for oysters. Come for the Watermen's Heritage Celebration in July or the Yorktown Tea Party in November (they throw tea into the river).

YORKTOWN AND YORKTOWN BATTLEFIELD

Williamsburg (Yorktown) - 1000 Colonial Pkwy (I-64 exit 242B, Rte. 199 east to Colonial Pkwy) 23690. Phone: (757) 898-2410. www.nps.gov/colo. Hours: 9:00am-5:00pm daily except Christmas & New Years. All park grounds are closed at sunset. Admission: $15.00 adult (16+). FREE for those under 16. Note: In our opinion, the battlefield tour is too long for the young ones.

This is the site of the last major battle of the American Revolutionary War and the surrender of Lord Cornwallis to General George Washington in 1781 (Moore House open 1:00-5:00pm daily in summer and weekends in the spring and fall, is site of surrender negotiations and can be toured). Ranger guided programs are offered from the Visitor Center which has a short film presentation, a museum with George Washington's original field tents and a children's exhibit, a bookstore and great Battlefield overlook. Yorktown Battlefield Shuttle Tour (55 minutes) is a ride through history along the Yorktown Battlefield tour roads. The tour highlights major portions of the siege lines and includes an extensive stop at the site of the surrender of the British army. Points of interest will be highlighted with audiotape information. The driving tour includes the earthworks, Moore House and Surrender Field. On the Battlefield, kids can volunteer in the non-firing artillery demonstration. You can stop by the Nelson House (home of one of the signers of the Declaration of Independence open 10:00am-4:30pm (summer) and 1:00-4:30pm (rest of year) and chat with Thomas or Lucy Nelson.

South East Area

CIVIL WAR WEEKEND

Yorktown. National Park Service. (757) 898-2410. www.nps.gov/colo. This event features tactical demonstrations, encampments and a Confederate field hospital to interpret the role Yorktown played during the Peninsula Campaign. A special Memorial Day ceremony takes place at the Yorktown National Cemetery and Confederate Cemetery. (May, Memorial Day weekend)

JULY 4TH

Yorktown. (757) 890-3300. The Road to Independence. Rides, parade, food, entertainment, concert and fireworks. FREE.

YORKTOWN CELEBRATES CHRISTMAS

Yorktown. (757) 890-4970. Three centuries of private homes and historic buildings are professionally decorated for the holidays. Period entertainment is also featured. Illumination of lights, trees and Santa. LIGHTED BOAT PARADE. Enjoy hot cider and musical performances in the glow of a beach bonfire, starting at 6:00pm, while awaiting the magnificent parade of lights. Decorated in holiday spirit, area boaters parade the York River in competition for "Best of Show." The parade starts at 7:00pm. Yorktown Beach. FREE. www.yorkcounty.gov/tourism. (December, first Saturday).

Chapter 6
South West

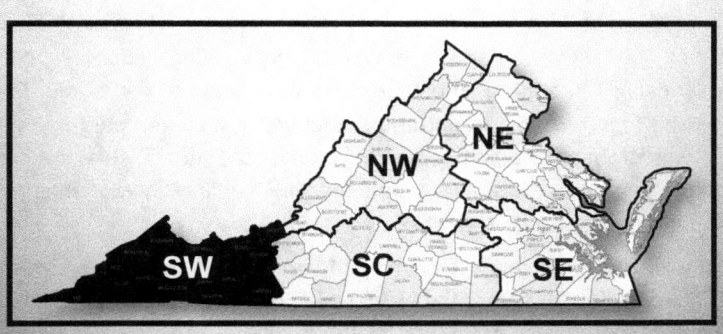

A Quick Tour of our Hand-Picked Favorites Around...

South West Virginia

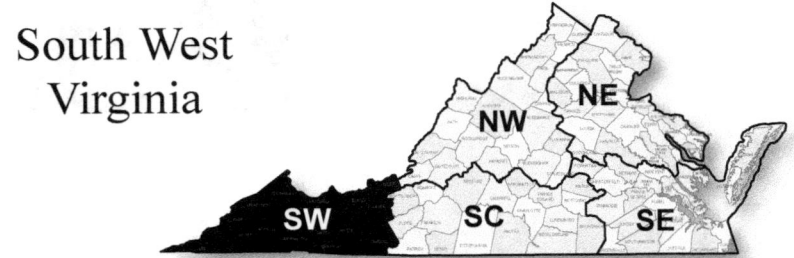

Nature and mountain music take center stage as well as crafts and folklore in Virginia's Blue Ridge Highlands and Appalachia. At **Historic Crab Orchard Museum & Park** in Tazewell, see Native American artifacts unearthed during the construction of Highway US 19/460, many of which date back to the Paleo people who hunted the Woolly Mammoth!

North of Tazewell is the **Pocahontas Exhibition Mine & Museum**, the first exhibition mine in the nation. The Town of Pocahontas was developed for the miners and their families. See the old country store, Silver Dollar Saloon and the Opera House.

Travel southwest to Big Stone Gap, site of the John Fox Jr. Museum. Author of 14 novels and 500 short stories, Fox was an avid outdoorsman who served with Teddy Roosevelt as a Rough Rider. His novel, **Trail of the Lonesome Pine**, is performed as a musical throughout the summer at the Trail of the Lonesome Pine Outdoor Amphitheater. The play tells the story of the great boom in this part of Virginia when the discovery of coal and iron ore forced the proud mountain people into making drastic changes. Hope you get picked as a member of the jury during the drama!

Just south of here, in Duffield, is a natural wonder – **Natural Tunnel**. More than 850 feet long and as high as a 10 story building, Natural Tunnel was naturally carved through a limestone ridge thousands of years ago. Fossils can still be found in and around the tunnel walls. It's been said that Daniel Boone was probably the first person to discover the tunnel. Take the chairlift ride to the tunnel floor. It's an adventure slowly "floating" in your chairlift seat to the bottom platform (the way back up seems steeper!).

And finally, at the very southern tip of Virginia (before you travel one mile into Kingsport, Tennessee) is the **Homeplace**. The mountains of Southwest Virginia still echo voices of the first pioneer settlers. They seek to create the

For updates visit: www.KidsLoveTravel.com

feeling of an early pioneer mountain farmstead, including the activities of everyday living. Watch a small boy pushing an old horse-drawn corn planter, or maybe an old-time mountain broom maker, or a sorghum miller, a cider miller, or a quilter or furniture maker.

Sites and attractions are listed in order by City, Zip Code, and Name. Symbols indicated represent: 🍽 Restaurants   🛏 Lodging

BARTER THEATRE

Abingdon - 133 West Main Street (I-81 exit 17) 24210. Phone: (276) 628-3991. www.bartertheatre.com. Performances: Thursday at 7:30pm, Friday-Saturday at 8:00pm with matinees Wednesday, Thursday, Saturday at 2:00pm and Sunday at 3:00pm. Admission: $25.00-$45.00. Reservations recommended.

Comedies, musicals, and dramas (like Snow White or the Christmas Show). "The State Theatre of Virginia" was founded in 1933 on the theory that drama could be bartered for food. During the Depression, the owner convinced several handfuls of Broadway actors that it was better to eat in Virginia than to starve in New York. Cash is now accepted replacing barters for tickets of milk, ham or poultry.

VIRGINIA HIGHLANDS FESTIVAL

Abingdon - (276) 676-2282, (800) 435-3440. www.vahighlandsfestival.org. Attractions include antiques, art and photography exhibits, drama, music, dance, storytelling, a gardening symposium, creative writing workshops, nature walks, historical tours & lectures, hot air ballooning & youth events. (first 10 days in August)

WOLF CREEK INDIAN VILLAGE & MUSEUM

Bastian - Rte. 1, Box 1530 (off I-77 exit 58, US 32 south) 24314. Phone: (276) 688-3438. www.indianvillage.org. Hours: Monday-Saturday 9:00am-5:00pm. Closed New Years, Thanksgiving and Christmas. Admission: Both Museum and Village: $15.00 adult, $10.00 child (5-17). Museum only $6.00. Note: While in Bland County, contact Virginia Highland Llamas. The children will thank you for hiking with furry llamas, although llamas are known to occasionally spit!

It was around the year 1215 that a group of Native Americans went in search of a new tribal home. Their journey led them to a valley nestled between two mountains (a natural protection from the harsh winter winds, a constant source of fresh water, and abundant collection of trees, game, nuts, herbs and clay, and fertile land to grow their crops).

So nearly 100 primitive Indians constructed a barricaded circular village. Where they came from, where they went, and exactly who they were remains somewhat of a mystery. The recreated village is near the site of the original McCord archeological excavations. Notice the domed, rather thatched huts vs. teepees you might expect? The Village has in costume re-enactors of the original crafts of the Eastern Woodland Indians. The museum has many artifacts and Indian related objects. Take a walk on the nature trails and picnic on the grounds.

SOUTHWEST VIRGINIA MUSEUM HISTORICAL STATE PARK

Big Stone Gap - 10 W. First Street North (West First St and Wood Ave, off US 23) 24219. Phone: (276) 523-1322. www.dcr.virginia.gov/state-parks/southwest-virginia-museum#general_information. Hours: Monday-Friday 10:00am-4:00pm, Saturday 10:00am-5:00pm, Sunday 1:00-5:00pm (Memorial Day-Labor Day). Closed Mondays (September-December, March-May). Closed Thanksgiving and Christmas. Admission: $3.00-$5.00 (age 6+).

Southwest Virginia Museum Historical State Park features a beautiful Victorian mansion that serves as the museum. By the mid-1700s, settlers looking for a fresh start were traveling south out of Pennsylvania and Maryland into the valley of Virginia. In 1775, Daniel Boone pushed the Wilderness Road through Cumberland Gap, opening the way west. Braving the unknown and constantly facing the threat of Indian attacks, pioneer settlers were almost totally dependent on the land, their own skills and the contents of their wagon for their every need. The people who stayed in this region are the Heart of Appalachia itself, learning to survive by their own determination, wits and skills. The first floor of the museum features exhibits about the area's coal and iron ore deposits, part of the "boom and bust" era. Kids like the "Daniel Boone-like" artifacts. Ask the front desk for a student scavenger hunt worksheet.

TRAIL OF THE LONESOME PINE STATE OUTDOOR DRAMA

Big Stone Gap - 518 Clinton Ave. East (June Tolliver Playhouse) 24219.

South West Area

Phone: (276) 523-1235. www.trailofthelonesomepine.com. Hours: Thursday-Saturday in July and August only. Curtain time 8:00pm. Pre-show 7:15pm. Admission: $15.00 adult, $10.00 senior (55+), child (6-12) and military. Note: Before the drama, you might visit the June Tolliver House and Craft Shop, where the heroine of "Lonesome Pine" actually lived while attending school. Also in town is the John Fox, Jr. Museum. Here, the author of "Lonesome Pine" wrote 15 novels and more than 500 short stories (small admission, open Weds-Sun afternoons).

Staged on the historic site where the story was actually lived, the drama tells an exciting and tender love story of a beautiful Virginia mountain girl and a handsome young mining engineer from the East. It tells the story of the great boom in Southwest Virginia when the discovery of coal and iron ore forced the proud mountain people into making many drastic changes in their way of life. Witty and humorous characters intermingle with tragedy, suspense and folk music. The main characters draw you into the dilemmas that develop and the love that underlies. Try to participate as a member of the jury (male volunteers are chosen from the audience). We really liked this quaint, wholesome and easy-to-follow story. Parents, they sneak in history, too.

NATURAL TUNNEL STATE PARK

Big Stone Gap (Duffield) - Rte. 3 Box 250 (US 23 then to Rte. 871) 24244. Phone: (434) 940-2674. https://www.dcr.virginia.gov/state-parks/natural-tunnel. Hours: Daily 8:00am-dusk. Visitor Center Friday-Monday 10am-4pm. Chairlift service begins around 10:00am until about 4:00-6:00pm, depending on the season. Admission: Small fee for the pool and chairlift ($5.00 round trip). $5.00 per vehicle to enter park grounds. Note: Lighting of the Tunnel event begins the last Saturday in May through December in the evening (last Saturdays each month only). It showcases the beauty of the Tunnel through the magic of lights. Summer Concessions open.

Amazing...trains still travel through. Be listening closely for approaching train whistles...

More than 850 feet long and as high as a 10-story building, Natural Tunnel was naturally carved through a limestone ridge thousands of years ago. The tunnel was carved by what is now Stock Creek and many fossils can still be found in and around the tunnel walls! It's been said that Daniel Boone was probably the first person to discover the tunnel. Other scenic features include the view of the steep stone walls and several pinnacles or "chimneys". Natural Tunnel State Park offers seven walking trails, the longest one being 1.1 miles long. These trails lead to the unique features of the park: the tunnel floor, Lover's Leap, Tunnel Hill and Gorge Ridge. A 500-foot boardwalk and observation deck provide accessibility to guests with disabilities. Most trails are open to mountain bikes with bike rentals available at the campground host campsite. The park also offers cave tours and canoe trips on the Clinch River. Cove Ridge Center has limited overnight camping, new cabins, picnicking, swimming pool, amphitheater and chairlift to the tunnel floor. It's an adventure slowly "floating" in your chairlift seat to the bottom platform (the way back up seems steeper!). Hear the sound of a train whistle? Don't be mistaken, trains still ride on the tracks of Natural Tunnel. On the platform, just outside the tunnel, there are informational kiosks.

The chairlift ride down and back was more than half of the thrill...

BREAKS INTERSTATE PARK

Breaks - PO Box 100 (off SR 80 on eastern edge of Cumberland Mountains) 24607. Phone: (276) 865-4413 or (800) 982-5122. www.breakspark.com. Hours: Park: Daily 7:00am-dark. Visitor Center: Thursday-Sunday 9:00am-5:00pm (March-August). Admission: $3.00 per car. Swimming pool, pedal boats extra $3.00-$8.00. Note: Picnicking, hiking, boating, swimming, fishing (12 acre lake), boat rentals, horseback riding, biking. Canyon Rim Zipline. Lodge with 58 rooms. Many summer bluegrass festivals. Restaurant open seasonally.

Aptly called the "Grand Canyon of the South", the Russell Fork of the Big Sandy River has cut a "break" (1600 foot deep gorge) through the surrounding mountain. A paved road leads from the entrance to the canyon rim with many overlooks providing views of palisades, rock formations, caves, springs and rhododendron in bloom annually. The Visitors Center contains natural science and historical displays and is the place to pick up maps of the park's trails.

South West Area

WHITE WATER RAFTING AT BREAKS INTERSTATE PARK

Breaks. The Breaks Interstate Park. During the first four weekends in October, John Flannagan Reservoir provides white water releases into the Russell Fork River. This creates some of the best white water rafting in the Eastern United States. (October)

MOUNTAIN TOP LIGHTS

Breaks. Breaks Interstate Park. Self-guided auto tour through lighted mountains, light displays, nature and holiday themes. Evenings. Admission fee. (mid-November/December)

RALPH STANLEY MUSEUM AND TRADITIONAL MOUNTAIN MUSIC CENTER

Clintwood - Chase House, 249 Main St, 24228. www.ralphstanleymuseum.com. Phone: (276) 926-5591. Hours: Tuesday-Saturday 10:00am-4:00pm (late March-early December). Admission: $10.00 general.

Combining the career of Dr. Ralph Stanley with the history of traditional mountain music, this state-of-the-art, interactive museum will allow you to see and hear this particular style of Appalachian American music in its original setting – the mountains of southwestern Virginia. Located in a historic Victorian home, the collection includes exhibits on Dr. Stanley, the region's musical roots, and on popular successors like Ricky Skaggs and Patty Loveless. A short film highlights the best of Dr. Stanley's career.

CUMBERLAND GAP NATIONAL HISTORICAL PARK

Cumberland Gap - Rte. 58 (The park can also be accessed from Virginia by traveling west on Highway 58 to its intersection with 25E in Tennessee) 37724. Phone: (606) 248-2817. www.nps.gov/cuga. Educators: Experience the story of westward movement firsthand through the interactive CD Within the Shadows of Cumberland Gap. These CDs are copyright free and free to order.

Go back in time when the gap - a natural passage through the mountain barrier - had been used by Indians, and then discovered by pioneers - including Daniel Boone. Hensley's Settlement is part of Cumberland Gap National Historical Park, which lies in three states: Virginia, Kentucky and Tennessee. The preserved settlement is located atop Brush Mountain where the Hensley's first settled in 1903. In the early part of the century, the Hensley's settled on the mountain, forsaking settled areas for an entirely self-sufficient way of life. This truly rural Appalachian settlement continued, without electricity, indoor plumbing, roads or any modern conveniences until the last inhabitant left in 1951.

Approximately 25 of the original buildings have been restored and the surrounding land has been returned to the original farming and pasture scene of its original appearance. Presently, transportation to the settlement is still somewhat limited in order to maintain the area's authenticity. Guided tours occur twice daily from mid-May through October for a fee of $5-$10.00.

GAP CAVE TOURS: Join park rangers on a two-hour adventure exploring this majestic underground cathedral! Discover glistening stalagmites and flowstone cascades, or catch a glimpse of a bat. The moderately strenuous, 1.5 mile tour explores four levels of the cave via 183 steps. The tour includes a 1 mile hike along the historic Wilderness Road. For the safety of all, no children under the age of five are permitted. Appropriate hiking footwear is required. No sandals or open toed shoes are allowed. Meet at the Daniel Boone parking area. Tickets must be purchased at least 15 minutes in advance. $4.00-$8.00 (April-September).

CLAYTOR LAKE STATE PARK

Dublin - 4400 State Park Road (off I-81 exit 101) 24084. Phone: (540) 643-2500. www.dcr.virginia.gov/state_parks/cla.shtml. Admission: $7.00 per vehicle. Hours: Daily 6:00am-10:00pm. **New: Three family lodges, three-bedroom cabins and a marina complex with a meeting room, gift shop and snack bar.**

Claytor Lake State Park in the New River Valley covers 4,500 acres and is 21 miles long. The lake was formed in 1939 by the Appalachian Power Company as a hydroelectric plant before it became a recreation area in 1946. Wooded hills and a sparkling lake provide an ideal setting for boating, swimming, camping, hiking and picnicking, plus sport fishing. About three miles of hiking trails with easy to moderate ratings are open year-round. Cabins overlook the 4500 acre lake and the historic Howe House which features interactive exhibits describing the ecology of the lake and surrounding areas.

WILDERNESS ROAD STATE PARK

Ewing - Rte. 2, Box 115 (off US 58 at intersection of rte. 923) 24248. Phone: (276) 445-3065. www.dcr.virginia.gov/state_parks/wil.shtml. $5.00 per vehicle fee.

Open for picnicking and hiking, canoeing plus visitors can enjoy the 10 mile stretch of the Wilderness Road for additional hiking, biking, and equestrian trails. In the shadow of the Cumberland Gap along the old Wilderness Road, is the reconstructed Martin's Station (site of a Civil War Battle). Consisting of several 18th century frontier cabins, outbuildings, and a stockaded fort, the property regularly holds living history demonstrations with blacksmithing, surveying, farming and militia musters. These activities, combined with the annual Raid on Martin's Station reenactment (in May) and the Trade Fair, bring the Wilderness Road era to life. Park open 8:00am-dusk; Visitors Center open 10:00am-5:00pm.

NEW RIVER TRAIL STATE PARK

Galax (Foster Falls) - 176 Orphanage Dr. (access points to the trail at Ivanhoe, Fries, Galax, Draper, Pulaski and Foster Falls) 24360. Phone: (276) 699-6778. www.dcr.virginia.gov/state_parks/new.shtml. Hours: Dawn-dusk Admission: $7.00 per car. Note: New River Adventures (276) 699-1034 or www.newriveradventures.com.

The park parallels the scenic and historic New River for 39 miles and serves as a link to a number of other recreational areas. The gentle slope of the trail makes it great for visitors to hike, bike or ride horses. Horse, boat and bike rentals, a boat launch, camping, a concession stand, fishing and picnicking.

CARTER FAMILY FOLD & MUSEUM

Hiltons - Carter Family Fold & Museum (I-81 to Rte. 23 north to Hwy. 58 east to 709 to 614) 24258. Phone: (276) 386-6054. www.carterfamilyfold.org. Hours: Shows are Saturdays from 7:30-11:00pm, year-round. Museum opens at 6:00pm Admission: Shows - $10.00 adult, $2.00 child (6-11). Museum - small donation.

The Carter Family Fold is a rustic, 1000 seat music "shed" offering traditional music every Saturday night. In keeping with the traditional music style, no electrical instruments are allowed (everything is acoustic). There's lots of dancing and fun for the entire family. Shows are family-oriented; no alcohol is permitted at concerts. Visit the A.P. Carter Museum in Hiltons, home of the Carter family - A.P., Sara, Maybelle and June Carter Cash - who are considered Country Music's First Family. The museum opens an hour prior to the show, and visitors can explore the role of the Carter family in the development of traditional bluegrass and country music. Artifacts include photos, books, and musical instruments, show clothes, 78rpm recordings and many other memorabilia, such as items donated by family members June and Johnny Cash. Located next door to the museum, is the old log cabin where A.P. was born. Recently restored, it showcases life in southwest Virginia during the early 1900's and includes many family antiques and collectibles.

HUNGRY MOTHER STATE PARK

Marion - 2854 Park Blvd. (I-81 exit 47 to Rte 11 to SR 16) 24354. Phone: (276) 781-7400. www.dcr.virginia.gov/state_parks/hun.shtml. Admission: $7.00 per car. Fees waived for overnight guests.

Named for a little child's cry of "Hungry, Mother" legends. Today, the mountain he cried from is Molly's Knob. Beautiful woodlands and a placid 108 acre lake in the heart of the mountains. The park features a sandy beach with bathhouse, pleasure boats and boat launch, a fishing pier, campgrounds, cabins, a lake overlook restaurant, a visitors center, a six bedroom guest lodge, hiking and biking trails and guided horseback trail rides.

GRAYSON HIGHLANDS STATE PARK

Mouth of Wilson - 829 Grayson Highland Lane (I-81 exit 45 to rte. 16 to US 58 west) 24363. Phone: (276) 579-7092. www.dcr.virginia.gov/state_parks/gra.shtml. Admission: $7.00 per vehicle, except for overnight guests.

Located near Virginia's highest point, this park offers views of "Swiss" peaks more than 5,000 feet high. Facilities include a visitor center, campgrounds, hiking trails and picnic areas. The park has nine hiking trails averaging a mile in length. These trails lead to panoramic vistas, scenic waterfalls and a 200 year old pioneer cabin. The park also offers access to the Appalachian Trail and trails in the surrounding Jefferson National Forest. Many Bike rental shops are in the area. Scenic horse trails and a horse camping area with stables and parking for trailers.

GRAYSON HIGHLANDS FALL FESTIVAL

Mouth of Wilson. Grayson Highlands Park. Visitors can enjoy a colorful autumn weekend in the Heart of the Highlands and go back to a time when horses and mules ground cane into juice to be boiled in sorghum or molasses, when apple cider was the soft drink of the time, when fresh apples were cooked in a copper kettle over an open fire all day long to render apple butter. Saturday night was reserved for fiddlin' and making music with the neighbors. In addition to all this, there is a pony auction and Sunday gospel music. Admission fee. (September, last weekend)

POCAHONTAS EXHIBITION MINE AND MUSEUM

Pocahontas - 300 Centre Street (CR 644 to CR 659) 24635. Phone: (276) 945-2134. http://pocahontasva.org. Hours: Wednesday-Saturday 10:00am-5:00pm, Sunday 1:00-5:00pm (summer). Weekends only (April-May). Admission: $10.00 adult, $8.50 child (6-12) Note: Temperature in mine is 52 degrees year round, wear a light jacket.

Opened in 1882, this coal mine has a spectacular 13 foot tall coal seam. The Mine operated for 73 years and produced more than 44 million tons of coal (would fill a train 6000 miles long). The walking tour allows you to step into the mine; listen as guides explain the story of mining at Pocahontas No. 3 Coal, and learn how the hand-loading era slowly gave way to mechanization. The Town of Pocahontas was developed for the miners and their families. See the old country store, Silver Dollar Saloon and the Opera House.

RADFORD HIGHLANDERS FESTIVAL

Radford - Radford University's Campus. www.radford.edu/festival. An evening ceilidh (celebration) will be held in downtown Radford. Events include a parade, Scottish Highland games, Celtic and Appalachian music, arts and crafts vendors, a gathering of the clans, children's activities, genealogy research and food. (October, second Saturday)

MUSEUM OF THE MIDDLE APPALACHIANS

Saltville-123PalmerAve,downtown 24370. https://museumofthemiddleappalachians.org/. Phone: (276) 496-3633. Hours: Monday-Saturday 10:00am-4:00pm. Sunday 1:00-4:00pm. Admission: $3.00-$5.00 per person (age 6+). Note: Nearby is SALT PARK - See a replica of a salt furnace where the 100 gallon capacity salt kettles are authentic. See an original Walking Beam Pump used as one of the various modes of extraction of the underground salt water. The pioneer cabin and blacksmith shop are typical structures appearing in this area during that early salt production developing years.

Salt Park - The site of an attempt to mine salt (using pick and shovel) dated the oldest such site in the United States.

The Museum of the Middle Appalachians is a collection of the paleo-archeological findings from annual digs. The earliest visitors to Saltville were drawn by the saline springs and their need for salt. Excavations as early as 1882 have revealed prehistoric mammals. The Museum showcases five permanent displays: The Ice Age, Woodland Indians, The War Between the States, The Company Town and Rocks & Minerals of the Appalachian Area. The first salt mine in the country was here and the town also served as the main source of salt for the Confederacy. Exhibits also cover battles in the area, natural history and nearby excavations. Children can delight in the full-size replicas of Ice Age mammals that once roamed the area, explore the interactive model of the Saltville Valley and uncover fossils in a hands-on exhibit. Self-guided tour brochure available.

BATTLE OF SALTVILLE

Saltville. Main Street. www.saltvilleva.com. Four days of music, food and family fun. During the week before Labor Day, residents heat up the town's old salt kettles and boil brine to make salt, just as it was done in the 18th & 19th centuries. (August, third weekend)

BURKE'S GARDEN / GARDEN MTN FARM

Tazewell - Rte. 3, Box 784 (Rte. 623, Banks Ridge Road) 24651. Phone: (276) 472-2511. https://visittazewellcounty.org/burkes-garden-2/

Sometimes referred to as "God's Thumbprint", this mountain-ringed bowl is 10 miles in diameter and filled with some of the most fertile farmland in the state. The area, which is the highest mountain valley in Virginia, was designated a National and Virginia Rural Historical District. The community can be viewed from the Appalachian Trail or by car from state route 623. Visitors can bike on area roads, hike and hunt in nearby Jefferson National Forest. The most noteworthy working farm here features pastured poultry and environmentally friendly methods of production. Organically grown product tours are available.

BURKE'S GARDEN FALL FESTIVAL

Tazewell - (800) 588-9401. Visit Virginia's largest historical district and national landmark for a day filled with fun, music, great food and crafts. Also hike part of the Appalachian Trail, bird watch or bike on scenic by-way described as the "Garden of Eden", bowl-shaped paradise. (September, last Saturday)

HISTORIC CRAB ORCHARD MUSEUM

Tazewell - 3663 Crab Orchard Rd (Rt. 19 & 460) 24651. www.craborchardmuseum.com. Phone: (276) 988-6755. Hours: Tuesday-Saturday 9:00am-5:00pm. Open Sunday afternoons (April-October). Admission: $5.00 adult, $4.00 senior, $3.00 child (7-12) For self-guided tours of the Museum Gallery and the Pioneer Park. Note: Gift Shop sells hand-made crafts, old-fashioned toys, distinctive books, snacks and souvenirs.

Historic Crab Orchard Museum & Pioneer Park in Tazewell features Southwest Virginia from prehistoric times to the present. Kids can take a guided tour through the park's log buildings and learn how people lived during the pioneer days of the region. The site includes Native American artifacts from nearby Crab Orchard archeological site, exhibits on Revolutionary and Civil Wars, and agricultural and mining displays. You'll also see animals like the infamous "Varmint," a coyote credited with killing 410 sheep in the 1950s and the hide of the 500-pound black bear named "Old Hitler," who was shot in the early 1940s after killing dozens of cattle and sheep. 14 log cabins from the 1800s show what daily life was once like in the "wild, wild west." Horse-drawn carriages, hearse, McCormick farm equipment and a Model T are featured in the Red Barn. Highway construction unearthed nearly all of the Native American artifacts seen in the exhibits, many of which date back to the Paleo people who hunted the Woolly Mammoth! Sometimes, bluegrass bands perform on the porches, and folks picnic on the grounds on Saturdays.

INDEPENDENCE DAY CELEBRATION

Tazewell - Traditional live music, mountain games, kids games, pioneer skills demonstrations. Colonial militia drills and afternoon reenactment. Join residents for a 4th of July celebration of their coal mining heritage. The event features a fireworks display, food and music. FREE. (July 4th)

FRONTIER CHRISTMAS

Tazewell - Pioneer apprentices singing carols, musical performances throughout the Pioneer Park cabins, storytelling, hot cider and cookies, Santa and more. Admission is a can of food for the local Food Pantry or a gently used children's book for the Reach Out and Read Program. (first Saturday evening in December)

HOMEPLACE MOUNTAIN FARM AND MUSEUM

Weber City - Wadlow Gap Road (Hwy. 93N - John B. Dennis By-Pass Hwy. 58-Rte. 224) 24251. Phone: (540) 386-2465 or (540) 386-6300. Hours: 10:00am-5:00pm Monday-Saturday, 1:00-5:00pm Sunday (April-December) Admission: $3.00 adult, $2.00 child (age 5+)

The mountains of Southwest Virginia still echo voices of the first pioneer settlers. This is a replica of a working 1860's farm that brings to life the stories of yesteryear. Watch a small boy pushing an old horse-drawn corn planter, or maybe an old-time mountain broom maker, or a sorghum miller or cider miller, or a quilter or furniture maker. Southern soldiers gather in mid-summer to do battle with Northern forces holding Moccasin Gap. They seek to create the feeling of an early pioneer mountain farmstead, including the activities of everyday living. The Clinch Mountain Cultural Center contains primitive artifacts and displays to aid understanding of the Appalachia people.

CIVIL WAR RE-ENACTMENT

Weber City. The Homeplace Mountain Farm & Museum & Malone Horse Farm . (276) 386-2465. This event is a re-enactment of the 1863 Civil War Battle for Moccasin Gap. (last weekend in July)

BIG WALKER LOOKOUT

Wytheville - 8711 Stony Fork Road - Star Route (I-77 OR I-81 exit US-52, 12 miles North on Byway) 24382. www.scenicbeauty-va.com. Phone: (276) 228-4401. Hours: Daily 10:00am-5:00pm (May-October). Admission: $3.50-$5.00 per person. Tower Admission includes the Swinging Bridge.

The Overlook of the Big Walker National Forest Scenic Byway provides great views from the Scenic tower and swing bridge attraction. This 100-foot tower looks out over patchwork farm valleys and mountain wilderness.

Facilities include an ice cream shop and craft/gift shop with locally made Appalachian Crafts. Located in the historic pass of the mountain where Molly Tynes made her famous midnight ride to warn Wytheville of impending Civil War raid by John Toland. Location of the short hiking trail to Monster Rock Overlook (15-20 minute hike.). Fee to climb tower.

ROCK HOUSE MUSEUM & BOYD HOUSE

Wytheville - 975 Tazewell Street 24382. http://museums.wytheville.org/. Phone: (276) 223-3330. Hours: Wednesday-Friday 10:00am-4:00pm. (April-December). Admission: $2.00-$4.00 (age 6+) - each museum. Tours: 30 minute, guided tours of Rock House.

ROCK HOUSE - The home of Wytheville's first resident physician, the Rock House has played a significant role in Wytheville's and the county's history since its construction. Dr. John Haller served his community as a country doctor, county coroner, and delegate to the Virginia Legislature. The home has been used as an infirmary and school during the Civil War years and as a boarding house when Wytheville became a popular summer resort. As you walk through this home you will learn about Dr. Haller, his wife and children; his great granddaughter Fannie Gibboney, pioneer of women's independence; and great, great granddaughter Kathleen Campbell, the last family member to own the house. There is even an area for children to test their knowledge of medicine in Wythe County and experience grinding herbs in a mortar and pestle, just like a 1800s apothecary. 205 E Tazewell Street.

THOMAS BOYD MUSEUM - Located in the Thomas J. Boyd Museum, the Discovery Corner offers ten interactive stations where students will learn math and science, as well as area history. Younger guests can participate in an activity of dressing up in reproduction Civil War uniforms. Guests also see replicas of items a solder would have carried and real Civil War items used by local citizens. Another highlight is the original weathervane from the Wytheville courthouse. The two remaining portions of the weathervane bear the scars of Toland Raid on the town. Children get a "feel" for the past by actually touching artifacts to learn how they were used.

HOMESTEAD LIVING HISTORY FESTIVAL

Wytheville - Vendors demonstrate making dulcimers, spinning, weaving, knitting, rug hooking, quilting, soup making, blacksmith, wood and leather works. Food offered over pit fires are beans and cornbread or pressed apple juice. Old time gospel and bluegrass entertainment. Admission. (September, fourth Saturday)

AMUSEMENTS

- **NE** Alexandria, *Great Waves At Cameron Run Regional Park*, 4
- **NE** Manassas, *Splashdown Waterpark*, 36
- **NW** Harrisonburg (McGaheysville), *Massanutten Resort*, 76
- **NW** White Post, *Dinosaur Land*, 99
- **SE** Richmond (Doswell), *Kings Dominion*, 177
- **SE** Virginia Beach, *Ocean Breeze Waterpark*, 181
- **SE** Virginia Beach, *Virginia Beach Boardwalk*, 184
- **SE** Williamsburg, *Busch Gardens Williamsburg*, 189
- **SE** Williamsburg, *Great Wolf Lodge Indoor Waterpark Resort*, 193
- **SE** Williamsburg, *Watercountry USA*, 188

ANIMALS & FARMS

- **NE** Herndon, *Frying Pan Park: Kidwell Farm & Spring Meeting House*, 31
- **NE** Leesburg, *Leesburg Animal Park*, 34
- **DC** Washington, *National Zoo*, 47
- **NW** Brownsburg/Raphine, *Wade's Mill*, 66
- **NW** Lexington, *Virginia Horse Center*, 99
- **NW** Luray, *Luray Zoo*, 81
- **NW** Natural Bridge, *Natural Bridge Zoo*, 85
- **NW** Natural Bridge, *Virginia Safari Park*, 85
- **NW** Steeles Tavern (Montebello), *Montebello State Fish Hatchery*, 94
- **SC** Roanoke, *Mill Mountain Zoo*, 124
- **SE** Chincoteague, *Chincoteague Pony*, 139
- **SE** Hampton, *Bluebird Gap Farm*, 143
- **SE** Newport News, *Peninsula SPCA Petting Zoo*, 148
- **SE** Norfolk, *Virginia Zoo*, 154
- **SE** Richmond, *Maymont*, 170
- **SE** Richmond (Chesterfield), *Metro Richmond Zoo*, 182
- **SE** Richmond (Glen Allen), *Meadow Farm Museum*, 177
- **SE** Virginia Beach, *Hunt Club Farm*, 181
- **SW** Tazewell, *Burke's Garden / Garden Mountain Farm*, 214

HISTORY

- **NE** Alexandria, *Christ Church*, 7
- **NE** Alexandria, *Fort Ward Museum & Historic Site*, 3
- **NE** Alexandria, *Freedom House*, 7
- **NE** Alexandria, *Friendship Firehouse Museum*, 7
- **NE** Alexandria, *Gadsby's Tavern & Museum*, 8
- **NE** Alexandria, *Stabler-Leadbeater Apothecary Museum*, 10
- **NE** Alexandria (Mason Neck), *Gunston Hall*, 13
- **NE** Alexandria (Mount Vernon), *Mount Vernon, George Washington's*, 14
- **NE** Ashland (Beaverdam), *Scotchtown, Historic Home Of Patrick Henry*, 19
- **NE** Colonial Beach, *George Washington Birthplace Nat'l Monument*, 20
- **NE** Fredericksburg, *Fredericksburg And Spotsylvania Civil War Battlefields*, 25
- **NE** Fredericksburg, *Fredericksburg Area Museum*, 21
- **NE** Fredericksburg, *George Washington's Ferry Farm*, 26
- **NE** Fredericksburg, *Historic Kenmore*, 22
- **NE** Fredericksburg, *Hugh Mercer Apothecary Shop*, 23
- **NE** Fredericksburg, *Mary Washington House*, 23
- **NE** Fredericksburg, *Rising Sun Tavern*, 24
- **NE** Fredericksburg (Falmouth), *White Oak Museum*, 29
- **NE** Harpers Ferry, *Harpers Ferry National Historical Park*, 30
- **NE** Irvington, *Historic Christ Church*, 32
- **NE** Leesburg, *Loudoun Museum*, 34
- **NE** Manassas, *Manassas National Battlefield Park*, 35
- **NE** Montpelier Station, *Montpelier, James Madison's*, 39
- **NE** Montpelier Station (Orange), *James Madison Museum*, 36
- **NE** Quantico, *National Museum Of The Marine Corps*, 42

Activity Index

HISTORY *(cont.)*

- **NE** Reedville, *Reedville Fishermen's Museum*, 38
- **NE** Stratford, *Stratford Hall Plantation / Stratford Mill*, 39
- **DC** Washington, *Capitol Building, United States*, 56
- **DC** Washington, *Ford's Theatre*, 44
- **DC** Washington, *Franklin D. Roosevelt Memorial*, 49
- **DC** Washington, *Frederick Douglass NHS*, 49
- **DC** Washington, *Jefferson Memorial*, 51
- **DC** Washington, *Library Of Congress*, 57
- **DC** Washington, *Lincoln Memorial*, 51
- **DC** Washington, *National Archives*, 55
- **DC** Washington, *Naval Museum*, 54
- **DC** Washington, *Pres. Lincoln's Cottage*, 55
- **DC** Washington, *Smithsonian Institution*, 58
- **DC** Washington, *United States Holocaust Memorial Museum*, 50
- **DC** Washington, *Washington Monument*, 54
- **NW** Charlottesville, *Ashlawn-Highland: Home Of James Monroe*, 66
- **NW** Charlottesville, *Lewis And Clark Exploratory Center*, 67
- **NW** Charlottesville, *Michie Tavern*, 67
- **NW** Charlottesville, *Monticello*, 68
- **NW** Front Royal, *Belle Boyd Cottage*, 72
- **NW** Lexington, *Lee Chapel & Museum*, 76
- **NW** Lexington, *Stonewall Jackson House*, 78
- **NW** Lexington, *VMI, Virginia Military Institute*, 79
- **NW** Middletown, *Cedar Creek & Belle Grove National Historical Park*, 82
- **NW** New Market, *New Market Battlefield State Historical Park*, 87
- **NW** Staunton, *Frontier Culture Museum*, 91
- **NW** Staunton, *Woodrow Wilson Birthplace Museum*, 92
- **NW** Steeles Tavern, *Cyrus McCormick's Farm*, 93
- **NW** Strasburg, *Hupp's Hill*, 95
- **NW** Winchester, *George Washington's Office Museum*, 96
- **NW** Winchester, *Museum Of The Shenandoah Valley*, 97
- **NW** Winchester, *Stonewall Jackson's Headquarters Museum*, 98
- **SC** Appomattox, *Appomattox Court House National Historical Park*, 104
- **SC** Appomattox, *Clover Hill Village*, 105
- **SC** Ararat, *Laurel Hill - J.E.B. Stuart Birthplace*, 106
- **SC** Bedford, *National D-Day Memorial*, 106
- **SC** Bedford (Forest), *Poplar Forest, Thomas Jefferson's*, 107
- **SC** Blacksburg, *Historic Smithfield*, 109
- **SC** Brookneal, *Red Hill-Patrick Henry National Memorial*, 109
- **SC** Ferrum, *Blue Ridge Institute & Farm Museum*, 113
- **SC** Green Bay, *Sailor's Creek Battlefield Historic State Park*, 112
- **SC** Hardy, *Booker T. Washington National Monument*, 113
- **SC** Meadows of Dan, *Mabry Mill*, 118
- **SC** Randolph, *Staunton River Battlefield State Park*, 119
- **SC** Roanoke, *History Museum Of Western Virginia*, 120
- **SC** Roanoke, *Roanoke Star*, 124
- **SC** Roanoke, *Virginia's Explore Park Visitors Center (BRPkwy)*, 122
- **SE** Chincoteague, *Museum of Chincoteague*, 138
- **SE** Hampton, *Hampton History Museum*, 143
- **SE** Hampton (Fort Monroe), *Casemate Museum At Fort Monroe*, 147
- **SE** Hopewell, *City Point Open Air Museum Walking Tour*, 147
- **SE** Hopewell, *Weston Manor*, 148
- **SE** Newport News, *Endview Plantation*, 150
- **SE** Newport News, *Huntington Park / Virginia War Museum*, 152
- **SE** Newport News, *Mariners' Museum*, 150
- **SE** Newport News (Fort Eustis), *U.S. Army Transportation Museum*, 152
- **SE** Norfolk, *MacArthur Memorial*, 156
- **SE** Petersburg, *Pamplin Historical Park & The National Museum Of The Civil War Soldier*, 160
- **SE** Petersburg, *Petersburg National Battlefield*, 162

KIDS LOVE VIRGINIA

HISTORY *(cont.)*

- **SE** Petersburg (Fort Lee), *Quartermaster Museum*, 163
- **SE** Portsmouth, *Lightship*, 164
- **SE** Portsmouth, *Naval Shipyard Museum*, 164
- **SE** Richmond, *American Civil War Museum*, 174
- **SE** Richmond, *Maggie L. Walker National Historic Site*, 166
- **SE** Richmond, *Museum Of The Confederacy*, 167
- **SE** Richmond, *Richmond National Battlefield Park*, 173
- **SE** Richmond, *St. John's Church*, 168
- **SE** Richmond, *Valentine Museum-Richmond History Center*, 168
- **SE** Richmond, *Virginia Historical Society*, 172
- **SE** Richmond, *Virginia State Capitol*, 169
- **SE** Richmond (Chester), *Henricus Historical Park*, 175
- **SE** Smithfield, *Fort Huger*, 178
- **SE** Smithfield, *Isle Of Wight County Museum*, 178
- **SE** Surry, *Smith's Fort Plantation*, 180
- **SE** Virginia Beach, *Military Aviation Museum*, 185
- **SE** Virginia Beach, *Surf & Rescue Museum*, 182
- **SE** Williamsburg, *Colonial Williamsburg*, 190
- **SE** Williamsburg (Charles City), *Berkeley Plantation*, 194
- **SE** Williamsburg (Charles City), *Sherwood Forest Plantation*, 195
- **SE** Williamsburg (Charles City), *Shirley Plantation*, 195
- **SE** Williamsburg (Jamestown), *Historic Jamestowne*, 196
- **SE** Williamsburg (Jamestown), *Jamestown Settlement*, 197
- **SE** Williamsburg (Yorktown), *Watermen's Museum*, 200
- **SE** Williamsburg (Yorktown), *Yorktown And Yorktown Battlefield*, 200
- **SE** Williamsburg (Yorktown), *Yorktown American Revolution Center*, 198
- **SW** Bastian, *Wolf Creek Indian Village*, 205
- **SW** Big Stone Gap, *Southwest Virginia Museum Historical State Park*, 206
- **SW** Cumberland Gap, *Cumberland Gap National Historical Park*, 209
- **SW** Saltville, *Museum Of The Middle Appalachians*, 213
- **SW** Tazewell, *Historic Crab Orchard*, 214
- **SW** Weber City, *Homeplace Mountain Farm And Museum*, 215
- **SW** Wytheville, *Rock House Museum & Boyd House*, 216

MUSEUMS

- **NE** Alexandria, *Alexandria Archaeology*, 5
- **NE** Alexandria, *Alexandria Seaport*, 4
- **NE** Alexandria, *United States Patent And Trademark Office Museum*, 11
- **NE** Fredericksburg, *CMoR*, 23
- **NE** King William, *Pamunkey Reservation*, 33
- **DC** Washington, *International Spy Museum*, 45
- **NW** Charlottesville, *University of Virginia*, 70
- **NW** Charlottesville, *Virginia Discovery*, 70
- **NW** Harrisonburg, *Explore More Discovery Museum*, 74
- **NW** Harrisonburg, *James Madison University Campus*, 74
- **NW** New Market (Shenandoah Caverns) *American Celebration On Parade*, 88
- **NW** Schuyler, *Walton's Mountain*, 89
- **NW** Winchester, *Shenandoah Valley Discovery Museum*, 97
- **SC** Lynchburg, *Amazement Square, The Rightmire Children's Museum*, 115
- **SC** Roanoke, *Virginia Museum Of Transportation*, 122
- **SC** South Hill, *South Hill Model Railroad Museum*, 128
- **SE** Richmond, *Children's Museum Of Richmond*, 169
- **SE** Richmond, *Federal Reserve Money Museum*, 166
- **SE** Waverly, *Miles B. Carpenter Museum Complex*, 187

For updates visit: www.KidsLoveTravel.com

Activity Index

OUTDOOR EXPLORING

NE Alexandria, *Atlantic Canoe & Kayak Co*, 6
NE Delaplane, *Sky Meadows State Park*, 21
NE King George, *Caledon Natural Area*, 32
NE Lancaster, *Belle Isle State Park*, 33
NE Mason Neck (Lorton), *Mason Neck State Park*, 37
NE McLean, *Theodore Roosevelt Memorial & Island*, 38
NE Montross, *Westmoreland State Park*, 37
NE Spotsylvania, *Lake Anna State Park*, 39
NE Woodbridge, *Leesylvania State Park*, 40
DC Washington, *National Mall*, 54
DC Washington, *Rock Creek Park And Nature Center*, 49
NW Basye, *Bryce Resort*, 65
NW Bentonville, *Shenandoah River State Park, Andy Guest*, 65
NW Cumberland, *Bear Creek Lake State Park*, 72
NW Cumberland, *Cumberland State Forest*, 72
NW Gladstone, *James River State Park*, 73
NW Hot Springs, *Homestead Resort*, 78
NW Luray, *Shenandoah National Park & Skyline Drive*, 81
NW Millboro, *Douthat State Park*, 83
NW Natural Bridge, *Natural Bridge*, 84
SC Appomattox, *Appomattox-Buckingham State Forest / Holliday Lake St Park*, 105
SC Clarksville, *Occoneechee State Park*, 110
SC Green Bay, *Twin Lakes State Park*, 112
SC Huddleston, *Smith Mountain Lake State Park*, 115
SC Roanoke, *George Washington & Jefferson National Forests*, 123
SC South Boston (Scottsburg), *Staunton River State Park*, 129
SC Stuart, *Fairy Stone State Park*, 129
SC Vinton, *Blue Ridge Parkway*, 129
SE Cape Charles, *Eastern Shore Of VA National Wildlife Refuge Visitors Center*, 135
SE Cape Charles, *Kiptopeke State Park*, 136
SE Chincoteague, *Assateague Island National Seashore/ Chincoteague Wildlife Refuge*, 137
SE Gloucester Point, *Gloucester Point Beach Park & VIMS Wetlands*, 142
SE Hampton, *Buckroe Beach*, 142
SE Hampton, *Sandy Bottom Nature Pk*, 144
SE Newport News, *Newport News Pk*, 149
SE Norfolk, *Norfolk Botanical Garden*, 159
SE Richmond, *Canal Walk*, 165
SE Richmond, *Lewis Ginter Botanical Garden*, 174
SE Richmond (Chesterfield), *Pocahontas State Park*, 176
SE Suffolk, *Great Dismal Swamp National Wildlife Refuge*, 179
SE Surry, *Chippokes Plantation State Park*, 179
SE Virginia Beach, *False Cape State Park & Back Bay National Wildlife Refuge*, 185
SE Virginia Beach, *First Landing State Park*, 180
SE Wakefield, *Airfield 4-H Center*, 186
SE Williamsburg, *York River State Pk*, 194
SW Big Stone Gap (Duffield), *Natural Tunnel State Park*, 207
SW Breaks, *Breaks Interstate Park*, 208
SW Dublin, *Claytor Lake State Park*, 210
SW Ewing, *Wilderness Road State Pk*, 210
SW Galax (Foster Falls), *New River Trail State Park*, 211
SW Marion, *Hungry Mother State Park*, 212
SW Mouth of Wilson, *Grayson Highlands State Park*, 212
SW Wytheville, *Big Walker Lookout*, 215

SCIENCE

NE Chantilly, *National Air And Space Museum / Udvar-Hazy Center*, 19
NE Mineral, *North Anna Nuclear Info Center*, 35
NW Front Royal, *Skyline Caverns*, 72
NW Grottoes, *Grand Caverns*, 73
NW Luray, *Luray Caverns*, 79
NW New Market, *Endless Caverns*, 86
NW New Market (Shenandoah Caverns), *Shenandoah Caverns*, 88
SC Danville, *Danville Science Center*, 110
SC Martinsville, *Virginia Museum Of Natural History*, 116

KIDS LOVE VIRGINIA

SC Roanoke, *Science Museum Of Western Virginia*, 121
SC Roanoke (Salem), *Dixie Caverns*, 125
SE Chincoteague (Wallops Island), *NASA Visitor Center*, 139
SE Hampton, *Virginia Air & Space Center*, 145
SE Newport News, *Virginia Living Museum*, 148
SE Norfolk, *Nauticus*, 157
SE Portsmouth, *Children's Museum Of Virginia*, 164
SE Richmond, *Science Museum Of Virginia*, 171
SE Richmond, *Three Lakes Nature Center*, 174
SE Virginia Beach, *Virginia Aquarium*, 182

SPORTS

SC Danville (Alton), *Virginia International Raceway*, 111
SC Martinsville, *Martinsville Speedway*, 118
SC South Boston, *South Boston Speedway*, 125
SC Stuart, *Wood Brothers Racing*, 128
SE Hampton, *Langley Speedway*, 144
SE Norfolk, *Norfolk Sports*, 153
SE Petersburg (Dinwiddie), *Virginia Motorsports Park*, 163
SE Richmond, *Richmond International Raceway*, 171
SE Richmond, *Richmond Kickers Soccer*, 171
SE Virginia Beach, *Mount Trashmore Park*, 186

THE ARTS

NE Alexandria, *Alexandria Symphony Orchestra*, 5
NE Alexandria, *Torpedo Factory Art Center*, 11
NE Fredericksburg, *Riverside Center Dinner Theatre*, 24
NE Manassas, *Pied Piper Theatre*, 35
DC Washington, *National Gallery of Art*, 61

NW Lexington, *Hull's Drive In Theatre*, 78
NW Waynesboro, *P. Buckley Moss Museum*, 95
SC Lynchburg, *Lynchburg Symphony Orchestra*, 116
SC Martinsville, *Piedmont Arts Association*, 116
SC Roanoke, *Art Venture*, 119
SC Roanoke, *Mill Mountain Theatre*, 120
SE Eastern Shore (Onley), *Turner Sculpture*, 141
SE Newport News, *Peninsula Fine Arts Center*, 151
SE Norfolk, *Chrysler Museum Of Art*, 155
SE Norfolk, *Virginia Stage Company*, 158
SE Norfolk, *Virginia Symphony/Virginia Youth Symphony Orchestra*, 154
SE Richmond, *Richmond Symphony*, 167
SE Richmond, *Childrens Theatre*, 172
SE Richmond, *Virginia Museum Of Fine Arts*, 173
SW Abingdon, *Barter Theatre*, 205
SW Big Stone Gap, *Trail Of The Lonesome Pine State Outdoor Drama*, 207
SW Clintwood, *Ralph Stanley Museum And Traditional Mountain Music Center*, 209
SW Hiltons, *Carter Family Fold & Museum*, 211

TOURS

NE Alexandria, *Alexandria Walking Tours*, 6
NE Alexandria, *Old Town Scavenger Hunt*, 9
NE Alexandria, *Potomac Riverboat Company*, 10
NE Arlington, *Arlington National Cemetery*, 18
NE Fredericksburg, *Fredericksburg Trolley Tours*, 21
NE Great Falls, *Colvin Run Mill*, 29
NE Reedville, *Tangier Island Cruise*, 38
DC Washington, *Bureau Of Engraving And Printing Tour*, 53
DC Washington, *DC Signature Tours*, 48
DC Washington, *Old Town Trolley*

For updates visit: www.KidsLoveTravel.com

Activity Index

	Tours, 44
DC	Washington, *The Lights Tours*, 47
DC	Washington, *White House*, 48
NW	Lexington, *Lexington Carriage Company*, 77
NW	Middletown, *Route 11 Potato Chips*, 83
NW	Scottsville, *Hatton Ferry*, 90
SC	Meadows of Dan, *Nancy's Candy Company*, 118
SE	Cape Charles, *Chesapeake Bay Bridge Tunnel*, 134
SE	Chincoteague, *Assateague Explorer*, 136
SE	Chincoteague, *Captain Barry's Back Bay Cruises*, 138
SE	Fort Story, *Cape Henry Lighthouses*, 142
SE	Norfolk, *American Rover Tall Ship Cruises*, 155
SE	Norfolk, *Elizabeth River Ferry*, 153
SE	Norfolk, *Naval Station Norfolk*, 154
SE	Norfolk, *Victory Rover*, 158
SE	Surry, *Jamestown-Scotland Ferry*, 180
SE	Virginia Beach, *Naval Air Station Oceana*, 186
SE	Virginia Beach, *Rudee Boat Tours*, 183
SE	Williamsburg (Yorktown), *Alliance Tall Ship Day Sails*, 199
SW	Cumberland Gap, *Gap Cave Tours*, 210
SW	Pocahontas, *Pocahontas Exhibition Mine And Museum*, 212
NW	Natural Bridge, *Natural Bridge Hotel*, 85
NW	Schulers, *Lovington Village Inn*, 90
SC	Meadows of Dan, *Mabry Mill*, 117
SE	Eastern Shore, *Hopkins & Bros*, 140
SE	Richmond, *Embassy Suites*, 175
SE	Williamsburg, *Kingsmill Resort*, 188

Note: For all **NE-DC** listings, area is coded as **DC**

SUGGESTED LODGING & DINING

NE	Alexandria, *Bugsy's Pizza*, 12
NE	Alexandria, *Embassy Suites Old Town*, 13
NE	Alexandria, *Hampton Inn Old Town*, 13
NE	Alexandria, *King St Blues Restaurant*, 13
DC	Washington, *Clydes @the Gallery*, 43
NW	Charlottesville, *Michie Tavern*, 68
NW	Charlottesville, *DoubleTree Hotel*, 71
NW	Charlottesville, *Wintergreen Resort*, 99

www.ingramcontent.com/pod-product-compliance
Lightning Source LLC
Chambersburg PA
CBHW071958070526
44583CB00015B/1250